THE
TRUTH
MACHINE

Also by Michael J. Casey and Paul Vigna

*The Age of Cryptocurrency: How Bitcoin and
the Blockchain Are Challenging the Global Economic Order*

Also by Michael J. Casey

*The Unfair Trade: How Our Broken Financial System
Destroys the Middle Class*

Che's Afterlife: The Legacy of an Image

*The Social Organism: A Radical Understanding of Social Media
to Transform Your Business and Life* (with Oliver Luckett)

Also by Paul Vigna

Guts: The Anatomy of The Walking Dead

THE
TRUTH
MACHINE

THE BLOCKCHAIN
AND THE FUTURE
OF EVERYTHING

MICHAEL J. CASEY & PAUL VIGNA

HarperCollins*Publishers*

HarperCollins*Publishers*
1 London Bridge Street
London SE1 9GF

www.harpercollins.co.uk

First published in the US by St Martin's Press 2018
This UK edition published by HarperCollins*Publishers* 2018

1 3 5 7 9 10 8 6 4 2

A catalogue record of this book is
available from the British Library

ISBN 978-0-00-830177-4

Printed and bound in Great Britain by
CPI Group (UK) Ltd, Croydon, CR0 4YY

For Liz, Jenny, Sarah, and Di
— MC

For my mom and dad
— PV

Contents

Preface

In *The Age of Cryptocurrency*, we explored the digital currency bitcoin and its promise of a fairer global payments system, one that functions without banks and other financial intermediaries. As that book was going to print, Bitcoin's* wider application—how its core operating system can help resolve problems of trust between individuals and businesses when they trade assets, enter into contracts, assert claims to property, or share valuable or sensitive information—came to the fore. Within companies, governments, and the media, a groundswell of interest, including a fair bit of hype, turned toward what became known as "blockchain technology."

In resolving longstanding problems of trust and enabling a community to track its transactions without entrusting that record-keeping process to a central intermediary, the blockchain idea promised a way to bypass the various gatekeepers who control society's exchanges of value. It could, for instance, let a neighborhood of "prosumers"—households that both consume power and produce it with solar panels

---

* Throughout this book you will see a distinction between "bitcoin" written with a lowercase "b" and "Bitcoin" with an uppercase "B." The former refers to bitcoin's status as a currency, the latter is a reference to the overarching system and protocol that underpins that currency and other uses for the Bitcoin blockchain ledger.

on their roofs—trade energy among themselves within a decentralized marketplace and without a profit-driven utility company setting the rates. Similarly, property owners, buyers, and mortgage lenders would not have to trust an unreliable government registry as the only record of deeds and liens when a more trustworthy one could be built on an immutable database managed by a decentralized network with less risk of corruption, human failure, or theft. These are just some of the many new applications that attracted people's attention to this innovative idea.

The zeitgeist of public awareness had two big impacts on our lives. The first was that one of us—Michael Casey—got so excited about blockchain technology's potential to change the world that he quit a twenty-three-year career in journalism to work on it full time. Less than six months after *The Age of Cryptocurrency* was published, Mike left *The Wall Street Journal* for MIT's Media Lab. The lab's frenetic director, Joichi Ito, who is commonly known as Joi, had recognized parallels between Bitcoin's emergence and the software development he'd witnessed during the early days of the Internet. Sensing a similar enthusiasm for a new, decentralizing architecture, Ito hatched a plan to bring powerful academic and financial resources to the vital task of developing this nascent technology. The result was MIT's Digital Currency Initiative, a center where leading academics and students in the fields of cryptography, engineering, and finance could collaborate with Fortune 500 strategists, innovative startups, philanthropists, and government officials to design the digital architecture of a new "Internet of Value." When Mike received an offer to join this initiative, he saw a once-in-a-lifetime opportunity to get in on the ground floor of an economic revolution.

The second impact is the book you are reading. In *The Age of Cryptocurrency*, we focused primarily on a single application of Bitcoin's core technology, on its potential to upend currency and payments. Since the book's publication, though, we have learned there's a risk in writing about technology: it changes, while the words on the page do not. So much has changed in three years, in fact, that we were compelled to write another book. *The Truth Machine* expands the conversation we began in 2015 and takes it to a level higher. It explores how Bitcoin's technology and its various offshoots point to a general redesign of social organizations, fostering many more alternative applications.

In the modern economy, to control information is to control the world. This is seen in the ever-growing influence of tech behemoths like Google and Facebook, constantly accumulating data that's pertinent to who we are and how we interact with each other. In this twenty-first-century economy, power is defined by whoever has authority to collect, store, and share data. Currently, that authority is centralized. It is concentrated among a narrow number of giant tech companies. If you're wondering why that's problematic, just think of the influence that Facebook's hidden algorithm, which prioritizes the company's business model above all other objectives, has had on our politics. In incentivizing the creation and sharing of often-dubious information to trigger dopamine releases among social networks of like-minded people, its algorithm played an instrumental role in the bombshell U.S. elections of 2016.

The ideas behind the blockchain* have now unleashed a struggle to turn that structure of concentrated power on its head, to figure out how the capacity to control and manage information might shift to a decentralized system that *no one* controls. It lets us imagine a world that's not dominated by Google, Facebook, or, for that matter, the NSA, one

---

* Addressing an inconsistency in popular parlance, we generally employ three distinct usages of the word "blockchain": "The blockchain," which refers to Bitcoin's original distributed ledger; "a blockchain"—or, pluralized, "blockchains"—to cover a variety of more recent distributed ledgers that share Bitcoin's chain-of-blocks structure; and "blockchain technology," referring to the overall field. We also use "distributed ledger technology" to encompass both blockchain and non-blockchain distributed ledgers. We mostly avoid the popular construct of "blockchain" as a non-countable noun. We view a blockchain, like any ledger, as a distinct, identifiable thing, not a process. The book's title uses the definite article form to acknowledge the catalytic role that the original Bitcoin blockchain played in unleashing this field.

where we, the people, the core components of global society, get to say how our data is managed.

We felt it was important to get that message across. *The Truth Machine* is our attempt to convey it.

THE
TRUTH
MACHINE

Introduction

A SOCIETY-BUILDING TOOL

Sixty miles east of Amman, in a 5.6-square-mile block of dry, stony ground carved out of the Jordanian desert, lies the UN High Commission for Refugees' Azraq camp. Teeming with 32,000 desperate Syrians living in pre-fabricated shelters—rows and rows of white, corrugated steel cabins arranged in a military-like grid—Azraq poses the logistical challenges of a small city. Yet UNHCR and the other aid agencies that give the refugees food, shelter, and a modicum of hope can't count on the kinds of institutions and infrastructure that normal cities use to ensure order, security, and functionality for their residents.

All refugee camps are, by definition, short on what political scientists call "social capital," the networks of long-established relationships and bonds of trust that allow communities to function, to engage in social interaction and exchange. But Azraq can seem especially devoid of it. There are police in Azraq, but they are Jordanian. They are not of the people, not of the community. And while the crime rates in Azraq are lower than those in nearby Zaatari camp, where 130,000 Syrians live in conditions that a UN review once described as "lawless," this hot, dry, stony place is hardly welcoming. When Azraq was set up in 2014 as an alternative to Zaatari's chaos, refugees complained that it lacked life. Electricity was sparse, which meant they couldn't charge their cellphones, cutting them off from family and friends. The lack of a functioning, trustful community also heightened the refugees' fears of being abducted by the extremist organization Islamic State. Many initially refused to move to Azraq camp, and although the numbers have increased more recently, Azraq is still far below the 130,000 capacity for which it was built.

It's fitting then that this pop-up city, in real need of some functioning social capital, is now the scene of a radical experiment in new models of community governance, institution-building, and the management of resources. At the heart of that effort is blockchain technology, the decentralized ledger-keeping system that underpins the digital currency bitcoin and promises a more reliable, immediate way to trace transactions. The World Food Program (WFP), a UN agency that feeds 80 million people worldwide, is putting 10,000 Azraq refugees through a pilot that uses this system to better coordinate food distribution. In doing so, the WFP is tackling a giant administrative challenge: how to ensure, in an environment where theft is rampant and few people carry personal identifying documents, that everyone gets their fair share of food.

Among those participating in this project was forty-three-year-old Najah Saleh Al-Mheimed, one of the more than 5 million Syrians forced to flee their homes as the brutal, ongoing civil war has all but destroyed their country. In early June 2015, with mounting food shortages and reports of girls being kidnapped by militias in nearby villages, Najah and her husband made the drastic decision to leave her hometown of Hasaka, where their families had lived for generations. "It was an ordeal that I pray to God no human will ever witness," she said in an interview conducted on our behalf by WFP staffers working in the Azraq camp.

In leaving behind her home, her assets, her circle of neighbors and family, and her ties to what was once a more coherent Syrian nation, Najah was also losing something extremely powerful that the rest of us take for granted: a societal system of trust, identity, and record-keeping that ties our past to our present, anchors us as human beings, and lets us participate in society. The amalgamation of information that goes

into proving that we can be trusted as a member of society has histori-
cally depended upon institutions that record and affirm our life events
and credentials—bank accounts, birth certificates, changes of address,
educational records, driver's licenses, etc.—and keep track of our financial transactions. To lose all of that, as refugees often do when thrust
into "statelessness," is to be put in a highly vulnerable position, one
that's inherently easy for the worst of the world's criminals and terror-
ist organizations to exploit. If you are unable to prove who you are, you
are at the mercy of strangers. Among all the work that agencies such
as the UNHCR and the WFP do, this core function—the creation of
stand-in societal institutions—is just as important as the food they provide. In dusty tent cities filled with dislocated people around the world,
these humanitarian agencies must undertake the challenging task of
recreating systems of social trust. They are reconstructing societies,
building them all over again. And it turns out that blockchain technology provides a tool for doing just that.

It's in this realm, where human beings must depend on reliable
institutions to keep track of their social interactions and provide proof
that their claims are valid, that blockchain technology comes into its
own. With this system we would no longer have to trust institutions to
maintain transaction records and vouch for us, since blockchain-based
programs comprise an intricate set of features that result in something
that's never existed before: a transaction record that is visible to all and
can be verified at any moment, but that is not controlled by any one
central authority. This means two things: nobody can alter the data to
suit their own ends, and everybody has greater control over their own
data. You can see how this could be an empowering idea for millions
of Syrians living a scorched-earth existence.

Just as the blockchain-distributed ledger is used to assure bitcoin
users that others aren't "double-spending" their currency holdings—in
other words, to prevent what would otherwise be rampant digital
counterfeiting—the Azraq blockchain pilot ensures that people aren't
double-spending their food entitlements. That's a pretty important
requirement in refugee camps, where supplies are limited and where

organized crime outfits have been known to steal and hoard food for profit. And it means that refugees like Najah will always be able to prove that their accounts are legitimate. That would end the periodic and disturbing disruption to provisions that many have experienced under the cash-voucher system. In that system, any inconsistency tends to flag a concern to administrators, who often feel compelled to cut off the person's access to food until it is resolved.

Under this new pilot, all that's needed to institute a payment with a food merchant is a scan of a refugee's iris. In effect, the eye becomes a kind of digital wallet, obviating the need for cash, vouchers, debit cards, or smartphones, which reduces the danger of theft. (You may have some privacy concerns related to that iris scan—we'll get to that below.) For the WFP, making these transfers digital results in millions of dollars in saved fees as they cut out middlemen such as money transmitters and the bankers that formerly processed the overall payments system.

So whenever a refugee spends some level of his or her digital "cash" to buy flour, that transaction automatically registers on a transparent ledger that can't be tampered with. That ever-present, ever-updating, extremely reliable record-keeping model means WFP administrators can have full visibility of the flow of transactions at any time, even though the WFP has no centralized record of its own. The organization can support a camp-wide payment system without having to take on the centralized role of a bank or payment processor.

By contrast, the UNHCR's identity program, which is integrated into the WFP's blockchain solution, *is* maintained as a centralized database. That has raised some concerns among critics. Such systems are susceptible to hacking because, by accumulating large amounts of data in one big "honeypot," they offer what's known as a single attack vector. In this case, such risks could in theory put this particularly vulnerable group of human beings at risk—it's not hard to imagine the worst if a database of biometric identifiers ever fell into the hands of an ethnic cleansing–minded institution like ISIS. People in the blockchain space, who are often fierce advocates of privacy, are among the most vocal about these concerns, and some are trying to figure out how to use the same technology to decentralize control over self-identifying information so that people aren't vulnerable to break-ins of these big data honeypots. But until such "self-sovereign" solutions are available, the WFP and the UNHCR have made a determination that the risks are for now outweighed by the benefits of a seamless, cashless system.

According to WFP spokesman Alex Sloan, the pilot has already shown success: it has saved money and created a much more efficient way of dealing with inconsistencies in refugees' accounts. It's so successful, in fact, that the agency is looking to extend the service to a larger population of 100,000 refugees. In the not too distant future, Sloan says, 20 million food program beneficiaries who receive disbursements in cash could be eligible for the blockchain program. With the world facing the biggest refugee crisis in history, a result of greed, of the brutal pursuit of self-serving power, and of failed Western policies to contain it, we owe it to these people to bring some security back into their lives—to provide them with a platform of trust upon which to rebuild. Perhaps blockchain technology offers the best chance of delivering that.

The World Food Program's Azraq experiment is just one example of how international agencies are exploring blockchain solutions to the problems of the world's neediest. In early 2017, a group of blockchain enthusiasts at the UN's New York headquarters launched a Web site calling on other UN employees to work with them. The group rapidly grew to eighty-five UN staffers worldwide, and they are now working on multiple pilots addressing blockchain for development, in partnership with governments such as Norway's. At the World Bank, a new blockchain lab was created with fresh funding in June 2017 to explore how the technology could tackle poverty alleviation through incorruptible property registries and secure digital identities. The Inter-American Development, in concert with MIT Media Lab's Digital Currency Initiative, is looking at how poor Latin American farmers might be able to obtain credit on the basis of reliable, blockchain-proven records from commodity warehouses. Non-profit international organizations such as the World Economic Forum and the Rockefeller Foundation are also diving into this area.

What do these decades-old international organizations see in an arcane digital technology built by the crypto-libertarians and Cypherpunks who gave us Bitcoin? It's the prospect that this decentralized computing system could resolve the issue of social capital deficits that we discussed in the context of the Azraq refugee camp. By creating a common record of a community's transactions and activities that no single person or intermediating institution has the power to change, the UN's blockchain provides a foundation for people to trust that they can securely interact and exchange value with each other. It's a new, more powerful solution to the age-old problem of human mistrust, which means it could help societies build social capital. That's an especially appealing idea for many underdeveloped countries as it would enable their economies to function more like those of developed countries— low-income homeowners could get mortgages, for example; street vendors could get insurance. It could give billions of people their first opening into the economic opportunities that the rest of us take for granted.

But it's not just in developing countries, or in the realm of non-profit charity and development work, that blockchain technology shows potential. Far from it. In the developed world, too, and within the boardrooms of plenty of Fortune 500 for-profit companies, there is a scramble to unleash what many believe could be a major force for economic growth. That's because the blockchain is seen as capable of supplanting our outdated, centralized model of trust management, which goes to the heart of how societies and economies function.

Until now, we have relied on institutions such as banks, government registries, and countless other intermediaries to sit in the middle of our economic exchanges with each other. These "trusted third parties" maintain records on our behalf so that the rest of us have enough trust in the system to interact, exchange items of value, and, hopefully, build vibrant, functioning societies. The problem is that these fee-charging institutions, which act as gatekeepers, dictating who can and cannot engage in commercial interactions, add cost and friction to our economic activities. They also have a habit of failing us—we can think of the crisis of 2008 as a case of banks breaching their duty to maintain honest records—or of exploiting their toll-collecting power to price gouge and demand exorbitant rents. What's more, there are plenty of situations in which it's simply not economically viable for these costly, inefficient institutions to resolve whatever particular trust deficit is preventing people from doing business with each other. So, if we bypass those intermediaries, we will not only save money but also open up previously impossible business models.

The Internet put us on this disintermediating path some time ago, well before the blockchain came along. But it's worth noting that at the heart of each new Internet application that cuts out some incumbent middleman there has typically been a technology that helps humans deal with their perennial mistrust issues. Who would have thought a decade ago that people would feel comfortable riding in the car of some stranger they'd just discovered on their phones? Well, Uber and Lyft got us over that trust barrier by incorporating a reputation scoring system for both drivers and passengers, one that was only made possible because of the expansion of social networks and communication. Their model showed that if we can resolve our trust issues with technology and give people confidence to transact, those people are willing and able to go into direct exchanges with complete strangers. These ideas are setting us on a path to a peer-to-peer economy.

What blockchain technology says is, "Why stop at Uber?" Why do we even need this particular company, which takes 25 percent from each ride and has a reputation for abusing its "God's View" knowledge of passengers' rides? How about a totally decentralized solution, such as the Tel Aviv–based, blockchain-powered ride-sharing application Commuterz? In that case no one owns the platform, which like Bitcoin is just based on an open-source software protocol that anyone can download. There's no Commuterz, Inc. taking 25 percent. Instead, users own and trade a native digital currency system that incentivizes them to share rides to reduce traffic congestion and lower the cost of transportation for all.

The broad idea is that by deferring the management of trust to a decentralized network guided by a common protocol instead of relying upon a trusted intermediary, and by introducing new, digital forms of money, tokens, and assets, we can change the very nature of social organization. We can encourage new approaches to collaboration and cooperation that weren't possible before, transforming a wide array of industries and organizational settings. Indeed, the breadth of blockchain's potential is captured in the breadth of the ideas under consideration. Here is sampling of possible use cases, and it is by no means an exhaustive list:

- *Inviolable property registries*, which people can use to prove that they own their houses, cars, or other assets;
- *Real-time, direct, bank-to-bank settlement of securities exchanges*, which could unlock trillions of dollars in an interbank market that currently passes such transactions through dozens of specialized institutions in a process that takes two to seven days;
- *Self-sovereign identities*, which don't depend on a government or a company to assert a person's ID;
- *Decentralized computing*, which supplants the corporate business of cloud computing and Web hosting with the hard drives and processing power of ordinary users' computers;
- *Decentralized Internet of Things transactions*, where devices can securely talk and transact with each other without the friction of an intermediary, making possible big advances in transportation and decentralized energy grids;
- *Blockchain-based supply chains*, in which suppliers use a common data platform to share information about their business processes to greatly improve accountability, efficiency, and fi-

nancing with the common purpose of producing a particular good;

- *Decentralized media and content*, which would empower musicians and artists—and, in theory, anyone who posts information of value to the Net—to take charge of their digital content, knowing they can track and manage the use of this "digital asset."

Blockchain technology could help achieve what some commentators are calling the promise of "Internet 3.0," a re-architecting of the Net to assert the core objective of decentralization that inspired many of the early online pioneers who built the Internet 1.0. It turned out that simply giving networks of computers a way to share data directly wasn't enough to prevent large corporate entities from taking control of the information economy. Silicon Valley's anti-establishment coders hadn't reckoned with the challenge of trust and how society traditionally turns to centralized institutions to deal with that. That failure was clear in the subsequent Internet 2.0 phase, which unlocked the power of social networks but also allowed first-mover companies to turn network effects into entrenched monopoly power. These included social media giants like Facebook and Twitter and e-marketplace success stories of the "sharing economy" such as Uber and Airbnb. Blockchain technologies, as well as other ideas contained in this Internet 3.0 phase, aim to do away with these intermediaries altogether, letting people forge their own bonds of trust to build social networks and business arrangements on their own terms.

The promise lies not just in disrupting the behemoths of the Internet, however. Lots of large, twentieth-century, for-profit companies believe this technology can help them unlock value and pursue new money-making ventures, too. Some see big opportunities, others a major threat. Either way, many incumbent businesses now feel compelled to at least experiment with and explore the development of this technology to see where it goes.

In finance, the very industry that Bitcoin was designed to make redundant, bankers are waking up to the possibility that blockchain-related technologies could replace the cumbersome processes by which securities and money are transferred, cleared, and settled between banks. Using a reliable, distributed ledger that a consortium of banks can update simultaneously in real time could reduce back-office costs and unshackle large amounts of new capital for investment. That's great news for investment banks such as Goldman Sachs, but not so great for custodial banks like State Street or clearinghouses like the Depository Trust & Clearing Corporation, whose business model is based on handling those back-office functions. Still, the institutions on both sides of that disruption story all feel compelled to engage in research and development in this field.

R3 CEV, a New York–based technology developer, for one, raised $107 million from more than a hundred of the world's biggest financial institutions and tech companies to develop a proprietary distributed ledger technology. Inspired by blockchains but eschewing that label, R3's Corda platform is built to comply with banks' business and regulatory models while streamlining trillions of dollars in daily interbank securities transfers.

The non-finance corporate world is also getting engaged. Hyperledger is a distributed ledger/blockchain-design consortium looking to develop standardized, open-source versions of the technology for businesses to use in areas such as supply-chain management. Coordinated by the Linux Foundation, it brings together the likes of IBM, Cisco, Intel, and Digital Asset Holdings, a digital ledger startup led by former J.P. Morgan powerhouse Blythe Masters.

One mark of the business world's enthusiasm is seen in the trajectory of media company CoinDesk's Consensus conference, the marquee annual event for businesses interested in blockchain technology. It went from a turnout of 600 at the inaugural conference in 2015 to 1,500 attendees in 2016 to 2,800 in 2017 with a further 10,500 registered viewers of an online livecast. The attendees in 2017 came from ninety-six countries, and a cross-section of more than ninety sponsors and exhibitors was broad enough to include consulting firm Deloitte, the research arm of Toyota, the Australian government's trade office, and Cryptonomos, a startup marketplace for digital tokens.

But lest you think this technology has been entirely consumed by corporate suits and international development staffers, the months during which we worked on this book also coincided with a get-rich-quick mania that dwarfed even the 2013 surge in Bitcoin's price. This gold rush, spawned by a new blockchain-based crowdfunding tool for startups that's known as the ICO—initial coin offering—had all the hallmarks of the dot-com bubble of the late 1990s. Much like two decades earlier, the boom was characterized by both a risky, speculative furor and a sense that underneath the money madness lay a transformative new technology and new business paradigm.

The startups behind this ICO trend are touting a host of new decentralized applications that could disrupt everything from online advertising to medical research. Integral to those services are special tokens that are pre-sold to the public as a way to both raise money and build a network of users—kind of like Kickstarter, but in which contributors have the potential to make quick money in secondary trading markets. At the time of writing, the highest amount raised by one of these pre-sale ICOs was $257 million by Protocol Labs, which sold a token called Filecoin that's designed to incentivize people to provide hard-drive space for a new decentralized Web. While it's quite possible that many ICOs will fall afoul of securities regulations and that a bursting of this bubble will burn innocent investors, there's something refreshingly democratic about this boom. Hordes of retail investors are entering into early stage investment rounds typically reserved for venture capitalists and other professionals.

Not to be outdone, Bitcoin, the granddaddy of the cryptocurrency world, has continued to reveal strengths—and this has been reflected in its price. Despite a bitter fight between developers and the "miners" that validate transactions on the Bitcoin network, a feud that led the currency to split into two separate coins with different software codes, bitcoin's price surged to a record high of \$11,323 in late November 2017, taking its market capitalization to almost \$190 billion according to CoinDesk's Bitcoin Price Index. That marks a price gain of more than 4,800 percent since *The Age of Cryptocurrency* was published in January 2015 and a return of almost 19 million percent since bitcoin was first tradable on a semi-liquid exchange in July 2010. If you'd invested \$6,000 in bitcoin, you'd be a millionaire right now. Such results give credence to crypto-asset analysts Chris Burniske and Jack Tatar's description of bitcoin as "the most exciting alternative investment of the 21st century."

In essence, the blockchain is a digital ledger that's shared across a decentralized network of independent computers, which update and maintain it in a way that allows anyone to prove the record is complete and uncorrupted. The blockchain achieves this with a special algorithm embedded into a common piece of software run by all the computers in the network. The algorithm consistently steers the computers toward a shared consensus on what new data to add to the ledger, incorporating all manner of economic exchanges, claims of ownership, and other forms of valuable information. Each computer updates its own version of the ledger independently but does so by following the all-important consensus algorithm. Once new ledger entries are introduced, special cryptographic protections make it virtually impossible to go back and change them. The computers' owners are either paid in a digital currency, which incentivizes them to work on protecting the system's integrity, or they do their work as part of a commitment to a consortium agreement. The result is something unique: a group of otherwise independent actors, each acting in pure self-interest, coming together to produce something for the good of all—an immutable record that everyone can trust and that's not managed by a single, centralized intermediary.

A bunch of computers managing data with fancy math tools might not seem like a big deal. But as we'll explain in the next chapter, record-keeping systems, and specifically ledgers, are at the heart of how societies function. Without them we wouldn't generate sufficient trust to enter into exchanges, to do business, to build organizations and form alliances. So, the prospects of improving that core function and of not having to rely on a centralized entity to perform it have profound implications.

This model should enable true peer-to-peer commerce, eliminating middlemen from all sorts of business operations. And because it has the capacity to inspire trust in our data records so that individuals and businesses can engage in the economy without fear of being duped, it could herald a new age of open data and transparency. Essentially, it should let people share more. And with the positive, multiplier effects that this kind of open sharing has on networks of economic activity, more engagement should in turn create more business opportunities.

Blockchains point the entire digital economy toward something people are calling the Internet of Value. Whereas the first version of the Internet allowed people to send information directly to each other, in the Internet of Value people can send anything of value to each other, be it currencies, assets, or valuable data that was previously too sensitive to transmit online. If the first phases of the Internet created huge opportunities for wealth creation and new business models by helping people jump the fences and get on the playing field, this next one promises to remove the fences altogether. In theory, it means that everyone with access to a device and the Internet can participate directly in the global economy. Thus, the hope is that we will greatly expand the pool of open-source innovation from which all sorts of powerful ideas will emerge.

Think of how disintermediation has already transformed the global economy in the earlier Internet era and you get a sense of how sweeping this next phase could be. Consider, for example, how the outsourcing of technical advice, Web design, and even accounting services disrupted jobs in Western countries and fostered economic growth in places like Bangalore, India. Or think of how Craigslist, which allowed people to post ads for anything at zero cost on a site that had global reach, completely decimated the classified ads business and, ultimately, shuttered hundreds of local newspapers. If blockchain technology lives up to its promise to decentralize and disintermediate so much of our economy, these prior disruptions may seem minuscule by comparison.

As we'll discuss in the pages ahead, there's still much work to do to get this technology ready for prime time. In fact, it may never be scalable to the size needed to make a difference. Nonetheless, people across every industry are coming to recognize its potential power. They're starting to realize that resolving trust barriers could allow all of us to do more with what we have: to deploy our assets, our ideas, our creativity into whatever productive endeavor takes our fancy. If I can trust another person's claims—about their educational credentials, for example, or their assets, or their professional reputation—because they've been objectively verified by a decentralized system, then I can go into direct business with them. I can give them a job. I can collaborate on a joint venture. I can share sensitive business information with them. All without having to rely on middlemen like lawyers, escrow agents, and others who add costs and inefficiencies to our exchanges. These kinds of agreements are the stuff of economic growth. They fuel innovation and prosperity. Any technology that reduces friction and makes such collaborations happen should benefit everybody, in other words.

Still, there's nothing to say this will assuredly play out in a way that's best for the world. We've seen how the Internet was co-opted by corporations and how that centralization has caused problems—from creating big siloes of personal data for shady hackers to steal to incentivizing disinformation campaigns that distort our democracy. So, it's crucial that we not let the people with the greatest capacity to influence this technology shape it to suit only their narrow interests. As with the early days of the Internet, there is much work to be done to make this technology sufficiently safe, scalable, and attendant to everyone's privacy concerns.

Blockchains are a social technology, a new blueprint for how to govern communities, whether we're talking about frightened refugees in a desolate Jordanian outpost or an interbank market in which the world's biggest financial institutions exchange trillions of dollars daily. By definition, getting blockchain technology right requires input from all sectors of society. You can treat that as a clarion call to take an interest, to get involved.

One

THE GOD PROTOCOL

It might surprise you to read this, but the most subversive, controversial, anti-authoritarian idea in the world of finance, an idea so powerful every government on the planet is trying to figure out whether to co-opt it or outlaw it, the dream of the most fervent libertarian, dark-Web denizens, is a ledger.

Like, an accounting book.

The genesis of that subversive idea was, of course, Bitcoin, which, when boiled down to its most basic concept, is founded on the upkeep of a digitized ledger, a record of exchanges and transactions. What makes this ledger so radical, so controversial, is the way in which this record of transactions, known as a blockchain, is created and maintained. Bitcoin, released in 2009 by a person or persons using the pseudonym Satoshi Nakamoto, was designed to be an end-around to the banks and governments that have for centuries been the guardians of our financial systems. Its blockchain promised a new way around processes that had become at best controlled by middlemen who insisted on taking their cut of every transaction, and at worst the cause of some man-made economic disasters.

You probably bought this book expecting to read crazy, wild ideas about our digitized future . . . and here we are, giving you ledgers. But ledgers have been integral in underpinning the development of civilization for millennia. The trinity of writing, money, and ledgers made it possible for human beings to do business beyond kinship groups and thus form larger settlements. And while the contributions of money and writing are well appreciated, ledgers tend to be known only by those who studied the dry science of accounting.

The advent of the first ledger technology can be traced back to roughly 3000 BCE, in ancient Mesopotamia (modern-day Iraq). Of the tens of thousands of clay tablets the Mesopotamians left behind, most are, well, ledgers: records of taxes, payments, private wealth, worker pay. The famous Code of Hammurabi—the Babylonians' system of law—was written on one of these ledgers, but most of the kings had their own rules set out as well. The rise of these ledgers matched the rise of the first large-scale civilizations.

Why have ledgers been so important throughout history? Exchanges of goods and services have defined the expansion of societies, but this was possible only if people could keep track of the exchanges. It wasn't so difficult for everyone in a small village to remember that someone had killed a pig and to *trust*—a word we'll encounter throughout this book—that all who ate of it would find some way to later repay the hunter, perhaps with a new arrowhead or some other thing of value. It was another to manage these cross-societal obligations across a larger group of strangers—especially when moving outside of kinship boundaries made it harder to trust each other. Ledgers are record-keeping devices that help deal with those problems of complexity and trust. They help us keep track of all the multiple exchanges upon which society is built. Without them, the giant, teeming cities of twenty-first-century society would *not exist*. That said, ledgers are not truth itself—not in an absolute sense—for when it comes to matters of value, an element of judgment and estimation is always present in the recording process. Rather, they are tools for getting closer to the truth, to an approximation of it that's acceptable to all. Problems arise when communities view them with absolute faith, especially when the ledger is under control of self-interested actors who can manipulate them. This is what happened in 2008 when insufficient scrutiny of Lehman Brothers' and others' actions left society exposed and contributed to the financial crisis.

Money itself is intrinsically linked to the idea of a ledger. Physical currency like gold coins and paper money are, similarly, record-keeping devices; they too aid with societal memory. It's just that rather than existing within a written account of transactions, a currency's record-keeping function is abstracted into the token—the gold coin, the dollar bill. That token is communally recognized as conveying some right to goods or services that the bearer has earned from tasks performed in the past.

Once human beings started to engage in exchanges of money across distances, tokens' capacity to play this record-keeping function broke down. There was no way for the payer to physically deliver the tokens to the payee without having to trust a courier who might well steal it. The solution came with the advent of a new form of ledger-keeping known as double-entry bookkeeping, an approach that was pioneered, as we'll discuss lower down, by a clique of Renaissance bankers. In adopting this bookkeeping, they thrust banking into the payments business and, for centuries, helped to greatly expand the capacity for human exchange. It's not an overstatement to say that this idea of banking built the modern world. But it also amplified a problem that had always dogged ledgers: can society trust the record-keeper?

Bitcoin tackled this problem by reimagining the ledger itself. It confronted the problem that bankers themselves are not necessarily to be trusted and might rip you off with hidden fees and opaque charges. Bitcoin did this by, for the first time, entrusting responsibility for confirming and maintaining the ledger of transactions to a community of users who checked each other's work and agreed on a common record to represent their shared approximation of the truth. A decentralized network of computers, one that no single entity controlled, would thus supplant the banks and other centralized ledger-keepers that Nakamoto identified as "trusted third parties." The ledger they collectively produced would become known as the blockchain.

With Bitcoin's network of independent computers verifying every-thing collectively, transactions could now be instituted peer to peer, that is, from person to person. That's a big change from our convoluted credit and debit card payments system, for example, which routes transactions through a long sequence of intermediaries—at least two banks, one or two payment processors, a card network manager (such as Visa or Mastercard), and a variety of other institutions, depending on where the transaction takes place. Each entity in that system maintains its own separate ledger, which it later must reconcile with every other entity's independent records, a process that takes time, incurs costs, and carries risks. Whereas you might think that money is being instantly transferred when you swipe your card at a clothing store, in reality the whole process takes several days for the funds to make all those hops and finally settle in the storeowner's account, a delay that creates risks and costs. With Bitcoin, the idea is that your transaction should take only ten to sixty minutes to fully clear (notwithstanding some current capacity bottle-necks that Bitcoin developers are working to resolve). You don't have to rely on all those separate, trusted third parties to process it on your behalf.

The key architectural feature of Bitcoin and other cryptocurrency systems that lets these peer-to-peer transactions happen is the *distrib-uted* nature of the blockchain ledger. That decentralized structure is made possible because of a unique software program that uses strong cryptography and a groundbreaking incentive system to guide the ledger-keepers' computers to reach consensus. It does so in a way that makes it virtually impossible for anyone to change the historical record once it has been accepted.

The result is something remarkable: a record-keeping method that brings us to a commonly accepted version of the truth that's more reli-able than any truth we've ever seen. We're calling the blockchain a Truth Machine, and its applications go far beyond just money.

To see how the blockchain's "God's-eye" view could be valuable, let's turn the lens away from Bitcoin for now and onto the traditional banking system. It's there that we can see the problems blockchains are supposed to solve.

The Trust Bubble

On January 29, 2008, the Wall Street firm Lehman Brothers reported its financial statement for the fiscal year of 2007. It had been a good year for Lehman, despite some rumblings in the stock market and a downturn in the housing market, which had been red-hot for years and a major source of revenue for investment and commercial banks. The firm, founded 167 years earlier in Alabama and one of the bedrock institutions of Wall Street, posted record revenue for 2007, $59 billion, and record earnings, $4.2 billion. The amount was more than twice what the company had brought in and earned just four years earlier. Lehman's "books" had never looked better.

Nine months later, Lehman Brothers was out of business.

Lehman Brothers is often Exhibit A in the breakdown of trust in the twenty-first century. A lion of Wall Street, the firm was revealed to be little more than a debt-ravaged shell kept alive only by shady accounting—in other words, the bank was manipulating its ledgers. Sometimes, that manipulation involved moving debt off the books come reporting season. Other times, it involved assigning arbitrarily high values to "hard-to-value" assets—when the great selloff came, the shocking reality hit home: the assets had no value.

The crash of 2008 revealed most of what we know about Wall Street's confidence game at that time. It entailed a vast manipulation of ledgers. The recorded value of the assets those ledgers were supposed to track—including those havoc-causing credit default swaps—turned out to be largely vapor. The shock of Lehman wasn't so much that it happened, but that even most experts trusted the ledgers so completely until it was too late.

Governments and central banks around the world spent trillions to clean up the mess, but all they really did was restore the old order, because they misdiagnosed the problem. The accepted wisdom was that this was a crisis of liquidity, in which the market broke down due to a lack of short-term funding. If you've ever been short a couple of hundred to cover your monthly bills, you understand what this looks like. The reality is, banks were sitting on trillions of purportedly valuable assets they could not even remotely value in the real world. They'd simply assigned poorly substantiated values and put them on their books. We all believed them because we trusted them. We trusted what the ledgers told us. The real problem was never really about liquidity, or a break-down of the market. It was a failure of trust. When that trust was broken, the impact on society—including on our divided political culture—was devastating.

The authorities swore in the wake of the crisis that they had a handle on the problem—they passed legislation to bring the banking sector to heel and rein in Wall Street's worst speculative habits. But to many in the public, it seemed they'd done little more than save the banks and corporations. Anger festered and turned into the Tea Party and Occupy Wall Street. Through all of the years since, the general public's trust has never been restored. Look no further than the election of a reality-show TV star to the U.S. presidency. It may have felt good to cast that protest vote for Donald Trump and stick it to the elites, but it seems pretty clear—to us at least—that all Trump was offering was the same old warmed-over economic ideas with a dash of hot sauce. We are no better off now than we were in 2008.

By various measures, the U.S. economy has recovered—at the time of writing, unemployment was near record lows and the Dow Jones Industrial Average was at record highs. But those gains are not evenly distributed; wage growth at the top is six times what it is for those in the middle, and even more compared to those at the bottom. That's a dynamic that's been building for decades, but it was made worse by the financial crisis, as well as the policies imposed since then to prop up the financial markets in which the rich hold their assets. It's one reason people both within and outside the United States believe they've been shortchanged by the institutions that had throughout the twentieth century delivered progress and prosperity. This is clear in Pew Research's ongoing longitudinal study of trust in government in the United States, which puts trust near historic lows (about 20 percent in May 2017). A separate survey by Gallop showed that only 12 percent of U.S. citizens trusted Congress in 2017, down from 40 percent in 1979; that about 27 percent trusted what they heard from newspapers, compared with 51 percent thirty-eight years earlier; and that 21 percent trusted big business, down from 32 percent.

At the time of writing, even traditional Republicans are wondering (1) how on earth Donald Trump was ever elected president, and (2) why so many people seem to fall prey to blatant disinformation and conspiracy theories. Trump's manifestly a liar, someone who lies even when evidence disproving the lie is readily available. But here's the bigger problem: in a world where trust has eroded sharply, where our government doesn't work, and where companies that once guaranteed jobs for life are now either outsourcing them or hiring robots, Trump's lies can seem minor in comparison to the more systemic breach of trust voters are feeling. Once-trusted news organizations are now thrust into competition with dubious online purveyors of disinformation, with both being accused of peddling "fake news." The public's store of trust in institutions is being depleted, and without resolving that breakdown, our democracy will continue to deteriorate at the hands of politicians and media that tell them what they want to hear.

Trust—particularly trust in our institutions—is a vital *social resource*, the true lubricant of all human interaction. When it works, we take it for granted—we wait our place in line, follow road rules, and assume everyone else will do the same. The trust behind these interactions is not present in our conscious minds. But when trust is lacking, things really, really break down. Today, it's seen most starkly in places like Venezuela, where people have lost faith in the stewardship of their government and its money, leading to hyperinflation, goods shortages, starvation, violence, rioting, and massive social upheaval. But it's evident in more subtle ways across the Western world. As government officials and central bankers seek to boost investment and create jobs, printing more money or bestowing more favor on connected players as they go, citizens everywhere are calling foul on the whole enterprise. It brought the United States Donald Trump and the United Kingdom Brexit. But it also created economic dysfunction. If people don't trust our economic systems, they don't take risks; they don't spend. The loser is economic growth and development.

This trust problem is intrinsically connected with ledgers and record-keeping. To comprehend that, we'll explore the little-known story of a Franciscan friar with a love of math who developed a system that fueled Europe's explosion out of the Dark Ages more directly than the Medici bankers who financed that growth. From there, we can draw a line all the way forward to Lehman Brothers and show how a better ac-counting system, such as blockchain, could be the answer to society's deep funk.

Truth, Trust, and "the Books"

How is it possible that a business could earn $4.2 billion one year and be out of business the next? The reason is not just because Lehman Brothers was manipulating its ledgers but because it was taking advantage of the trust invested in it by shareholders, regulators, and the public at large. On the accounting side, Lehman resorted to myriad tricks to bolster its books, those all-important financial documents that investors and other stakeholders depend upon to ascertain the risk of dealing with an institution. Lehman's accountants would move billions of dollars' worth of debts off the bank's balance sheet at the end of a quarter and stash them in a temporary accounting facility called a repo transaction, a device that's supposed to be used to raise short-term capital, not hide debt. When it came time to report, the company didn't appear to be overly indebted. Once the report was in, the company brought the debt back on the books. Really, it was as if the company was maintaining two sets of books—one it showed the public, one it kept private. Most people accepted what was reported in the public-facing books, Leh-man's version of "the truth." Just how severely skewed Lehman's books were would become clear in September 2008. But the problem really started with the public's trust, in the blind faith given to the com-pany's numbers. And that problem—quite literally one of *faith*—goes way, way back.

Double-entry accounting was popularized in Europe toward the end of the fifteenth century, and most scholars believe it set the table for the flowering of the Renaissance and the emergence of modern capitalism. What is far less well understood is the *why*. Why was something as dull as bookkeeping so integral to a complete cultural revolution in Europe?

Over nearly seven centuries, "the books" have become something that, in our collective minds, we equate with truth itself—even if only subconsciously. When we doubt a candidate's claims of wealth, we want to go to his bank records—his personal balance sheet. When a company wants to tap the public markets for capital, they have to open their books to prospective investors. To remain in the market, they need accountants to verify those books regularly. Well-maintained and clear accounting is sacrosanct.

The ascendance of bookkeeping to a level equal to truth itself happened over many centuries, and began with the outright hostility European Christendom had to lending before double-entry booking came along. The ancients were pretty comfortable with debt. The Babylonians set the tone in the famous Code of Hammurabi, which offered rules for handling loans, debts, and repayments. The Judeo-Christian tradition, though, had a real ax to grind against the business of lending. "Thou shalt not lend upon usury to thy brother," Deuteronomy 23:19–20 declares. "In thee have they taken gifts to shed blood; thou hast taken usury and increase, and thou hast greedily gained of thy neighbors by extortion, and hast forgotten me, saith the Lord God," Ezekiel 22:12 states. As Christianity flourished, this deep anti-usury culture continued for more than a thousand years, a stance that coincided with the Dark Ages, when Europe, having lost the glories of ancient Greece and Rome, also lost nearly all comprehension of math. The only people who really needed the science of numbers were monks trying to figure out the correct dates for Easter.

It was only during the twelfth century and the Crusades, when Europeans began trading with the East, that they encountered the mathematics that had developed in the Arab world and Asia. In the thirteenth century, an Italian merchant named Fibonacci made trips to Egypt, Syria, Greece, and Sicily, where he collected numerous mathematical papers. His *Liber Abaci*, a book filled with integers and fractions, square roots and algebra, showed how this new math had commercial applications, such as currency transfers and profit calculations. Before Fibonacci, European merchants simply couldn't calculate the things we take for granted today; he taught them how to measure proportions, how to divide, say, a bale of hay and charge accurate prices. He taught them how to divide profits in an enterprise. Fibonacci's math gave them precision in business matters that people did not previously have.

Fibonacci's new numbering system became a hit with the merchant class and for centuries was the preeminent source for mathematical knowledge in Europe. But something equally important also happened around this time: Europeans learned of double-entry bookkeeping, picking it up from the Arabians, who'd been using it since the seventh century. Merchants in Florence and other Italian cities began applying these new accounting measures to their daily businesses. Where Fibonacci gave them new measurement methods for business, double-entry accounting gave them a way to record it all. Then came a seminal moment: in 1494, two years after Christopher Columbus first set foot in the Americas, a Franciscan friar named Luca Pacioli wrote the first comprehensive manual for using this accounting system.

Pacioli's *Summa de arthmetica, geometria, proportioni et proportionalita*, written in Italian rather than Latin so as to be more accessible to the public, would become the first popular work on math and accounting. Its section on accounting was so well received that the publisher eventually published it as its own volume. Pacioli offered access to the precision of mathematics. "Without double entry, businessmen would not sleep easily at night," Pacioli wrote, mixing in the practical with the technical—Pacioli's *Summa* would become a kind of self-help book for the merchant class.

That a member of the clergy took an interest in double-entry bookkeeping was important, because Pacioli's method helped the merchants overcome the church's disdain for usury. The merchants had to prove to the church that their businesses were not, in fact, sinful, that they provided a benefit to mankind. During the Middle Ages, writes author James Aho, "the very thought that a person might be profit-hungry and yet Christian was an outrage." Double-entry accounting, completely unintentionally, provided a way around this. How? The answer lies in the Book of Revelations, Christianity's tale of a final reckoning, where it is said:

> And I saw the dead, small and great, stand before God; and the books were opened; and another book was opened, which is the book of life; and the dead were judged out of those things which were written in the books, according to their works.

Interpretation: The dead stand before God and open their book. Then *God* opens *his* book. The second book. You might call this, oh, *double bookkeeping.* "Whosoever was not found written in the book of life was cast into the lake of fire." Through a simple method of accounting, the merchant class was able to perform a trick that had eluded them for a millennium: making it acceptable to engage in the business of making loans. Double-entry bookkeeping, Aho writes, "was itself complicit in the invention of a new 'field of visibility': the Christian merchant."

This deliberate connection between biblical records and accounting records is evident in Pacioli's writings. His very first instruction in describing his double-entry method directed: "Businessmen should begin their business records with the date AD, marking every transaction so that they always remember to be ethical and, at work, always act mindful of His Holy name."

Once usury was liberated from the Christian distrust of commerce, people began to take it up. The Medici of Florence came first, turning themselves into vital middlemen in the matching of money flows around Europe. The Medici's breakthrough was made possible because of their consistent use of double-entry ledgers. If a merchant in Rome wanted to sell something to a customer in Venice, these new ledgers solved the problem of trust between people who lived at great distances from each other. By debiting the payer's bank account and crediting that of the payee—with double-entry practices—the bankers were able to, in effect, move money without having to ship physical coins. In so doing, they transformed the whole enterprise of payments, setting the stage for the Renaissance and for modern capitalism itself. Just as important, they also established the 500-year practice of bankers creating an essential role for themselves as society's centralized trust bearers.

The value of double-entry bookkeeping, therefore, wasn't merely in dry efficiency. The ledger came to be viewed as a kind of moral compass, whose use conferred moral rectitude on all involved with it. The merchant was pious, the banker had sanctity—three popes in the sixteenth and seventeenth centuries came from the Medici family—and the trader discharged his business with veneration. Businessmen, previously mistrusted, became moral, upstanding pillars of the community. Aho writes: "Methodist Church founder John Wesley, Daniel DeFoe, Samuel Pepys, Baptist evangelicals, the deist Benjamin Franklin, the Shakers, Harmony Society, and more recently, the Iona Community in Britain, all insist that the keeping of meticulous financial accounts is part and parcel of a more general program of honesty, orderliness, and industriousness."

Thanks to mathematical concepts imported from the Middle East during the Crusades, accounting became the moral grounding for the rise of modern capitalism, and the bean counters of capitalism became the priests of a new religion. Most (though certainly not all) people today have a hard time seeing the Bible as literal truth; but they had no trouble seeing Lehman Brothers' books as literal truth—until the gaping inconsistencies were exposed.

The great irony of 2008 was that our belief in a system of accounting, a belief woven so deeply inside our collective psyche that we're not even aware of it, made us vulnerable to fraud. Even when done honestly, accounting is sometimes little more than an educated guess. Modern accounting, especially at the big, international banks, has become so convoluted that it is virtually useless. In a comprehensive dissection in

2014, the Bloomberg columnist Matt Levine explained how a bank's balance sheet is almost impossibly opaque. The "value" of a large portion of the assets on that balance sheet, he noted, is simply based on guesses made by the bank about the collectability of the loans they make, or of the bonds they hold, and the prices that they might fetch on the market, all measured against the offsetting and equally fuzzy valuation of their liabilities and obligations. If a guess is off by even 1 percent, it can turn a quarterly profit into a loss. Guessing whether a bank is actually profitable is like a pop quiz. "I submit to you that there is no answer to the quiz," he wrote. "It is not possible for a human to know whether Bank of America made money or lost money last quarter." A bank's balance sheet, he said, is essentially a series of "reasonable guesses about valuation." Make the wrong guesses, as Lehman and other troubled banks did, and you end up out of business.

Our goal here is not to trash double-entry bookkeeping or the banks. Were we to, you know, add up all the debits and credits, double-entry bookkeeping has done more good than harm. The goal really is to show the deep historical and cultural roots behind *why* we trusted this kind of accounting. The question now, in the wake of our fall, is whether a particular technology that allows a different kind of bookkeeping will help us renew our trust in our economic system. Can a blockchain, which is continuously open to public inspection and guaranteed not by a single bank but by a series of mathematically secured entries into a ledger that's shared and maintained by many different computers, help us rebuild our lost social capital?

The God Protocol

On October 31, 2008, while the world was drowning in the financial crisis, a little-noticed "white paper" was released by somebody using the pen name "Satoshi Nakamoto," and describing something called "Bitcoin," an electronic version of cash that didn't need state backing. At the heart of Nakamoto's electronic cash was a public ledger that could be viewed by anybody but was virtually impossible to alter. This ledger was essentially a digitized, objective rendering of the truth, and in the years to follow it would come to be called the blockchain.

Nakamoto combined several elements to come up with his Bitcoin. But like Fibonacci and Pacioli centuries before, he wasn't the only one working on the idea of leveraging the technology of the day to create better systems. In 2005, a computer expert named Ian Grigg, working at a company called Systemics, introduced a trial system he called "triple-entry bookkeeping." Grigg worked in the field of cryptography, a science that dates way back to ancient times, when coded language to share "ciphers," or secrets, first arose. Ever since Alan Turing's calculating machine cracked the German military's Enigma code, cryptography has underpinned much of what we've done in the computing age. Without it we wouldn't be able to share private information across the Internet—such as our transactions within a bank's Web site—without revealing it to unwanted prying eyes. As our computing capacity has exponentially grown, so too has the capacity of cryptography to impact our lives. For his part, Grigg believed it would lead to a programmable record-keeping system that would make fraud virtually impossible. In a nutshell, the concept took the existing, double-entry bookkeeping system and added a third book: the independent, open ledger that's secured by cryptographic methods so that no one can change it. Grigg saw it as a way to combat fraud.

The way Grigg described it, users would maintain their own, double-entry accounts, but added to these digitized books would be another function, essentially a time stamp, a cryptographically secured, signed receipt of every transaction. (The concept of a "signature" in cryptography means something far more scientific than a handwritten scrawl; it entails combining two associated numbers, or "keys"—one publicly known, the other private—to mathematically prove that the entity making the signature is uniquely authorized to do so.) Grigg envisioned his triple-entry accounting as a software program that would run within, say, a large company or organization. But the third ledger, containing the sequence of all those signed receipts, could be verified publicly, and in real time. Any deviation from its time-stamped records would be an indication of a fraud. Picture a fraud like Bernie Madoff's, in which Madoff was simply making up transactions and recording them in completely fictitious books, and you can see the value in a system that can verify accounts in real time.

Before Grigg, in the 1990s, another visionary had also seen the potential power of a digital ledger. Nick Szabo was an early Cypherpunk* and developed some of the concepts that underlie Bitcoin, which is one reason why some suspect he is Satoshi Nakamoto. His protocol has at its heart a spreadsheet that runs on a "virtual machine"—such as a network of interlinked computers—accessible to multiple parties. Szabo envisioned an intricate system of both private and public data that would protect private identities but provide enough public information about transactions to build up a verifiable transaction history. Szabo's system—he called it the "God Protocol"—is now more than two decades old. Yet it is remarkably similar to the blockchain platforms and protocols that we'll learn about in the chapters to come. Szabo, Grigg, and others pioneered an approach with the potential to create a record of history that cannot be changed—a record that someone like Madoff, or Lehman's bankers, could not have meddled with. Their approach might just help restore trust in the systems we use to transact with each other.

Big Math, Openness, and a New Tool for Agreeing on Facts

If communities are to engage in exchange and forge functioning societies, they must find a way to arrive at a commonly accepted foundation of truth. And in the digital age of the twenty-first century, when many

---

* For background on the Cypherpunk movement from the San Francisco Bay Area and the role it played in the development of cryptocurrencies, see our previous book, *The Age of Cryptocurrency*.

communities are formed online, where they transcend borders and legal jurisdictions, the old institutions we've used to establish those norms of truth won't function nearly as well.

Advocates of blockchain solutions say this truth-discovery process is best left to a distributed approach, one over which no single entity has control. That way the approach is not vulnerable to corruption, attack, error, or disaster.

Also, the results should be collated using the hard-to-crack math of cryptography, which prevents them from ever being overwritten in the future. Here's how cryptography can achieve what it does: it uses data-protecting codes drawn from a set of possible numbers so large that it's far, far beyond human imagination. The sheer quantity of possibilities makes it impossibly time-consuming to discover the hidden code through "brute force" guesswork—in other words, by testing and discarding each possible number. Consider that Bitcoin is now the most powerful computing network in the world, one whose combined "hashing" rate as of August 2017 enabled all its computers to collectively pore through 7 million trillion different number guesses per second. Well, it would still take that network around 4,500 trillion trillion trillion years to work through all the possible numbers that could be generated by the SHA-256 hashing algorithm that protects Bitcoin's data. Let the record show that period of time is 36,264 trillion trillion times longer than the current best-estimate age of the universe. Bitcoin's cryptography is pretty secure.*

Yet this system of honest accounting still needs something more than cryptography to work. It needs to open up its sequenced record of

---

* A noteworthy caveat is that, if and when scientists create a truly functioning quantum computer, this level of cryptography could indeed be crackable. But that idea is not only a long way off; if it were to arrive, it would render *all* cybersecurity systems, not just Bitcoin's, unworkable. Nonetheless, cryptocurrency designers are already working on quantum-proof systems that, in theory, will resist quantum attacks.

traceable, interlinked transactions to public scrutiny. This means that (1) the ledger should be public, and (2) the algorithm that runs it should adhere to open-source principles, with its source code on view for all to see and test.

At the same time, however, the system must allow sufficient privacy capabilities and protections for individuals and their data, as people won't use it if their personal identities and proprietary business secrets are open for the world to see. Bitcoin deals with this by displaying only the one-off alphanumeric "addresses" that are randomly assigned to users when they receive bitcoin and which tell you nothing about the identity of the people who control them. But it's not an entirely anonymous system—it's better described as "pseudonymous." In Bitcoin it's possible, by following transaction flows from one address to another, to trace the fund exchanges to an address where users can be identified—such as when they cash out into dollars at a regulated bitcoin exchange that keeps records of its customers' names, addresses, and other details. For certain cryptographers who take privacy very seriously, that's not good enough. So a few are developing alternative cryptocurrencies—examples include Zcash, Monero, and Dash—that add even more privacy protection than Bitcoin. These other cryptocurrencies keep enough information on the ledger so that validating computers can be assured that the accounts have not been corrupted or manipulated, but do a more complete job of obscuring identities.

Whether the solution requires these extreme privacy measures or not, the broad model of a new ledger system that we laid out above—distributed, cryptographically secure, public yet private—may be just what's needed to restore people's confidence in society's record-keeping systems. And to encourage people to re-engage in economic exchange and risk-taking.

For society to function, we need a "consensus on facts," says Tomicah Tillemen, a director at the New America Foundation in Washington and chairman of the Global Blockchain Business Council. "We need to establish a common reality that everyone can bind to. And the way we've done that in developed countries is we have institutions that are in charge of establishing those basic facts. Those institutions are under fire right now. . . . Blockchain has the potential to push back against that erosion and it has the potential to create a new dynamic in which everyone can come to agree on a core set of facts but also ensure the privacy of facts that should not be in the public domain."

Bitcoin showed how this idea works in one especially important context: money. By giving currency users a means of agreeing on the "facts" of their transactions, it allowed complete strangers to use an independent currency to pay each other securely over the Internet and still have a high level of confidence that counterfeiting was impossible, even in the absence of a centralized ledger-keeper like the Federal Reserve.

The more powerful revelation, however, was that a group of people could reach a consensus on facts without a central entity arbitrating the process. If we think about this as the Israeli historian Yuval Noah Harari would, in terms of how the power of human social organization comes from our ability to craft meaningful stories that we all believe in—notions of religion, nationality, common currency—we can see how important this is. The history of human civilization is not founded on absolute truths per se—after all, even scientific understandings are subject to revision—but on an even more powerful notion of the truth: a consensus, a common understanding on what we take to be the truth, a society-wide agreement that allows us to overcome suspicions, forge trust, and enter into cooperative endeavors. The best way to think about blockchain technology, then, is not as a replacement of trust—as a "trustless" solution, as some cryptocurrency fanatics damagingly describe it—but as a tool upon which society can create the common stories it needs to sow even greater trust, to build social capital, and to forge a better world.

This empowering idea helps explain the growing enthusiasm—sometimes excessive or misplaced—for blockchains as a solution to, well, just about anything. As people across a diverse range of fields start exploring its potential to disintermediate their industries and create new ways to unlock value, they are seeing in blockchain technology the potential for more than just a cash machine. If it can foster consensus in the way it has been shown to with Bitcoin, it's best understood as a Truth Machine.

Two

"GOVERNING" THE DIGITAL ECONOMY

One evening in September 2011, an entrepreneur named Peter Sims received a text message from a friend, Julia Allison, wondering if he happened to be in an Uber SUV near 33rd Street and Fifth Avenue in New York. It happened that this was exactly where he was, and Sims assumed the friend must have seen him from another car.

In fact, Allison wasn't even in the same state. She was at a party in Chicago, celebrating the launch of Uber in the Windy City. She'd watched as the Uber team performed one of its favorite party tricks: showing people what it called its "God's view," a live map revealing the locations of its cars and their passengers, by name. Uber was not only tracking its cars' movements, it was tracking people's movements. When Allison explained how she knew so much about his whereabouts, Sims flipped out and wrote a biting blog post about the experience.

Uber has become notorious for sexual harassment among its staff and has taken drastic action to try to resolve the problem, which was a significant factor in the forced resignation of its co-founder, CEO Travis Kalanick. But this privacy issue is just as important. Not only does the company control sensitive information about the journeys people take, but senior company officials, at least in the early days of the company, showed a willingness to abuse that power. In November 2014, Uber launched an investigation into the actions of its New York general manager, Josh Mohrer, after BuzzFeed journalist Johana Bhuiyan reported that he had used the God's view feature to monitor her movements. The outcry over this and other privacy concerns led to a settlement with New York Attorney General Eric Schneiderman in which Uber agreed to encrypt riders' names and geolocation data.

It's certainly not hard to see that Uber and its main competitor, Lyft, have quickly enmeshed themselves in our daily lives. When the name of your company becomes a verb—Xerox, Google, Uber—you know you've arrived. But for all the branding associated with democratizing transportation, and with allowing drivers and passengers to come together and "ride-share," Uber is really a centralization play. It's not about disintermediation at all. This for-profit company is the gatekeeper for every deal that gets struck between every driver and every passenger, and for that it takes 25 percent each time. And it is far from the only for-profit company that makes money the new-fashioned way: by controlling data. How Uber, and also Facebook, Google, and all the other twenty-first-century tech titans, treat that data has become a critical issue.

The Internet, in case you weren't aware, is *owned*. There are a handful of dominant companies that essentially control everything: Google, Amazon, Facebook, Apple (GAFA, some call them). We trust them to intermediate our e-mail and social media exchanges with each other, to manage our Internet searches, to store our data, etc. To varying degrees they do what seems to be a good job, but there is a huge cost in terms of the power we hand to these organizations. We, the general public, their unpaid product developers, literally create value for these companies, creating content and handing over our valuable data. We get services in return, yes, but the imbalance in the relationship is highly problematic. That's most evident in our system of democracy.

As became widely known after America's 2016 elections, Facebook and Google control what news you see. Consider how Facebook's secret algorithm chooses the news to suit your ideological bent, creating echo chambers of like-minded angry or delighted readers who are ripe to consume and share dubious information that confirms their pre-existing political biases. It's why during the 2016 U.S. presidential campaign, a group of teens in Macedonia could produce fake news articles, which made claims like that the pope had endorsed Donald Trump, which generated more likes, shares, and advertising dollars than real news items produced by fully funded and researched news outlets.

And it's not just that, for example, Facebook and Google have become such large social hubs. It's that these digital leviathans have unprecedented control over much of the most important socially influential data that flies across the Web. The "freemium" model, in which we view these companies' services as "free content," is a myth. While we might not be paying U.S. dollars to Google, Facebook, and co., we are handing over a much more valuable currency: our personal data. Control over that currency has turned these players, quite simply, into monopolies, the new incumbent powers of the digital age. Others have said this, of course. We revisit it to illustrate how this concentration of control over Internet information exposes the core problem of the centralized architecture of the Web and the unresolved trust issue that gives rise to it.

A Hacker's Dream

In the wake of the 2016 legal battle between Apple and the FBI over the latter's demand that the smartphone maker give the law enforcement agency access to customers' encrypted data, consumers would seem to be between a rock and a hard place. If we want to live in the digital economy, it seems, either we let private companies control the data with all the capacity for abuse that entails or we let governments control those private companies and expose ourselves to the kind of intrusions that Edward Snowden revealed at the NSA. But the choice need not be so stark. We hope to demonstrate that the solution may lie in a third way, one that involves reimagining the very structure of how online data is organized.

The ideas behind Bitcoin and blockchain technology give us a new starting point from which to address this problem. That's because the question of who controls our data should stem first from a more fundamental question about who or what institutions we must *trust* in order to engage in commerce, obtain services, or participate in modern society. We see compelling arguments for a complete restructuring of the world's data security paradigm. And it starts with thinking about how Internet users can start to directly trust each other, so as to avoid having to pour so much information into the centralized hubs that currently sit in the middle of their online relationships. Solving data security may first require a deliberate move from what we call the *centralized trust model* to one of *decentralized trust*.

In an age when technology is supposed to be lowering the cost of entry, the outdated centralized trust-management system has proven expensive and restrictive (think about the 2 billion people in the world who are unbanked). It has also failed—spectacularly. Even though the world spent an estimated $75 billion on cybersecurity in 2015, according to estimates by Gartner, total annual losses from online fraud theft were running at $400 billion that year, said Inga Beale, CEO of British insurance market Lloyd's of London. If you're alarmed by that figure—and you ought to be—try this one on for size: $2.1 trillion. That's the estimated fraud loss Juniper Research came up with after extrapolating from current trends into the even more digitally interconnected world projected for 2019. To put that figure in perspective, at current economic growth rates, it would represent more than 2.5 percent of total world GDP. To be clear, these numbers don't only represent the total amount stolen by hackers; they also include the cost of legal actions, security upgrades, and so forth—the business losses that are generated by countless attacks every year. Even so, the data suggest that black-hat hackers are among the most financially successful innovators of the Internet era.

This colossal failure to protect global commerce is directly attributable to a mismatch between the centralized way in which we process and store information and the decentralizing tendencies of a global "sharing" economy that's pushing for more peer-to-peer and device-to-device commerce. As more people connect over peer-to-peer social networks and use online services, and as more so-called Internet of Things (IoT) devices such as smart thermostats and refrigerators and even cars join the network, ever more access points are created. Hackers use these points to find their way into the Internet's ever-growing *centralized* data-stores and steal or otherwise mess with their contents.

The risks contained in these contradictory trends were brought home with the October 2016 attack on Dyn, a registered DNS (domain name system) provider. The attack started when a hacker figured out that users of mini computing systems such as game consoles and laptops weren't routinely downloading security patches as they did with home computers. Once compromised, those devices could then be used as launchpads to direct attacks on other parts of the Internet. When the hacker published a how-to list of instructions, some rogue actors inevitably gave their approach a whirl. Taking control of multiple devices, these malefactors launched a massive distributed denial of service (DDOS) attack against Dyn, a strategy that involved sending a relentless barrage of domain name queries to the firm's hosting service, so many that it paralyzed the Web sites of its clients, including Twitter, Spotify, Reddit, and many other heavy-traffic sites. This was a direct outcome of the paradox we've been talking about. Domain name registrations are managed by increasingly large, centralized, third-party providers while lightweight IoT devices are getting into the hands of an ill-prepared general public. That combination is a hacker's dream.

And what a pool of data we are gathering for those hackers to play with. In 2014, IBM estimated that human beings were creating 2.5 exabytes, otherwise expressed as 2.5 quintillion bytes of data, every day, most of them now stored permanently thanks to a cloud computing era in which storage has become so cheap that it no longer makes sense to destroy data. Let's lay that number out numerically, with all seventeen zeroes: 2,500,000,000,000,000,000. (Another way of expressing it: the equivalent of 2.5 trillion PDF versions of *The Age of Cryptocurrency*.) According to the IBM team, this number meant that human beings had created 90 percent of all data accumulated throughout history in just two years—most of it stored on the servers of cloud service providers like the ones IBM runs.

The only way to protect this data and slow down the force of attacks against it, we will argue, is to take it away from centralized servers and create a more distributed storage structure. Control of data needs to be put back into the hands of those to whom it belongs, the customers and end users of the Internet's services. If hackers want our data they'll have to come after each and every one of us, a far more expensive exercise than simply finding a weak entry point into a giant silo database that holds all of our data in one convenient place. To achieve this goal, we need to embrace the decentralized trust model.

Before we delve more deeply into this solution, let's reflect further on why it matters for humanity. It's about much more than dollars and cents. There is an intrinsic link between the challenge of protecting privacy, a necessary element of a functioning society, and data security. When that protection breaks down, as it does repeatedly, lives can be destroyed: people's money and assets are stolen, their identities and reputations are hijacked, they face extortion and blackmail, and they find that the intimate moments they've shared with others are thrust into the public domain. Online identity theft has been linked to depression and even suicide. And if this isn't bad enough, experts are convinced we'll soon experience cyber-murders, as Internet-enabled cars and other potentially lethal devices become targets of hacker hitmen. Murders may have already been committed; speculation that the mysterious disappearance of Malaysian Airlines flight MH370 was the result of a hacking attack on the plane's onboard computer is no longer the stuff of conspiracy theorists. We must get ahead of this problem.

Individuals aren't the only losers in this model. Companies and institutions lose out as well. The list of recent big cyber-attack targets includes some of the biggest names in the S&P 500—J.P. Morgan, Home Depot, Target, Sony, Wendy's. All paid a high cost in legal fees, restitution to their users, and investment in upgraded security systems. And it's not just corporate America. Governments, too, have been hit. Recall that security clearance data on 18 million people was compromised when the U.S. Office of Personnel Management was hacked in 2015. And, of course, the alleged Russian hacks of the Democratic National Committee in 2016 have unleashed an all-out political crisis during the Trump administration's first year.

These constant attacks are expensive, ongoing headaches for the IT departments at companies and other institutions. Every new trick deployed by a rogue hacker prompts a new patch to a security system, which attackers inevitably figure out how to compromise. That prompts even more expensive investment in cybersecurity systems that will themselves, inevitably, get breached or require further upgrades. The companies keep spending more dollars to build ever-higher firewalls, only to learn their adversaries are constantly getting ahold of taller ladders.

Clearly, we need a new architecture for security. And the ideas contained within blockchain technology might help us get there. Within the distributed structure of a blockchain environment, participants do not depend on centralized institutions to maintain cybersecurity infrastructure such as firewalls to protect large groups of users. Instead, security is a shared responsibility. Individuals, not trusted intermediaries, are responsible for maintaining their own, most sensitive information, while any information that *is* shared is subject to a process of communal consensus to assure its veracity.

The potential power of this concept starts with the example of Bitcoin. Even though that particular blockchain may not provide the ultimate solution in this use case, it's worth recalling that without any of the classic, centrally deployed cybersecurity tools such as firewalls, and with a tempting "bounty" of more than $160 billion in market cap value at the time we went to print, Bitcoin's core ledger has thus far proven to be unhackable. Based on the ledger's own standards for integrity, Bitcoin's nine-year experience of survival provides pretty solid proof of the resiliency of its core mechanism for providing decentralized trust between users. It suggests that one of the most important non-currency applications of Bitcoin's blockchain could be security itself.

Security by Design

One reason why Bitcoin has survived is because it leaves hackers nothing to hack. The public ledger contains no identifying information about the system's users. Even more important, no one owns or controls that ledger. There is no single master version; with every batch of confirmed transactions, the so-called blocks of the blockchain, a new, updated version of the entire ledger is created and relayed to every node. As such, there is no central vector of attack. If one node on the network is compromised and someone tries to undo or rewrite transactions in that node's local version of the ledger, the nodes controlling the hundreds of other accepted versions will simply refuse to include data from the compromised node in the updates. The contradiction between the many clean versions and the one that's been altered will automatically label the compromised block as false. As we'll discuss further in the book, there are varying degrees of security in different blockchain designs, including those known as "private" or "permissioned" blockchains, which rely on central authorities to approve participants. In contrast, Bitcoin is based on a decentralized model that eschews approvals and instead banks on the participants caring enough about their money in the system to protect it. Still, across all examples, the basic, shared, and replicated nature of all blockchain ledgers, in which the common record of truth resides in multiple locations, underpins this core idea of distributed security, that the risk of failure is backstopped by multiple "redundancies."

This is not how big companies tend to think about security, however. In March 2016, at a symposium organized by the financial securities settlement and clearing agency Depository Trust & Clearing Corp., or DTCC, the audience, filled with bankers and representatives of companies that support them, was asked to vote on what IT sector they would invest in tomorrow if they had $10 million to deploy. From a menu of options, the votes came back, with the majority in favor of investing in "cybersecurity" services, and "blockchain" opportunities second. On stage at the time, Adam Ludwin, the CEO of blockchain/distributed ledger services company Chain Inc., took advantage of the result to call out Wall Street firms for failing to see how this technology offers a different paradigm. Ludwin, whose clients include household names like Visa and Nasdaq, said he could understand why people saw a continued market for cybersecurity services, since his audience was full of people paid to worry about data breaches constantly. But their answers suggested they didn't understand that the blockchain offered a solution. Unlike other system-design software, for which cybersecurity is an add-on, this technology "incorporates security by design," he said.

For the private "permissioned" blockchains that Wall Street is typically exploring—distributed ledger models in which all the validating computers must be pre-authorized to join the network—Ludwin's "by design" notion refers solely to the fact that the data is distributed among many nodes rather than held solely by one. The advantage is that this structure creates multiple redundancies, or backups, that can keep the network running if one node is compromised. A more radical solution is to embrace open, "permissionless" blockchains like Bitcoin and Ethereum, where there's no central authority keeping track of who's using the network. And in that case, the entire security paradigm—the question of what constitutes "security"—changes. It's not about building a firewall up around a centralized pool of valuable data controlled by a trusted third party; rather the focus is on pushing control over information out to the edges of the network, to the people themselves, and on limiting the amount of identifying information that's communicated publicly. Importantly, it's also about making it prohibitively expensive for someone to try to steal valuable information.

It's perhaps counterintuitive to think that a system in which people don't reveal their identities could be safe from attackers. But the fact is that the incentive and costs that these software programs impose on actors in the system have proven remarkably secure. Bitcoin's core ledger has never been successfully attacked. Now, it will undoubtedly be a major challenge to get the institutions that until now have been entrusted with securing our data systems to let go and defer security to some decentralized network in which there is no identifiable authority to sue if something goes wrong. But doing so might just be the most important step they can take to improve data security. It will require them to think about security not as a function of superior encryption and other external protections, but in terms of economics, of making attacks so expensive that they're not worth the effort.

Let's compare our current "shared-secret model" for protecting information with the new "device identity model" that Bitcoin's blockchain could facilitate. Currently, a service provider and a customer agree on a secret password and perhaps certain mnemonics—"Your pet's name?"—to manage access. But that still leaves all the vital data, potentially worth billions of dollars, sitting in a hackable repository on the company's servers. With a permissionless blockchain, control over the data stays with the customer, which means that the point of vulnerability lies with their device. So instead of Visa's servers containing the vital identifying information that's needed for hundreds of millions of cardholders to access its payments network, the right to access a network is managed solely by you, on your phone, your computer. A hacker could go after each device, try to steal the private key that's used to initiate transactions on the decentralized network, and, if they're lucky, get away with a few thousand dollars in bitcoin. But it's far less lucrative and far more time-consuming than going after the rich target of a central server.

The weak link—there is always one, it is a truism of cybersecurity—would now be the device itself. The onus in a blockchain system is on the customer to protect that device. Admittedly, that opens up new challenges in terms of education around the management of private keys and encryption strategies. Optimizing the cryptocurrency future will require people to take charge of their own security.

But even with this new challenge in terms of device protection, we should see a dramatic reduction in the number of attacks. The crucial point here is that the potential payoff for the hacker is so much smaller for each attack. Rather than accessing millions of accounts at once, he or she has to pick off each device one by one for comparatively tiny amounts. It's an incentives-weighted concept of security. It is security by design, not by patch.

It seems clear to us that the digital economy would benefit greatly from embracing the distributed trust architecture allowed by blockchains—whether it's simply the data backups that a distributed system offers, or the more radical idea of an open system that's protected by a high cost-to-payout ratio. Once we put our heads in that place, liberating new models for managing data emerge, models that restore control to the individuals who produce the data and then give the data itself significantly more protection.

One industry that would no doubt rejoice at such a solution would be the health care industry. Right now, highly sensitive health records are spread across separate siloed databases managed by insurance firms, hospitals, and laboratories, each sitting on their own pools of vulnerable data. These institutions are bound by strict non-disclosure rules laid out in well-intentioned but highly restrictive patient privacy legislation such as the Health Insurance Portability and Accountability Act, which imposes high penalties for failing to protect patient data, and they would love to be free of this liability.

Attacks have been mounting in the industry. A 2016 cyber-attack on insurer Anthem Health exposed 78 million customers' records. The so-called WannaCry ransom attacks, in which health records of patients in different hospitals around the world were encrypted by hackers who demanded bitcoin payments to unlock them, largely targeted hospitals and other places where the data is a life-or-death consideration.

The biggest losers are patients. This structure creates time-wasting, costly inefficiencies in their care—there are countless horror stories of critically ill patients unable to release vital records from their primary-care physicians to emergency staff so they can take the right measures. And because data isn't being freely shared, research into potentially lifesaving treatments is held back. Almost everything about how the U.S. health care system manages medical records is broken.

That's why initiatives like MedRec, an open-source program based on the Ethereum blockchain that was created by MIT Media Lab students Ariel Eckblaw, Asaph Azaria, and Thiago Yieira, are filled with such potential. The idea, one that's also being pursued in different forms by startups such as Gem of Los Angeles and Blockchain Health of San Francisco, is that the patient has control over who sees their records. Data would still reside with each provider, but patients would use their private cryptographic key—the same device used to authorize bitcoin payments—to release whatever specific aspects of their data are required by providers, to whom they authorize access.

Decentralized Economy with Centralized Trust

How do we get to a world of decentralized trust, so that it costs me close to nothing to safely and confidently engage in transactions with others online? Answers to that question lie in reflecting on how we went from the utopian concept of a level-playing-field Internet that led *New York Times* columnist Thomas Friedman to declare that the "world is flat" to one in which a handful of gargantuan gatekeepers have asserted almost total control.

Let's start with the pre-Internet offline economy, the one we inherited from the twentieth century, when the centralized trust model was the only one we could imagine. Under that system, which prevails to this day, we charge banks, public utilities, certificate authorities, government agencies, and countless other centralized entities and institutions with the task of recording everyone's transactions and exchanges of value. We trust them to monitor our activities—our check writing, our electricity consumption, our monthly payments for everything from newspaper delivery to telephone services—and to reliably and honestly update that information in ledgers that they, and only they, control. With that exclusive knowledge, those entities gain unique powers in determining our capacity to engage in commerce. *They* decide whether we can access an overdraft, draw power from the public utility grid, or make a phone call. And they invoice us for that privilege.

This system was inherently incompatible with the nobody's-in-charge, distributed framework of the Internet. The Net was designed to let anyone publish and send information, at near-zero cost, to anyone else anywhere. That opened up vast new economic opportunities, but it also posed unique challenges for trust management. The person you're dealing with might now have a picture of a dog as their avatar and use the moniker "Voldemort2017." How do you know they can be trusted to deliver on whatever contractual agreement you're entering into? Star ratings, at services like Yelp and eBay, have tried to step into the breach, but these are easily gamed by fake identities and fake reviews, much as Facebook "likes" can be. When it comes to high-value transactions, they cannot be trusted. Well, when Internet companies discovered they couldn't resolve those challenges, they were forced to invite centralized entities to intermediate on our behalf. It was perhaps a necessary solution, but a flawed one that is now exposing a host of other security and privacy concerns.

The distributed system made it easier for crooks to misrepresent their identities. They could also duplicate, forge, or counterfeit valuable information. So, when entrepreneurs pioneered e-commerce in the mid-nineties, they struggled to design an online payments model that wouldn't expose customers to fraud. Unable to assure customers and merchants that their bank account and credit card data were safe, they at first focused on privacy-protecting forms of electronic cash, the concept that Satoshi Nakamoto would tackle with Bitcoin. If cash were digital, they reasoned, people could make online payments without revealing personal identifying information, just as they did with banknotes. In pursuit of that goal, the aforementioned "Cypherpunks"—a loose association of programmers with a fiercely libertarian bent who were obsessed with using cryptography to protect privacy online—and other Internet adventurers toyed with private cryptocurrency concepts, while banks and governments stealthily experimented with sovereign currency-based e-cash. (In *The Age of Cryptocurrency*, we reported on one little-known e-cash pilot that the U.S. Treasury Department explored in conjunction with Citibank.)

These early digital currencies were bedeviled by the "double-spend" problem mentioned above—rogue users could always find ways to duplicate their currency holdings. Overcoming this was vital because, whereas we might happily make a copy of a Word document and send it to someone, digital counterfeiting of this kind would destroy any monetary system's inherent value. Technologists tried to make a system to verify that people weren't double-spending, but it proved much harder than you might think.

In the end, prior to the existence of Bitcoin, the e-commerce industry settled on a workaround: Firms such as Verisign pioneered a model for issuing SSL (Secure Sockets Layer) certificates to verify the trustworthiness of Web site encryption systems. Meanwhile, card-issuing banks beefed up their anti-fraud monitoring efforts. A version of the "trusted third party" was added to our complicated system of global value exchange. It was another jury-rigged solution that meant that the banking system, the centralized ledger-keeping solution with which society had solved the double-spend problem for five hundred years, would be awkwardly bolted onto the ostensibly decentralized Internet as its core trust infrastructure.

With customers now sufficiently confident they wouldn't be defrauded, an explosion in online shopping ensued. But the gatekeeping moneymen now added costs and inefficiencies to the system. The result was high per-transaction costs that made it too expensive, for example, to sustain micropayments—extremely low payments, maybe as little as pennies, that otherwise promised to open up a whole new world of online business models. That nixed a dream of early Internet visionaries, who saw that idea feeding into a global marketplace where software, storage, media content, and processing power would be bought and sold in fractional amounts to maximize efficiency. The compromise also meant that credit cards, once an elite-only instrument, became an integral, even necessary component of e-commerce infrastructure, making banks even more relevant to our payments system. Under this model, the banks charged merchants an interchange fee of around 3 percent to cover their anti-fraud costs, adding a hidden tax to the digital economy that we all pay in the form of higher prices.

Meanwhile, other aspects of Internet governance had to be entrusted to centralized entities as well. These include the domain name system (DNS) managers and hosting service providers, companies whose servers occupy URLs—those specially assigned areas of the World Wide Web around which we navigate our Internet surfing—and host the files that make up the clients' Web sites that point to those Internet addresses. Anyone who has set up a Web site has dealt with such outfits. All of them charge fees. The more files and pages that need hosting, the more they charge.

All these solutions worked for those who could afford them. But, inevitably, the added transaction costs translated into barriers to entry that helped the largest incumbents ward off competitors, limiting innovation and denying billions of financially excluded people the opportunity to fully exploit the Internet's many possibilities for advancement. It's how we've ended up with Internet monopolies. Those with first-mover advantages have not only enjoyed the benefits of network effects; they've been indirectly protected by the hefty transaction costs that competitors face in trying to grow to the same scale. In a very tangible way, then, the high cost of trust management has fed the economic conditions that allow the likes of Amazon, Netflix, Google, and Facebook to keep squashing competitors. Just as important, it has also meant that these monolithic players have become all-powerful stewards of our ever-growing pools of vital, sensitive data.

The Internet's Missing Piece

This was not the dream conveyed in the Cypherpunk manifesto of Tim May and his fellow band of libertarian advocates for cryptography, privacy, and an online world of individual empowerment. Those geeky rebels of the 1990s Bay Area wanted an Internet that was free of both government and corporatist control, a decentralized online economy where self-expression was devoid of censorship, where anyone could transact with anyone else under whatever identity they chose. Ideas like Ted Nelson's ill-fated Xanadu project, which never achieved anywhere near its lofty vision of a global network of independent, self-publishing, interlinked, fully autonomous computers, envisaged a network in which far more processing power and data was placed under the control of individual owners' computers. They were ideas that were far ahead of their time, conceived at a moment when resource, economics, and political realities simply weren't compatible with them.

But then, in 2008, with the Cypherpunk community seemingly having lost its mojo, along came Bitcoin—an idea for cryptomoney that was straight out of their playbook, even though few by then expected it would work. Now, the question of identifying who controlled the data didn't matter. Its integrity could be assured by a decentralized network that constantly updated itself through a process of unbreakable consensus. Once Bitcoin's implications were apparent, the revelation came as a bolt of lightning to many who'd been involved in building the Internet's early architecture. These people included Marc Andreessen, the venture capitalist and co-creator of the first commercial Web browser, Netscape, who told authors Don and Alex Tapscott that people like him suddenly recognized it as "the distributed trust network that the Internet always needed and never had."

As Andreessen and others in Silicon Valley's moneyed classes started to throw money at developers working on Bitcoin and its clones, the sheer breadth of what Bitcoin's underlying blockchain technology might achieve became apparent. For many of the new technologies that innovators are rolling out today, designers are thinking about how blockchain concepts will be part of the general enabling framework:

- Internet of Things solutions will require a decentralized system for machine-to-machine transactions;
- Virtual reality content creation, by which future imaginary worlds will be collaboratively produced by writers and coders, could use a blockchain system for divvying up royalties via smart contracts;
- Artificial intelligence and Big Data systems will need a way to as-

sure that the data they are receiving from multiple, unknown sources has not been corrupted;

- "Industry 4.0" systems for smart manufacturing, 3D printing, and flexible, collaborative supply chains need a decentralized system for tracking each supplier's work processes and inputs.

In short, the blockchains may provide the architecture framework that makes possible the so-called Fourth Industrial Revolution that brings "bits and atoms" together and thrives off massive amounts of processed, global information. It makes the aspirational goal of an Internet of "open data" possible. With this, we might free up the world's data so that smart people everywhere can work with it. Open access to data should better enable humankind to collectively figure out solutions to our many problems and make better products more efficiently. It is an extremely empowering concept.

Code Is Not Law

As we've said elsewhere, there's no guarantee that this sweeping vision of a new enabling platform for the global digital economy will come to fruition. In addition to various technological and internal governance challenges, which we'll address in coming chapters, there are numerous external barriers to adoption. There are also some thorny questions to resolve before blockchain technology or any other decentralized trust system can comprehensively underpin the world's transactions and information exchanges.

The challenges include those posed by regulators, who are struggling to keep up with the category-defying changes that cryptocurrency poses. It took two years for the New York Department of Financial Services to come up with its benchmark-setting BitLicense regulation for money transmission with digital currencies like bitcoin. By the time it was enacted in 2015, the crypto world had moved on to smart contracts and Ethereum; now it's all about utility tokens, initial coin offerings, and decentralized autonomous organizations—none of which were foreseen by the regulation's authors. One risk is that regulators, confused by all these outside-the-box concepts, will overreact to some bad news—potentially triggered by large-scale investor losses if and when the ICO bubble bursts and exposes a host of scams. The fear is that a new set of draconian catchall measures would suck the life out of innovation in this space or drive it offshore or underground. To be sure, institutions like the Washington-based Coin Center and the Digital Chamber of Commerce are doing their best to keep officials aware of the importance of keeping their respective jurisdictions competitive in what is now a global race to lead the world in financial technology. But we live in unpredictable political times in which, to say the least, policymaking is not being guided by rational, forward-thinking principles. The sheer lack of clarity on the intention of regulators and legislators is itself a limit to the technology's progress.

We are going to need regulations—a framework for understanding how the new organization and governance models of blockchain logic can be interpreted by traditional legal systems, whether based on old or new laws. How do we legally define ownership of a digital asset when rights to it come down to control over a private, anonymized key? Where do jurisdictional responsibilities lie when a blockchain ledger is shared around the world or when there's no way to know which computers within a global network will execute the randomly assigned instructions contained within a smart contract? Advocates for these new ideas might argue that new laws aren't needed, but they can't make the claim that they deserve some kind of exemption from regulation altogether. The online world is not a world unto itself; it exists as a subset of the broad framework of laws and norms that we've built up over the centuries.

Some libertarian-minded crypto enthusiasts who want to live entirely by the rules of a blockchain and free themselves from dependence on government are fond of citing the phrase "code is law," used by Harvard professor Lawrence Lessig. Some have over-interpreted this message. Lessig never meant that software code could be a substitute for real-world law, that all disputes would be resolved by these automatic machines, only that code shares some of the qualities of law in the way it proscribes the behavior of computing components. To see code as a substitute for the law is to reduce the latter to something far smaller than what it is. If the law were merely a set of instructions and rules, then yes, perhaps we could just have computers, working together in algorithmic concert, arbitrating and executing all of our digital exchanges with each other. But the law goes much, much deeper and much, much broader than that. The philosophical question of "what is law?" can prompt a host of different answers, but the more you dig into the concept the harder it is to separate law from what Carl Jung called our "collective unconscious," a set of ideas about how to treat each other that we've inherited from prior generations and iteratively altered over millennia. It's simply not something we can reduce to computer code.

No episode brought this lesson home more forcefully than the debacle of The DAO attack of June 2016. The DAO stands for The Decentralized Autonomous Organization. In using this name, the founders of The DAO appropriated an acronym that had until then been used as a generic description of a variety of new, and potentially valuable, systems of automated corporate management and attached it to an extreme expression of techno-anarchic ideals. The DAO was an investment fund established by Slock.it, a smart contracts development group founded by Ethereum's former chief commercial officer, Stephan Tual, and two others. This entity, The DAO, was to be entirely managed by software code—no CEO, no board of directors, no managers of any kind. This kind of thing had been talked about in theory, but these guys were the first ones to give it a shot. The basic idea was that the platform would allow the funds' investors to vote on how to allocate its money—that is, to select from a variety of proposed projects. The idea was that a more democratic, and supposedly superior, investment logic would emerge than that of traditional funds, where fund managers' interests don't always align with those of their principals.

It was pie in the sky to the moon, and then some. Investors were invited to buy DAO tokens with ether, Ethereum's native currency, giving them a stake in The DAO fund. Decisions on investments would depend on token holders' votes on submitted business proposals. After that, the contributions, dividends, and distributions would all be handled according to the Ethereum-based smart contract that ran The DAO. The concept sparked an inordinate amount of excitement among decentralization utopians within the crypto community, who saw it as a way to prove that effective economic decisions could be made without relying on third-party institutions, whether private or government.

Lawyers expressed concerns about the lack of redress in the event of losses, and respected cryptographers such as Zcash founder Zooko Wilcox-O'Hearn and Cornell professor Emin Gün Sirer gave grave warnings about flaws in the code that would allow a clever hacker to siphon off funds. Despite this, investors poured $150 million of ether into DAO tokens in just twenty-seven days. It was, at the time and at that valuation, said to be the biggest crowdfunding exercise in history.

As it turns out, the whole concept was doomed by defects unnoticed by founders and investors blinded by hubris and idealistic faith. In the pitch documents explaining the terms of the deal, Slock.it said, "The DAO's smart contract code governs the Creation of DAO tokens and supersede[s] any public statements about The DAO's Creation made by third parties or individuals associated with The DAO, past, present and future." This was a bold—and, as it would turn out, poorly conceived—statement. It pushed Lessig's "code is law" concept to an extreme interpretation, a *literal* interpretation. They wanted to eliminate humans, and their fuzzy, subjective notions of what is right and wrong, from the equation.

The flaw in this logic was soon made apparent. In the early hours of Friday, June 17, 2016, monitors of The DAO's ether account realized that it was being relentlessly drained of funds. A massive attack was under way by an unidentifiable participant who'd figured out that if he or she wrote a program to interact with the smart contract, it could constantly ask for and receive funds, sent to a copycat DAO that they controlled. The attacker built a virtual version of an out-of-control ATM, one that could not be turned off by the now autopilot-managed DAO system.

Before they locked the attacker out, he or she siphoned off almost $55 million worth of ether.

The panicked organizers now found themselves in legal no-man's-land since they had declared that nothing supersedes the code. Whatever the software does was supposed to be okay, and in this case the software, according to the rules of its own code, was redistributing investors' funds to one savvy user. "I'm not even sure that this qualifies as a hack," wrote Gün Sirer, the Cornell professor, on his blog post later that day. "To label something as a hack or a bug or unwanted behavior, we need to have a specification of the wanted behavior. We had no such specification for The DAO. . . . The 'code was its own documentation,' as people say. It was its own fine print. The hacker read the fine print better than most, better than the developers themselves. . . . Had the attacker lost money by mistake, I am sure the devs would have had no difficulty appropriating his funds and saying 'this is what happens in the brave new world of programmatic money flows.' When he instead emptied out coins from The DAO, the only consistent response is to call it a job well done." By The DAO founders' own terms, the attacker had done nothing wrong, in other words. He or she had simply exploited one of its *features*.

In the real world, the spirit of the law always supersedes its letter—the intent is more important than the code. In this case, the intent of the attacker was made clear in the mood of the token holders: they were angry; they believed they'd been *wronged*. They wanted their money back. But whom were they going to sue? There was no designated owner of this enterprise. They were all equal members of a decentralized system with no one in charge. As many lawyers argued, however, the law will always find a way to get around that problem. The law will seek out and find someone to hold responsible. And in this case those most likely to be fingered were the Slock.it team and various Ethereum founders and developers who'd encouraged and promoted The DAO. Even if they could avoid legal consequences, their reputations, and that of the system they supported, were on the line.

Sure enough, one year later, the law did take an interest. Conducting an investigation into the affair, the U.S. Securities and Exchange Commission ruled that the tokens that had been issued constituted unregistered securities and so would have been in breach of U.S. laws. To Slock.it's inevitable relief, the SEC decided not to pursue charges, but the press release explaining its decision was a shot across the bow. Not only did it make clear that the growing number of crypto-token issuers needed to be wary of regulatory action, but it was also a reminder of how far-reaching are the jurisdictional powers of regulatory institutions that carry the weight of U.S. law behind them.

A related matter is the question of how to incorporate relationships of human trust into a blockchain. Bitcoin purists believe that users need not trust anyone with whom they enter into a transfer of bitcoin currency. The record of their transactions is generated according to a distributed software program that no one controls, and when currency is transferred to other users, that exchange is verified by a decentralized system that requires no "trusted third party's" adjudication and has no need to identify the users. But in reality, Bitcoin users can't get away from having to trust someone or something. For one, the payment is only one part of the transaction; there's nothing in the software that ensures that the merchant delivers the goods or services offered in return. Bitcoin users also must trust that data being input into the record is reliable. How do you know the smartphone or PC you are using to give instructions to the Bitcoin network hasn't been compromised? How do you know that when you are typing "6f7Hl92ej" on your keyboard, those characters are the ones being conveyed to the Bitcoin network? We have little choice but to trust that Apple, Samsung, and other manufacturers are using strict supply-chain monitoring systems to ensure that attackers haven't put malware into the chips. This is not to sound paranoid, because the fact is that, even in the face of constant cyber-breaches, we all choose to trust our computers. But it is to say that it's inaccurate, and a little naïve, to think that blockchain systems operate within what some in the cryptographic community describe as a state of "trustlessness."

Once we go beyond bitcoin currency and start to transfer other rights and assets over a blockchain, the insertion of more trusted parties arises. The authenticity of a land title document that's represented in a blockchain will, for example, depend on the attestation of some authority figure such as a government registrar. This dependence on a trusted middleman, some cryptocurrency purists would argue, overly compromises a blockchain's security function, rendering it unreliable. For that reason, some of them say, a blockchain is inappropriate for many non-currency applications. We, however, view it as a trade-off and believe there's still plenty of value in recording ownership rights and transfers to digitally represented real-world assets in blockchains. We must, however, be aware of that trust component and establish acceptable standards for how data from such sources is gathered and entered into a blockchain-based system.

Blockchain technology doesn't remove the need for trust. In fact, if anything it's an enabler of more trustful relations. What it does do is widen the perimeter of trust. While the software removes centralized trust from the internal ledger-keeping process inside the blockchain, we must trust other people in the "off-chain" environment. We have to trust that a merchant will fulfill a promise to deliver goods on time, that a provider of some source of key information like a stock market price-feed is accurate, or that the smartphones or computers we use to input information haven't been compromised at the manufacturing stage. As we go about designing new governance systems based on this technology, we need to think hard about best practices as they exist at that outer rim—the "last mile" of verification, as some call it. Blockchain technology should be an impetus to develop standards and rules about how the fulfillment of contractual obligations is to be judged in ways that can be read and understood in this new digital context.

Finally, there's a potentially contentious issue around the market framework—the questions of which computers control the blockchain and how much power to dictate prices, access, and market dominance that allows. Permissioned blockchains—those which require some authorizing entity to approve the computers that validate the blockchain—are by definition more prone to gatekeeping controls, and therefore to the emergence of monopoly or oligopoly powers, than the permissionless ideal that Bitcoin represents. (We say "ideal" because, as we'll discuss in the next chapter, there are also concerns that aspects of Bitcoin's software program have encouraged an unwelcome concentration of ownership—flaws that developers are working to overcome.)

Permissioned systems integrate a trusted third party—the very kind of intermediary that Satoshi Nakamoto aimed to avoid—to authorize which computers can participate in the validation process. This option makes sense for various industries that are looking to adopt blockchain technology but whose current industry structures just don't allow a permissionless system. Until the law changes, banks would face insurmountable legal and regulatory opposition, for example, to using a system like Bitcoin that relies on an algorithm randomly assigning responsibility at different stages of the bookkeeping process to different, unidentifiable computers around the world. But that doesn't mean that other companies don't have a clear interest in reviewing how these permissioned networks are set up. Would a distributed ledger system that's controlled by a consortium of the world's biggest banking institutions be incentivized to act in the interests of the general public it serves? One can imagine the dangers of a "too-big-to-fail blockchain": massive institutions could once again hold us hostage to bailouts because of failures in the combined accounting system. Perhaps that could be prevented with strict regulation; perhaps there needs to be public oversight of such systems. Either way, it's incumbent upon us to ensure that the control over the blockchains of the future is sufficiently representative of broad-based interests and needs so that they don't just become vehicles for collusion and oligopolistic power by the old guard of finance.

The open-source development of permissioned ledger models that's being done by R3 CEV, a consortium dominated by major banks, and by the Hyperledger group, in which tech firms like IBM, Intel, and Cisco play hefty roles, is important. It's forcing the incumbents within them to see the spotlight that this new technology shines on the inefficiencies of their old, centralized work processes. And some of the ideas being developed there will no doubt be of great value to the wider ecosystem of blockchain development. But we believe the "permissionless" ideal first laid down by Bitcoin and since followed by countless alternative "altcoins" and blockchains is a vital one for the world to focus on.

As we stated in *The Age of Cryptocurrency*, Bitcoin was merely the first crack at using a distributed computing and decentralized ledger-keeping system to resolve the age-old problem of trust and achieve this open, low-cost architecture for intermediary-free global transactions. It may or may not be the platform that wins out. Perhaps something else will come along and fulfill for the age of cryptocurrency what the Transmission Control Protocol/Internet Protocol, or TCP/IP, pair of protocols did for the age of the Internet. Something will emerge as a standard, base-layer protocol that dictates how all computers everywhere exchange value with each other. Will it be Bitcoin, Ethereum, or something else entirely, perhaps a protocol that allows computers with digital assets on any one of these competing blockchains to trade directly with each other without going through a third party? Such is the threat and opportunity that open-source development offers: anyone can copy and then improve upon your idea. The good news is that boundless energy and innovation will go into figuring out how to iterate upon the ideas that currently exist and will build a potentially better system. That innovation might find its way back into Bitcoin, helping to cement its first-mover advantage. Or it might diffuse the value creation power across a wider array of platforms until something more popular comes along. In the next chapter we will ask such questions as we survey the frenetic pace of invention in the blockchain space.

Three

THE PLUMBING AND THE POLITICS

Building a decentralized economic system for a network of independent, anonymous computer owners in which everyone will work in the interests of the group poses a daunting technical challenge. It's also a major political challenge. Herding cats comes to mind. It turns out that building a network outside the traditional political system requires a lot of political decisions.

Success for a decentralized cryptocurrency or blockchain network comes down to designing the right rule set—the software protocol—by which participants interact with each other. Satoshi Nakamoto's Bitcoin breakthrough gave us the first working example of how to achieve this even when large amounts of money, business secrets, and other matters of value are at stake. But as the community of Bitcoin's users and computer owners has grown and changed, and as newcomers have demanded new functions and more powerful applications, there's been constant pressure to upgrade and change the protocol to facilitate those needs. The problem is that in a truly decentralized, open-source system where no one is in charge, it's extremely difficult to get all those people with their far-flung disparate interests to agree on what changes to make.

There are probably several thousand extremely bright programmers and entrepreneurs trying to make this software take off. In some ways, they're like the Founding Fathers in the United States: they've come across something new and intriguing that could change the world, if they could only configure it properly. "All men are created equal" did not just explode, sui generis, on the colonial landscape in July 1776. It was the synthesis of a classical-liberal school of thought that had been developing for decades—and still is, for that matter. The techno-philosophers of the blockchain movement are grappling with myriad iterations of an idea. They just have to find the best ones.

The Cypherpunks' Holy Grail

The starting point for understanding how blockchains work, as well as the technical and political debates they engender, is the first working blockchain: the Bitcoin blockchain. Bitcoin put the objective of pure, permissionless decentralization front and center. In guiding a community of autonomous users to reach agreement on transaction histories, it showed that software controlled by no individual or corporation could now supplant the "trusted third-party" role that institutional intermediaries such as banks have traditionally played in confirming our financial records. If society is to define a sensible path for adopting, or not, this highly disruptive technology, we must first understand what Bitcoin is and why it matters. So, we're going to peer under its hood.

Before we do that, however, let's start with this generic definition of a blockchain: a distributed, append-only ledger of provably signed, sequentially linked, and cryptographically secured transactions that's replicated across a network of computer nodes, with ongoing updates determined by a software-driven consensus.

What does that mouthful actually mean? Well, let's break down its key words:

1. "distributed": the ledger does not reside in one place but in many, with each bookkeeping node independently responsible for updating it in coordination with the others. Once one bookkeeper (in this case, a computer) updates the ledger, along with some proof that its work was sound, all others simultaneously up-

grade their own versions with that same update. What emerges is a constantly updated, commonly agreed record of truth with no centralized master copy.

2. "append-only": information can only be added, not removed. This is important because it means no one can go back and doctor the record. What's been agreed upon as the truth *is* the truth. There is no room for debate.

3. "provably signed": blockchains use the public key infrastructure encryption methodology for sharing and controlling information. With PKI, as it's known, users control two separate but mathematically linked strings of numbers and letters, or "keys." One is a secret "private key" that only they know, and the other is a public key, visible to all, that's associated with some form of valuable information. In Bitcoin, that information refers to an amount of bitcoin currency. When the user "signs" their public key with their private key, that action mathematically proves to outsiders that the user has control of the underlying information and can then assign, or send it, to another person's public key. In Bitcoin's case, that's the process by which a person sends currency from their "address" (their public key) to another. (Though it's not a perfect analogy, you can think of your private key as a secret password or PIN to manage your money and your address as an account.)

4. "sequentially linked and cryptographically secured": some other tools from the science of cryptography are used to represent entries into the ledger in a way that links them, with a series of unbreakable mathematical locks, into a fully verifiable sequence. This forms a never-ending, chronological series of blocks, or batches of transaction data, whose integrity is protected by cryptography. This structure provides an unfathomably high probability of confidence that nothing in the ledger has been altered from its agreed-upon state.

5. "replicated": the ledger is copied across participating nodes (as per the distributed pattern described in 1 above).

6. "software-driven consensus": a program that all the computers run independently sets certain requirements and incentives for them to behave in a way that systematically guides them to reach agreement on which transactions should or shouldn't be included in each updated version of the replicated ledger. "Consensus" is a key word in blockchain design, as it describes the process by which each participant's independently managed copy of the ledger is harmonized with everyone else's in keeping with a commonly agreed version of the truth. It typically boils down to how to get a majority to agree on updates.

Not so complicated, right? Well, if you're still struggling to understand, never fear, we'll dig deeper.

A key point to note here is that our generic blockchain definition doesn't capture the magnitude of Nakamoto's breakthrough. There are other elements to Bitcoin that, for all intents and purposes, achieved the Cypherpunks' Holy Grail: a fully decentralized cryptocurrency that no single person, entity, or consortium of members anywhere could control.

The Bay Area–based Cypherpunk community, which fought hard to achieve decentralization for two decades before Bitcoin arrived, knew that any digital system of money would need a common ledger to keep track of everyone's debits and credits. This was to ensure people weren't "double-spending"—in effect, counterfeiting—their currency balances. But for the system to be fully decentralized, it had to allow anyone to participate in managing that ledger. It had to be "permissionless," with a consensus system that no one party could influence. That way, no authorizing entity could block, retract, or decide what gets entered into the ledger, making it *censorship resistant*.

Before Bitcoin, all attempts to achieve this goal ran into an irresolvable dilemma: without a central authority affirming the identity of those validating the ledger, a fraudulent validator could secretly distort the consensus by creating multiple computing nodes under different aliases. (Think of all those fake Twitter aliases for a sense of how easy this is.) By replicating themselves, they could cast more than 50 percent of the votes and get their own false, "double-spent" transactions inserted into the shared record. This could be resolved by some authority identifying and authorizing each computer user, but that would just take things back to square one. It breached the Cypherpunks' ideals of "permissionlessness" and censorship resistance.

Satoshi Nakamoto's ingenious solution lay in a mix of carrot-and-stick incentives that encouraged those who were validating transactions to do so honestly. Any computer anywhere could participate in validation work, and, in fact, would be incentivized to do so with a lottery-like system of bitcoin rewards. These would be paid out every ten minutes, whenever one of those computers successfully added a new batch, or "block," of freshly validated transactions to the blockchain ledger. (These computers are known as "miners," because in seeking to win the ten-minute payout, they engage in a kind of computational treasure hunt for digital gold. At the time of writing, the ten-minute "block reward" was equal to 12.5 bitcoins—around $125,000—issued automatically by the decentralized software protocol to the winning miner. Miners also pick up transaction fees, which we'll get into later.)

Now, since it's a permissionless system, anyone could up their chance of winning the randomly assigned bitcoin reward lottery by adding more computing nodes to the network. So Nakamoto needed a non-centralized way to prevent a rogue miner from taking over more than 50 percent of the computing power. He achieved this by requiring every single competing computer to conduct an exercise called "proof of work": a difficult mathematical puzzle that requires heavy computation to find just one number within a mountainous digital haystack of other numbers.

Proof of work is expensive, because it chews up both electricity and processing power. That means that if a miner wants to seize majority control of the consensus system by adding more computing power, they would have to spend a lot of money doing so. Because of features such as a "difficulty adjustment," which makes the proof-of-work puzzle ever harder as overall network-wide computing power increases, Nakamoto's proof-of-work system ensures that the costs of a so-called 51 percent attack grow exponentially as an attacker gets closer to that consensus-controlling threshold. Double-spending and fraud are not illegal in Bitcoin; in other words, they are just "taxed" to such a degree that it's prohibitively expensive. At the time of writing, the GoBitcoin.io site was estimating that a 51 percent attack would require an outlay on hardware and electricity costs of $2.2 billion.

Over time, bitcoin mining has evolved into an industrial undertaking, with gigantic mining "farms" now dominating the network. Might those big players collude and undermine the ledger by combining resources? Perhaps, but there are also overwhelming disincentives for doing so. Among other considerations, a successful attack would significantly undermine the value of all the bitcoins the attacking miner owns. Either way, no one has managed to attack Bitcoin's ledger in nine years. That unbroken record continues to reinforce belief in Bitcoin's cost-and-incentive security system.

If we view the bitcoin currency from this angle—and not merely as it is popularly portrayed, as a strange new digital unit of value that some geeky guys think is a good alternative to dollars, euros, or yen—we can build a conceptual framework for understanding the wider implications of Satoshi's invention. The currency, *bitcoin (lowercase "b")*, is first and foremost a store of value that rewards people for securing *Bitcoin (uppercase "B")*, the system. That, and not the hope that it will become an everyday medium of exchange, is its primary purpose. Without its existence as an incentive for computer owners to honestly validate exchanges of valuable information, Satoshi's censorship-resistant distributed ledger simply wouldn't work.

Of course, for this all to tie together, the miners must regard bitcoin currency as having value—they must believe they'll be able to exchange it for other things of established value, be they goods and services or *fiat* currencies such as dollars. Fully exploring how they, and millions of others, came to conclude that bitcoins *did* have value requires a deeper dive into how human communities reach agreements on what constitutes a common medium of exchange, store of value, and unit of account—the three qualities of money. (For that dive, we again will shamelessly recommend *The Age of Cryptocurrency.*) What we can say is that, contrary to popular opinion, a currency need not be *backed* by anything, be it the commitment of a government or a fixed amount of commodity such as gold, only that it be sufficiently recognized as a useful means of measuring and clearing exchanges of value. This might seem counterintuitive because we tend to think of money as a physical *thing* that somehow contains value *within* the particular item—the paper note, or the gold coin. But in reality currencies only convey a symbolic tokenized value, one that's derived solely from the collective will of society to commonly accept the token as a marker of that value. This same malleability of thinking can be applied to any token, so long as enough people accept it. That's what happened to bitcoin.

The structure of the ledger is also important for keeping Bitcoin secure. Nakamoto conceived of his as an ever-growing, unbroken chain of *blocks*, each representing a batch of transactions strung together and validated within a ten-minute bitcoin reward period. Hence the word that's now on every CIO's lips: "blockchain." (Notably, the term "blockchain" never appeared in the original Bitcoin white paper—a good argument for why Bitcoin should have no exclusive claim to the term.)

Within each block period, every miner that's engaged in the proof-of-work race for the next bitcoin reward is simultaneously gathering new incoming transactions and arranging them into their own new block. The details of each transaction—date, time, addresses of senders and recipients, the amounts sent, etc.—are captured and run through a special cryptographic algorithm to produce an alphanumeric string known as a *hash*. A hashing algorithm can convert any arbitrary amount of original source data into a single, fixed-length string of letters and numbers, providing a means of mathematically proving the existence of that underlying information. Anyone in possession of the transaction information can easily run it through the same hashing algorithm to confirm that whoever made the original hash must be in possession of the same data.

A key feature of hashes is that they are hypersensitive to changes in the underlying data. Here's one we generated from the previous paragraph's raw text by running it through the highly secure SHA-256 algorithm that Bitcoin uses:

63f48074e26b1dcd6ec26be74b35e49bd31a36f849033bdee-4194b6be8505fd9

Now, note that when we simply remove the last period from that paragraph of text, the algorithm came back with a completely different alphanumeric string:

8f5967a42c6dc39757c2e6be4368c6c5f06647cc3c73d3aa2c0ab-dec3c6007a5

If you think about this in terms of someone trying to secretly change transaction data, you can see how this hypersensitivity is vital to the blockchain's integrity. If anyone tries to introduce changes to existing transactions, other miners will clearly recognize that the new hash output doesn't match what they have in their versions of the blockchain. So they will reject it.

Bitcoin also takes advantage of the fact that it's possible to take two hashes, combine them, and produce a root hash that encapsulates the two separate data proofs. This process can be repeated ad infinitum, creating hashes of hashes of hashes in a hierarchical structure known as a Merkle Tree. This is how transactions within each block are bundled and cryptographically tied together.

Bitcoin then takes this linking function one step further. Through another cryptographic hashing function, the winning miner ties their newly created block to the previous one. This turns the entire blockchain into a never-ending, mathematically linked chain of hashed transactions that goes all the way back to the "Genesis" block of January 3, 2009. Make a change to a transaction from January 15, 2011, and the blockchain's interlinked hash-based record of all the data recorded in the subsequent seven years will be completely altered. It's a bit like how banks use exploding dye to protect banknotes: any thief who tries to spend the stolen money is immediately exposed.

This unbroken record of transactions provides the foundation that miners use to verify the legitimacy of the transactions contained in the winning miner's new block. If a miner is satisfied with the contents of that block they will commit to connecting their next block to it if they are lucky enough to be the winner. If they're unsatisfied, they would attach their new block to an earlier block whose contents they trust, leaving the suspicious one as an "orphan." This decision-making forms the basis for Bitcoin's consensus logic, which is based on a convention known as the "longest chain." The idea is that if no miner has amassed more than 50 percent of total computing capacity, then mathematical probability will ensure that any attempt by a rogue minority to add a series of new ten-minute blocks to a previously rejected and orphaned one will soon fall behind the majority's longer chain and will be abandoned. The caveat, of course, is that if bad actors do control more than 50 percent of the computing power they can produce the longest chain and so incorporate fraudulent transactions, which other miners will unwittingly treat as legitimate. Still, as we've explained, achieving that level of computing power is prohibitively expensive. It's this combination of math and money that keeps Bitcoin secure.

These cobbled-together concepts comprise Satoshi Nakamoto's breakthrough: a decentralized, censorship-resistant record of the past. If we acknowledge that all accounting systems are merely estimates— that it's impossible to arrive at a perfect representation of reality—then this one, a system that collectively captures the shared opinions of a community with no central authority, results in the most objective representation of *the truth* yet devised.

In solving the double-spend problem, Bitcoin did something else important: it magically created the concept of a "digital asset." Previously, anything digital was too easily replicated to be regarded as a distinct piece of property, which is why digital products such as music and movies are typically sold with licensing and access rights rather than ownership. By making it impossible to replicate some-thing of value—in this case bitcoins—Bitcoin broke this conventional wisdom. It created *digital scarcity*. This was vital for how bitcoin is val-ued as a currency, but also for the many imitator crypto-assets that would come later.

Yet, Bitcoin, even if it is a better mousetrap, is far from being a per-fect mousetrap. Nothing made that clearer than a bitter internal fight over what seemed like a mundane issue. It started as a technical dis-agreement but blew up into a full-fledged fight over control of what was designed to be an uncontrollable network. It showed that managing Bitcoin was more than just managing the ledger itself; it was about gov-erning a community. It was about politics.

Bitcoin's "Civil War"

Major code changes have always been difficult for open-source proj-ects, and they are even harder for Bitcoin. There's no identifiable leader to adjudicate disputes and no way, in the absence of identifying infor-mation, to be sure of whom you're arguing with or how much of a stake they have in the system. What's more, there is real money on the table. Changes can deeply affect the value people have stored up in the digital currency. It's a toxic mix. And it means that people will argue, and ar-gue, and argue, and argue.

The biggest fight of all revolved around a small piece of code: the maximum data size of an individual block, which from 2010 on was hard-coded to a limit of one megabyte. That limit meant that only about seven transactions could be processed per second over the Bitcoin blockchain, a serious impediment for payment providers who have as-pirations for Bitcoin to compete with Visa, whose network handles about 65,000 transactions per second.

By 2016, there were too many bitcoin transactions over the net-work to fit inside the 1MB block limit. Transactions that were supposed to be settled in minutes were being settled in hours, or longer. To avoid that fate, users offered rising fee payments to miners to better their chances of having their transaction included in a block. An artificially created "fee market" was emerging, in other words, pitting user against user. By June 2017, the average fee on the Bitcoin network reached more than $5—okay for a $20,000 transfer but impossible for a $2 cup of coffee. That cost was borne by the user and became an additional source of revenue for miners on top of the Bitcoin software's routine 12.5-bitcoin block reward. Suddenly, the miners looked a bit like the banking gatekeepers that Bitcoin was supposed to disrupt. For users, a supposedly frictionless payments system was now saddled with friction.

Many startups that were trying to build a business on top of Bitcoin, such as wallet providers and exchanges, were frustrated by an inability to process their customers' transactions in a timely manner. "I've become a trusted third party," complained Wences Casares, CEO of bitcoin wallet and custodial service Xapo. Casares was referring to the fact that too many of his firms' transactions with its customers had to be processed "off-chain" on faith that Xapo would later settle the transaction on the Bitcoin blockchain.

Action was needed. Some simply argued in favor of increasing the block size. But this otherwise trivial coding change was not uniformly viewed as the best solution. Making blocks bigger would require more memory, which would make it even more expensive to operate a miner, critics pointed out. That could drive other prospective miners away, and leave Bitcoin mining even more concentrated among a few centralized players, raising the existential threat of collusion to undermine the ledger. On the surface, it seemed both arguments had merits. "Big blockers," as they were known, were on the side of making sure anyone could afford to use bitcoin—that high transaction fees wouldn't make it impossible to pay for a cup of coffee. "Small blockers" were all about protecting two big-picture objectives: decentralization and security. Their differences were irreconcilable, all the more so because of how much money was now at stake. Bitcoin had grown from a small, hobbyist's project into a global experiment with a market value of more than $50 billion by the fall of 2017. Without an owner, or board of directors, or management, who was to say which side had the right idea for protecting this pool of value?

A number of solutions were proposed, but none could attract consensus—a word that has almost holy connotations in Bitcoin circles. In part, it's because there was no mechanism for determining how much of a stake the supporters of each idea held. The pseudonymous nature of Bitcoin, where there is no formal identification of people and the bitcoin addresses they control, is a vital design feature, with an emphasis on privacy and permissionless participation. But it makes it hard to organize a vote on policy changes. Without a tally of who's who and who owns what, there was no way to gauge what the majority of the Bitcoin community, composed of users, businesses, investors, developers, and miners, wanted. And so, it all devolved into shouting matches on social media.

The big-blockers and small-blockers were hopelessly, er, blocked. The arguments got so bad that at one point the Bitcoin community on Reddit split in half, with two separate sub-reddits serving each constituency. And since agreement seemed impossible, more and more people came around to adopting a similarly divisive but almost inconceivable solution: splitting Bitcoin in half.

The idea was to "fork" Bitcoin. That's a software term that just means you're upgrading a program, like a new version of Microsoft Word. There are two kinds of forks, hard and soft. In a soft fork, the older version of the software lacks the new features but is still compatible with the newer version; in a hard fork, the new software is "backwards incompatible," which means it can't interoperate with older versions. A hard-fork-based software change thus poses a do-or-die decision for users on whether to upgrade or not. That's bad enough for, say, word processing software, but for a currency it's downright problematic. A bitcoin based on the old version could not be transferred to someone running software that supports the new version. Two Bitcoins. Two versions of the truth.

Then, out of the creative mind of Bitcoin developer Pieter Wuille came an alternative approach: a code change called Segregation Witness, or SegWit, that could be achieved with just a soft fork. It wouldn't double the block-size limit per se, but it would make the transaction data more efficient, which meant that more or less double the information could be jammed into a 1MB block. Even more important, SegWit fixed some longstanding coding quirks that had made it difficult to implement a very important new invention: the Lightning Network.

Lightning, which might one day allow Bitcoin to compete with Visa's 65,000 transactions per second, was created by Thaddeus Dryja and Joseph Poon. It allows people to jointly sign smart contracts that create time-locked, two-way payment channels based on a pre-agreed amount of money that the payer seeds with a single bitcoin transaction. They can then move funds to and from each other within that pre-established balance. Also, through an interlocking system of secondary channels, they can transfer funds to third parties, creating a network of traced payments that need not be confirmed in the Bitcoin blockchain. So, there are no miners' fees to pay and no limit on how many transactions can be done at any time. The smart contracts prevent users from defrauding each other while the Bitcoin blockchain is used solely as a settlement layer, recording net balance transactions whenever a channel is opened or closed. It persists as the ultimate source of proof, a guarantee that all the "off-chain" Lightning transactions are legitimate.

Many in the coder community lined up behind the SegWit/Lightning solution, especially those associated with Bitcoin Core, whose developers, such as Wuille, were affiliated with the influential Bitcoin infrastructure company Blockstream. The SegWit/Lightning combination was in their minds the responsible way to make changes. They had a duty, they believed, to avoid big, disruptive codebase alterations and instead wanted to encourage innovators to develop applications that would augment the powers of the limited foundational code. It's a classic, security-minded approach to protocol development: keep the core system at the bottom layer of the system simple, robust, and hard to change—some use the words "deliberately dumb"—and thus force innovation "up the stack" to the "application layer." When it works you get the best of both worlds: security *and* innovation.

But a group of miners with real clout was having none of it. Led by a Chinese company that both mined bitcoin and produced some of the most widely used mining equipment, this group was adamantly opposed to SegWit and Lightning. It's not entirely clear what upset Jihan Wu, CEO of Bitmain, but after lining up with early Bitcoin investor and prominent libertarian Roger Ver, he launched a series of lobbying efforts to promote bigger blocks. One theory was that Bitmain worried that an "off-chain" Lightning solution would siphon away transaction fees that should rightly be going to miners; another was that because such payment channel transactions weren't as traceable as on-chain transactions, Chinese miners were worried that their government would shut them down. Bitmain's reputation suffered a blow when revelations emerged that its popular Ant-miner mining rigs were being shipped to third-party miners with a "backdoor" that allowed the manufacturer-cum-miner to shut its opponents' equipment down. Conspiracy theories abounded: Bitmain was planning to subvert SegWit. The company denied this and vowed to disable the feature. But trust was destroyed.

The standoff continued through the spring of 2017. Then, eventually, after multiple soft- and hard-fork coding change proposals, a group of businessmen led by longtime bitcoin investor Barry Silbert came up with the SegWit2x compromise. Backed by a who's who of the Bitcoin business community (Blockstream was a notable exception), the two-step plan was to get a certain threshold of miners to commit by the end of July to first implement SegWit and then, in November, double the block size to 2MB. For the big-blockers it looked like nothing more than a face-saving exercise, since there was no way in an open-source setting that anyone could hold others to the block size doubling four months later. Nonetheless, the ploy worked. Shortly before the SegWit2x deadline it was revealed that more than 80 percent of the computing power was now signaling that they would implement SegWit after July 31, enough to declare it a done deal. And yet, even then, in the eleventh hour, Silbert's team was denied a clear victory: a breakaway group in China that Bitmain was suspected of supporting said it would launch a hard fork after all. And so, on August 1, just when it seemed that Bitcoin might avert a painful divorce, the split finally happened.

On that date, a new version of Bitcoin, calling itself Bitcoin Cash, with a new currency bearing the symbol BCH (compared with bitcoin's BTC) was launched with an 8MB block capacity. Once a few anti-SegWit miners started mining blocks with those characteristics, the fork was on. It was like a stock split—technically, all holders of bitcoin were entitled both to their original BTC and an equal share of BCH—except that, unlike a stock split, both sides were mutually incompatible. If that idea of equal-but-different money is confusing to you, you're not alone. It was new to bitcoin exchanges, too. But once some agreed to start trading BCH, the market didn't seem to know what to do with this new rebel bitcoin. The price initially jumped from an opening near $300 to $700, but then, amid signs that only one major mining outfit was backing it, it dropped back to just above $200 and eventually steadied around $350 over the summer. Meanwhile, original bitcoin went on a tear, rallying by more than 50 percent to a new high above $4,400 over a two-week period. The comparative performance of the pair suggested that small-block BTC and the SegWit reformers had won.

Bitcoin Cash continues to trade, though it doesn't appear capable of supplanting Bitcoin. And the original SegWit2x compromise, which was supposed to increase Bitcoin's block size to 2MB, was eventually abandoned in November 2017, after it failed to achieve an overwhelming consensus, leaving one side bruised and one side gloating. Bitcoin had gone through a ridiculous circus, one that many outsiders naturally assumed would hurt its reputation and undermine its support. Who wants such an ungovernable currency? Yet here was the original bitcoin currency surging to new heights and registering a staggering 650 percent gain in less than twelve months.

Why? Well, for one, Bitcoin had proven itself resilient. Despite its civil war, its blockchain ledger remained intact. And, while it's hard to see how the acrimony and bitterness was an advantage, the fact that it had proven so difficult to alter the code, to introduce a change to its monetary system, was seen by many as an important test of Bitcoin's immutability. Solid censorship resistance was, after all, a defining selling point for Bitcoin, the reason why some see the digital currency becoming a world reserve asset to replace the outdated, mutable, fiat-currency systems that still run the world. In fact, it could be argued that this failure to compromise and move forward, seen by outsiders as Bitcoin's biggest flaw, might actually be its biggest feature. Like the simple, unchanging codebase of TCP/IP, the gridlocked politics of the Bitcoin protocol were imposing secure rigidity on the system and forcing innovation *up the stack*.

Another lesson from the BTC/BCH split concerned the question of where money goes when blockchain engineering talent is hard to find. It showed that the funds go to where the developers are, where the innovation is most likely to happen, and where the security measures are most likely to be properly implemented, updated, and tested. That's what BTC, the original Bitcoin, promises with its depth of talent at Core and elsewhere. BTH can't access such rich inventiveness because the community of money-focused bitcoin miners can't attract the same kinds of passionate developers. This is not to say that Core developers are saints; many businesses are rightly frustrated with Core's intransigent position when a quick, small, block-size increase might have reduced stress in the system, and some worry that venture-capital-backed Blockstream wields too much influence over the group's work.

Regardless, Bitcoin is far from the only blockchain game in town. In the corporate world of established enterprises, both finance and non-finance companies are in many cases opting for permissioned blockchains. Under these arrangements, some authority, such as a consortium of banks, chooses which entities get to participate in the validation process. It is, in many respects, a step backward from Nakamoto's achievement, since it makes the users of that permissioned system dependent, once again, on the say-so of some trusted third party. Some prefer to describe these private network arrangements as "blockchain-inspired" rather than as blockchains per se, and tend to use the generic term "distributed ledger technology" to describe them. But they do use many of the revolutionary features that Bitcoin introduced, and they can tackle the many issues of trust that the approved members of these permissioned systems would otherwise encounter in sharing information with each other. Most importantly, permissioned blockchains are more scalable than Bitcoin's, at least for now, since their governance doesn't depend upon the agreement of thousands of unidentified actors around the world; their members can simply agree to increase computing power whenever processing needs rise. But, as we'll discuss in chapter six, these permissioned systems may be inherently more constrained in terms of the kind of innovation that can be harnessed within them.

To us, permissionless systems pose the greatest opportunity. While there may well be great value in developing permissioned blockchains as an interim step toward a more open system, we believe permissionlessness and open access are ideals that we should strive for—notwithstanding the challenges exposed by Bitcoin's "civil war." It's why we spend so much time in this book looking at them.

There has been a feverish pace of development in permissonless blockchains, too, as new models emerge that try to advance or augment what Bitcoin offers. Many of them address much more than Bitcoin's straightforward currency proposition to embrace a wider concept of decentralized computing. Whether we think of these as competitors to Bitcoin or interesting spin-offs, they illustrate how dynamic the exploration of new ideas has become since Bitcoin has arrived on the scene.

Ethereum: An Unstoppable Global Computer . . . With Bugs

One platform that has, arguably, attracted as much interest as Bitcoin is Ethereum, a project conceived by Russian-born Canadian whiz kid Vitalik Buterin. One of the first proverbial "big ideas" to come out of Bitcoin was that a blockchain network could be used to transfer more than just currency without an intermediary. Anything that could be digitized—a land title, a contract, medical records, copyrights, legal contracts, personal IDs, even the registration of a corporation—and transferred across a network could be inserted into a blockchain transaction and recorded in an immutable setting. And what that meant was that an entirely new, automated economy of peer-to-peer exchanges could be possible. The problem was that Bitcoin's single-purpose currency design wasn't ideally suited for these non-currency applications. So, Buterin took the core decentralized concepts and designed a new program optimized for "smart contracts" that would run specialized, decentralized applications, or Dapps, allowing users to exchange anything.

The idea is that computers on Ethereum's network would compete for the right to carry out the Dapps' encoded instructions to issue and transfer digital assets. The computers would earn Ethereum's currency, ether, in return for that computing work. Because the network was decentralized, the Dapps could run in an entirely impartial fashion that users could trust to execute as the contract stipulates. If it lived up to all that Buterin and others imagined, the system would amount to a global, decentralized *virtual machine*, one that always implemented users' coding instructions without any control by any one computer.

When Buterin released his white paper in December 2013, people were immediately entranced by the idea, recognizing that it was the first truly extensible platform for building decentralized applications. In a few years, the open-source project grew to attract a wide tent of enthusiastic app developers. "You're just as likely to find a web developer, a systems engineer, an academic, or an MBA. A transsexual, an avid Trump supporter, a Chinese entrepreneur, a New York City venture capitalist, or a techie in a hoodie who has 5 million dollars' worth of ether. It's a safe space for eccentric personalities," wrote a blogger using the moniker "owaisted" about the preeminent Ethereum developers' conference, Devcon.

And it's no wonder; the ideas that spin off of this decentralized platform are just as wide and eclectic. Here are just a few: digital "self-sovereign" identity; decentralized medical record sharing; automated, market-driven solar microgrids; decentralized commodity exchanges; crowdfunded, ownerless investment funds; blockchain-certified marriage certificates; provably secure online voting systems; decentralized supply-chain and logistics platforms; security for the Internet of Things. The list goes on and on. Ethereum's internal programming language is described as being "Turing complete"—which essentially means it has great versatility, allowing people to write an unlimited variety of programs.

The key breakthrough was that this structure, beyond its easy-to-use programming language, would enable smart contracts. As they were first raised in the pre-Bitcoin era by crypto-systems theorist Nick Szabo, smart contracts are a way to express, in a piece of computing code, instructions for executing transactions according to previously agreed contractual conditions. Lawyers often bristle at the use of the word "contract" in this context; contracts, after all, refer to legally binding agreements between humans. Machines can only execute the clauses outlined in those agreements. Still, the "smart contracts" misnomer shouldn't distract from the idea that trustfully executed agreements could be extremely useful.

Here's a simple example: Two parties enter into a "contract for difference," an agreement that's a bit like a stock option. If a data feed from a stock exchange alerts the computer that the price of a given equity has fallen or risen above a pre-agreed level—usually the initial purchase price—then one party must pay the other party the difference. With an Ethereum-based smart contract, those kinds of deals can be executed automatically without the intervention of lawyers, third-party certifiers, escrow agents, or the like, since both parties trust that the tamper-proof system will function as advertised. Smart contracts could, for example, immediately trigger a transfer of title to goods in return for a digital-currency payment when a chip with GPS capability detects that a shipment has been transferred to a designated warehouse. As such, these computerized contracts could revolutionize how businesses manage their supply-chain relationships with each other.

After launching Ethereum at the North American Bitcoin Conference in January 2014, Buterin told the authors he wanted to create an

"Android for decentralized apps." It would be an open platform, much like Google's smartphone operating system, on which people could design any new application they wanted and run it, not on a single company-owned server but in a decentralized manner across Ethereum's ownerless network of computers. At the time, Buterin was just nineteen years old; he had dropped out of a computer science program at the University of Waterloo when he realized that Bitcoin and the cryptocurrency worlds were taking off and weren't going to wait for him. Now he was building a universally accessible, decentralized global supercomputer. It was an audacious, revolutionary idea. Now, with more than six hundred decentralized applications, or Dapps, running on Ethereum, he is looking vindicated. In just the first eleven months of 2017, the system's internal currency, ether, rose from just over $8 to more than $400. By then the entire market cap for ether stood at $39 billion, a quarter that of Bitcoin's. The success has made the wunderkind Buterin an instant multi-millionaire and turned him into a cultlike figure for the holders of ether and related tokens who've become rich. But in an industry that is constantly obsessed with the risks of centralizing too much attention in one institution, there are some who worry that that cult of Vitalik has gone too far.

Ethereum's technology is young, underdeveloped, and buggy. Because it's so versatile and open to such a variety of computing possibilities, it leaves open doors for attackers to cause mischief, or worse. The network is constantly under distributed denial of service (DDOS) attacks, for example, in which malicious hackers exploit weaknesses in its code to blast its network of ledger-validating nodes with excessive transactions, paralyzing the system. Because it was designed as an all-things-for-all-comers platform, with countless programs built on top of it, there's an inordinately large number of possible attack vectors through which rogue actors can try to harm the network.

Ethereum co-founder Joseph Lubin only added to the complexity when he set up ConsenSys, a Brooklyn-based think tank–like business development unit tasked with developing new use cases and applications of the technology. Lubin's team's work is important: it has helped demonstrate the great potential of this technology, which has in turn inspired developers and expanded the world's blockchain talent pool; ConsenSys has also driven the concept of a decentralized architecture more deeply into the mainstream, partnering with companies such as Microsoft to provide a suite of tools that allow developers from startups and more established companies to develop their own Ethereum-powered decentralized applications. But the proliferation of these projects, creating new wallets and smart contracts across hundreds of new applications, also means there are even more ways for malicious actors to mess with things or, in worst-case scenarios, commit theft. For example, the Parity Wallet, which was designed by Ethereum co-founder and lead architect Gavin Wood as a way to seamlessly engage, via a browser, with Ethereum smart contracts, lost $30 million in a hack.

While these failures would overwhelm a bank's mission-critical service, the spirit of open-source development views such attacks as teaching moments, opportunities to make the system stronger. The idea is that everyone using Ethereum is doing so on a caveat emptor basis. As long as that's agreed, this roiling process is viewed as an exercise in group improvement, in making Ethereum stronger, more dynamic, and adaptable. At least that's the theory. In practice, when there's a lot of money at stake, people get quite defensive about their rights to that money, which in turn means that successful open-source projects like Ethereum can, like Bitcoin, become quite politicized. That has left Buterin and the other early Ethereum founders—people like Lubin, Wood, and chief communications officer Stephan Tual—open to criticism that they are putting their personal interests first. Such divisions are to be expected, of course; what's interesting is how differently the Ethereum community has dealt with them compared to the Bitcoin community.

From the beginning, Ethereum was a project led by an identifiable group of people with a deliberate strategy to develop and profitably market a product. Ethereum's creators had much more of a startup mentality than that of the early Bitcoin community. Bitcoin emerged almost by stealth, with an unidentified creator slowly introducing it to a narrow subset of early volunteer users and developers until it slowly, but surely, caught on in the wider world. And whereas bitcoin tokens were started from day one at a zero balance, with anyone who knew about it eligible to participate, Ethereum started by "pre-mining" some 70 million tokens, which were sold and allocated to raise money for development, management, and marketing, and to reward the founders. In what was then one of the biggest crowd sales of its kind, Ethereum raised about $18.4 million in 2014 by "pre-selling" most of these tokens. Separately, another tranche of pre-mined ether tokens—16.5 percent of the total, worth about $3.5 million at the time—was set aside for founders and developers. For members of the team allotted ether from that pool, it turned out to be a bonanza. Those same tokens were worth $4.7 billion as of late November 2017—a staggering increase of more than 100,000 percent in just three years.

These kinds of dynamics, with large amounts of money at stake, can foster concerns that founders' interests are misaligned with other users. Ethereum's answer was the not-for-profit Ethereum Foundation, which was tasked with managing the pool of ether and other assets from the pre-mine and pre-sale—a model since used by many of the ICO token sales. For the time being, so many people are getting so rich with Ethereum that the top guys are mostly seen as heroes by other token holders. If anything, the biggest problem is the cult of success and the expectation that the developers can do no wrong. More so than Bitcoin, Ethereum's lead developers function like senior managers. They don't have the same execution authority as a regular company's C-suite, mostly because the community of users can, as with Bitcoin, reject updates to the software. But in practice, they exert significantly more political influence over the governance of Ethereum than do Bitcoin's developers.

This was best illustrated in the fallout from the $55 million DAO attack discussed in the previous chapter. White-hat developers plugged the hemorrhaging DAO account before the attacker could drain the whole investment fund, but the problem remained: what to do about the $55 million? Ethereum's leaders knew that by making software adjustments they could alter rights to the funds and so get the money back, so long as they acted before a twenty-seven-day lockup on The DAO tokens expired. The question was: should they? After a few modest coding changes failed, they settled on a drastic fix: Ethereum's core developers "hard-forked" the Ethereum blockchain, implementing a backward-incompatible software update that invalidated all of the attacker's transactions from a certain date forward. It was a radical move. To many in the cryptocurrency community, it threw into question Ethereum's all-important claim to immutability. If a group of developers can force a change in the ledger to override the actions of a user, however unsavory those actions are, how can you trust that the ledger won't be tampered with or manipulated again in the interests of one group over another? Does that not destroy the whole value proposition?

Well, in many respects, the Ethereum team operated as policymakers do during real-world crises. They made hard decisions that hurt some but were ultimately taken in the interests of the greater good—determined, hopefully, through as democratic a process as possible. The organizers went to great lengths to explain and gain support for the hard fork. And, much like the Segwit2x and other Bitcoin reform proposals, it wouldn't have come into effect if a majority of the Ethereum miners didn't accept it. For all intents and purposes, the fix *was* democratic—arguably, much more so than non-participatory democratic models through which crisis policymaking is enacted by national governments. And since Ethereum is more of a community of software engineers than of cryptocurrency investors, it was less contentious than Bitcoin's struggle over hard-fork proposals.

What's more, it turned out that disgruntled Ethereum participants weren't entirely powerless, either. A group decided to continue mining and trading the older, non-forked version of ether, with The DAO attacker's coins still there in the transaction history. They called it Ethereum Classic, adopted the code ETC for its currency, and traded it alongside the forked Ethereum's ETH ether. You now had two versions of Ethereum. This created much confusion and some interesting arbitrage opportunities—as well as some lessons for bitcoin traders when their own currency split two years later—but it can also be viewed as the actions of a dissenting group non-violently exercising their right to secede. More than a year later, Ethereum Classic is still around, though it trades at a small fraction of Ethereum's value, which means The DAO attacker's funds—whose movements on the public Ethereum blockchain have been closely watched—are of lower value than if they'd been preserved in ETH.

These hacks, and the scrambles to fix them, seem nuts, right? But let's put them in perspective. First, is this monetary chaos anything less unsettling than the financial crisis of 2008? Or the audacity of the subsequent Wall Street trading scandals? Also, as these wild hacks and rescues have occurred, each has provided a learning opportunity, leading to improvements in Ethereum's model and increasing confidence in it. They have given rise to new innovations such as Plasma, personally created by Buterin and Lightning Network co-creator Joseph Poon, which, much as Lightning does for Bitcoin, aims to shift resource-heavy transactions and smart-contract executions into a secure "off-chain" environment that reduces the burden on the Ethereum blockchain. If it works, it could make Ethereum ready for true, enterprise-level usage. Against this explosion of ideas, all fed by a multi-billion-dollar rush of money into this space, the hacking attacks seem insignificant.

Nonetheless, the trials of both Bitcoin and Ethereum show that the governance of open-platform, decentralized systems is hard. It requires disparate groups with competing interests to agree in order to make any changes. Still, in the inventive minds of the developers attracted to this space, limitations create an insatiable desire to fix them. That's why one of the most exciting aspects of blockchain innovation is found in the great ideas now being floated to deal with some of the early blockchain platforms' shortcomings.

In the early years of the Internet, plenty of doomsayers argued that autonomous computers would never safely talk to each other—mainly because encryption, legal, and other protections weren't in place. Eventually, the amount of brainpower dedicated to those problems vanquished them. The rest is history. We believe the same outcome will likely occur here. We close this chapter looking briefly at a few more of the most recent solutions that push us toward such goals.

A Better Bitcoin?

One major flaw of Bitcoin and other early cryptocurrencies is a source of obsession among cryptographers but often overlooked by the general public: a lack of privacy. Despite the prevailing perception of Bitcoin as an anonymous instrument and its occasional, well-publicized use by criminals and hackers to hide their identities, the reality is that the Bitcoin blockchain is a very public ledger. And although you won't see any names, only alphanumeric strings as addresses, having every transaction visible to everyone and traceable means that people—and the law—can eventually track you down, especially now that regulated bitcoin exchanges must comply with know-your-customer (KYC) requirements. This fuels nervousness among all who care deeply about the fundamental human right of privacy. Without true privacy, unhindered open economic access and social interaction will remain a pipe dream, privacy advocates say, since unwanted public exposure limits people's capacity to engage in free expression and free commerce. That's why various programmers are designing digital currencies that are less traceable.

You might ask, why shouldn't we be able to catch those odious ransomware hackers when they cash out for dollars? Well, for one thing, the forever-recorded block history of a specific coin's brushes with the law can undermine its value relative to another. As Zooko Wilcox-O'Hearn, founder of a new cryptocurrency called Zcash, explains, it's all about ensuring a currency's "fungibility"—the principle that "if you're going to pay someone with something, and you have two of them, it doesn't matter which one you give them." In other words, every dollar, or yen, or pound is worth the same regardless of the serial number on the relevant banknote. This isn't always the case with bitcoin. When the FBI auctioned the 144,000 bitcoins (worth $1.4 billion as of late November 2017) that it seized from Ross Ulbricht, the convicted mastermind of the Silk Road illicit goods marketplace, those coins fetched a significantly higher price than others in the market. The notion was that they had now been "whitewashed" by the U.S. government. In comparison, other bitcoins with a potentially shady past should be worth less because of the risk of future seizure. That's hardly fair: imagine if the dollar notes in your wallet were hit with a 10 percent tax because the merchant knew that five years ago, unbeknownst to you, they had been handled by a drug dealer. To avoid these distortions and create a cryptocurrency that works more like fungible cash, Wilcox's Zcash uses sophisticated "zero-knowledge proofs" to allow miners to prove that holders of the currency aren't double-spending without being able to trace the addresses.

Zcash, along with other new, cryptographically secured anonymous cryptocurrencies, such as Dash and Monero, have sparked a great deal of interest. And not just from libertarians and others who want to hide from snoopers. Banks are also drawn to this technology, for pretty straightforward reasons: they don't want their or their clients' trades revealed to the marketplace, since it would undermine their ability to do deals. In fact, there's a surge of interest in privacy solutions for the financial sector beyond these new "privacy coins." In February 2017, seven of the world's biggest banks, including J.P. Morgan and UBS, joined forces with the CME Group, Intel, and Microsoft to found the Ethereum Enterprise Alliance to "define enterprise-grade software" that's compatible with the high demands for both performance and, most importantly, privacy that large companies demand.

And then there are those thorny problems faced by Bitcoin and Ethereum: how to achieve scalability securely—namely, how to handle more transactions per second without creating an overly centralized or hackable platform—and, on a related matter, how to establish a democratic governance structure to address such issues. Two new blockchain offerings, Tezos and EOS, attack both of these. Over the course of twelve days in July, they raised $232 million and $185 million, respectively, to briefly claim records as the biggest and second-biggest crowdfunding exercises in history. (Filecoin's subsequent offering topped these deals, pulling in $252 million, most of it in just one hour.)

EOS is the brainchild of Daniel Larimer, an early pioneer in decentralized applications and distributed organizations. It also includes the well-respected cryptographer Ian Grigg—he of triple-entry bookkeeping. Block.one, the company behind EOS, lets miners verify records and confirm transactions by reviewing messaging data, a significantly lighter task than reviewing the historical balances that other permissionless blockchains require. With easier computation demands, EOS has been tested to handle 50,000 transactions a second and should eventually be able to hit millions per second, EOS says.

Tezos is structured to allow the community to more easily arrive at consensus over protocol changes. The system lets holders of the Tez token vote their stakes in support of special delegates empowered to approve staged protocol changes and incorporates flexible, dynamic rules that let users define and develop their own governance model over time. As we were going to print, Tezos's viability was in question as an ugly internal spat, discussed in chapter four, undermined people's confidence. Still, Tezos's contribution to the development of more robust governance systems has been an important one.

Every new idea will have shortcomings, yet, if developed by serious engineering teams, each idea can move the ball forward toward decentralization, functional governance, scalability, and privacy. This has been so with altcoins such as Litecoin, whose alternative approach to the proof-of-work algorithm showed that it was possible to stall the entrance of high-powered, industrial players into the mining network. Others—notably Vertcoin, discussed in chapter four—have improved on Litecoin's model. Vertcoin has avoided Bitcoin's unwelcome experience, in which the unrestrained competition for block rewards fostered a concentration of computation-heavy, electricity hungry mining operations.

There are also various iterations of the so-called proof-of-stake algorithm, which sets a user's right to validate transactions according to how many coins they hold. The core idea behind proof of stake is that with this "skin in the game," validators are disincentivized to undermine a record-keeping system that's vital to maintaining the value of their assets. One criticism of the model has been that without the electricity-consumption costs of proof of work, attackers in a proof-of-stake system would simply mine multiple blocks to boost their chances of inserting a fraudulent one into the ledger. But, more recently, a modified delegated proof-of-stake model has been developed—notably it is employed by EOS—with a more robust level of security. Called delegated proof-of-stake, it lets users appoint certain computer owners as delegates to vote on the performance and honesty of the miners—a kind of representative legislative branch to curtail the power of the executive.

Our comparison to constitutional government isn't coincidental. The protocol rules of a blockchain, as we've stressed, act as a form of governance over our economic behavior. Many businesses are betting that this technology will provide a new governance layer for the entire digital economy. That's why figuring out how best to govern the platforms themselves is also critical. The good news is that with this open-source, ad hoc, global process of competing ideas and innovations, solutions are being discovered. Perhaps the established blockchains such as Bitcoin and Ethereum will learn from the upstarts' improvements and absorb them into their models. Or perhaps they have too much at stake to change and will themselves be disrupted. Or perhaps some overarching cryptographic tool will come along that provides interoperability across all these disparate models, keeping them all alive but leaving no single player dominant.

We'll have to see. The point is, the competition between these different systems matters. Who decides what changes get made to these newly emerging economic systems does not just concern bitcoin mining companies in China or nerdy cryptographers in Palo Alto. It affects the future for all of us.

Four

THE TOKEN ECONOMY

On May 31, 2017, at 2:34 p.m. GMT, Brave Software Inc., a San Francisco–based firm specializing in Web infrastructure, opened an online sales window. They offered only one item for sale that day, and all of twenty-four seconds later, the entire stock of one billion was sold out, leaving many potential customers bitter about being left out. The object of this ravenous demand? Brave had raised the equivalent of $35 million in the initial coin offering, or ICO, of its basic access tokens, or BATs.

Over the end of the spring into the summer of 2017, ICO mania took hold. In the first seven and a half months of 2017, almost $1.5 billion flowed into this new investment class. Like bitcoin, BATs involved a unique, tradable digital asset whose transactions were proven via a public, decentralized blockchain. But, unlike bitcoin, these tokens were typically designed for exchanges within a specific industry or among a community using a particular Dapp. Most weren't mined on an ongoing basis, either; they were brought into existence through these one-off ICOs.

Other ICOs would raise as much as six times Brave's haul to successively establish new records for the biggest crowdfunding exercises in history. But what was striking about the Brave sale, which unlike many other larger ICOs was deliberately capped in size, was the sheer speed of incoming orders. It was clear that investors bought into Brave's promise of a token that could fundamentally change the broken online advertising industry. Brave took in Ethereum's ether as the incoming currency for the rapid-fire sale, which raised some concerns about heavyweight investors muscling less nimble players out of the pool. But it also said something about the appeal of Brave's unique value proposition. It represented the first effort to put a value on a resource that all of us are constantly giving up for little to no return: our attention. Here was the real power of this new idea of tokens. They offered a way to redefine and revalue the very exchange of resources around which economies function.

A Brave New Advertising Economy

Anyone who's been confronted by annoying pop-up ads that freeze their browser and prevent them from reading articles they've clicked on knows that the online advertising and publishing market is broken. We were promised improved precision, better analytics, direct-to-customer marketing, and greater revenue for quality content. It's fair to say each of the three stakeholder segments of the online content economy—publishers, advertisers, and users (readers/viewers)—has something to complain about. For users, the scourge of banner ads and unsolicited promotional videos is not only deteriorating the Web site experience, it is literally costing them bandwidth. (By one estimate, $23 a month of people's mobile phone bill pays for ads they don't want.) For advertisers, "bots" that generate fake traffic data have inflated rates for unworthy Web sites—resulting in $7.2 billion in losses for the industry in 2016, according to the Association of National Advertisers. Meanwhile, plunging CPMs, the standard costs-per-impression measure by which ad charge-out rates are set, are hurting mainstream publishers as their sites compete with the relentlessly expanding supply of alternative online content from blogs and social media. Perhaps inevitably, consumers are turning to ad-blocking software, with some 600 million mobile and desktop devices using these services as of early

2017, a trend that will leave labor-intensive newsrooms starved for the funds they need to produce quality journalism.

The result of all this is an ever-diminishing quality of information and a distorted set of incentives that makes it profitable for "fake news" providers to capture markets and earn ad dollars—essentially by lying, both with the false content they deliver to readers and the false Internet traffic data they share with advertisers. This in turn gives outsized influence to people who deliberately misinform for power or profit. Whatever your politics, we can all agree that plunging confidence in the quality of information, in an environment in which once undisputed facts are subject to bias and debate, is insidiously harmful to the democratic process and society at large.

Which brings us back to Brave's highly successful offering. The Brave team, led by Brendan Eich, inventor of the ubiquitous JavaScript Web programming language, is betting that tokens that put a value on audience attention can upend the distorted economics of this industry. The idea is to create price signals that entice participants to create better content and provide accurate information about audience behavior. As with many token issues, it's about using this new tool to provide incentives for companies and individuals to behave in ways that serve the common interest.

How do tokens work? Just as Bitcoin's protocol steers users and participants into certain actions that serve the community's interest—in its case, creating a secure, reliable ledger that all can trust—the programs that run tokens incorporate incentives and constraints that encourage certain pro-social behavior. A new concept—token economics—is emerging. It encapsulates the idea that we can embed into these "programmable" forms of money a way to steer communities toward desired common outcomes. Tokens might help us solve the Tragedy of the Commons. In other words, they could be a big deal.

The Tragedy of the Commons concept stems from a 1968 essay by the ecologist Garrett Hardin. Hardin tells the story of nineteenth-century farmers over-grazing the public land they shared because none of them could trust their counterparts not to let their livestock eat more than their fair share. It has long been used as a cautionary tale about the need for government to regulate access to a public resource—in the farmers' case, land. Ever since then, the "commons" has become a catchall for any "space" of public value, tangible or intangible, that needs protection. It is why, for example, people talk about free speech and copyright-free content on the Internet belonging to a "creative commons" zone that should be protected by laws, contractual agreements, and community activism. The issue is closely related to the classic economic problem of "externalities"—that capitalism can't easily put a price on the costs that everyone bears when a public resource is depleted, such as when a factory pollutes the air.

How does this relate to the ad and content industry? Well, like farmers sharing a commons, the online content industry has its own misused public resource, one that it struggles to put a fair price on: something Brave calls "user attention." Everyone in the publishing and advertising space is competing over access to readers' and viewers' eyeballs so that they can steer them toward content and entice them to buy something, whether it's a newspaper subscription or an advertised product. But the industry does a lousy job of identifying and paying for that attention—starting with the way it compensates readers and viewers, who provide the resource. In theory, we are "paid" for our attention to advertising with access to the news and other information that we want to consume—falsely described as "free"—while advertisers pay the publishers for the privilege of siphoning off a portion of our attention, often against our wishes, toward their product pitches. There's almost something dishonest about it.

Poor or fake page-view metrics and an ever-growing supply of available content have made the pricing of attention even more imprecise than it was already. Meanwhile, the real cost to users of giving up their attention is arguably much higher. As we discussed in chapter two, users are handing over exabytes' worth of valuable personal data—part of a new asset class that *The Economist* described as a twenty-first-century resource on par with oil in the previous century. We are giving up this valuable new data currency and getting a deteriorating experience in return. Meanwhile, publishers and advertisers—unable to accurately measure user attention, let alone capture it—are blindly working with meaningless numbers to devise pricing schemes that don't reflect the reality of how much of the user attention resource they have access to. These failures are the underlying reason for the distortions, abuses, and industry dysfunction highlighted above.

Brave applies a two-pronged strategy to this problem. It has created a new browser designed to work seamlessly with its tokens. The browser blocks all ads by default and, with sophisticated analytics, collates and anonymizes data from users that indicate how much time they spend looking at certain content. That way it can come up with a useful record of the amount of time we all spend at Internet sites without identifying us. As a user of the Brave browser, you are offered the potential to earn BATs for selectively turning off the ad blocker to view ads; tokens are delivered to an integrated wallet that you uniquely control. You can in turn use those tokens to reward publishers of content that you appreciate—in effect, tipping them with donations. Meanwhile, to place ads with publishers of content on the system, advertisers must first acquire BATs and then pay those tokens to publishers, with the price for those ads dictated by the attention metrics associated with the latter's content.

Together, these features have the potential to create an ecosystem in which attention is more directly and precisely compensated. It won't necessarily end the phenomenon of "clickbait" journalism—presumably, if stories on Kim Kardashian continue to draw people's attention, they will fetch the highest payouts in BATS. But the option to tip publishers could send more nuanced, informative signals to them. We don't know for sure how people will behave, but perhaps they'll be more inclined to tip BATs for a work of insight and effort than for a sexy photo they felt compelled to click on.

Whether we end up with higher-quality content or not, the BATs model seems like an intrinsically fairer way to price user attention than the existing one, since it directly rewards the attention givers. Users earn tokens for choosing to look at an ad, and if demand for BATs-priced ads expands, those tokens will rise in value as more and more advertisers enter the market, providing a capital gain to users. This is a better alignment of results than the current system, built as it is on the conceit that we get wanted content for "free" in return for viewing ads, when in fact we are giving up both time and large amounts of valuable data about ourselves and our Internet surfing habits.

An effective token strategy is one where the exchange of that token within a particular economy impacts human economic behavior by aligning users' incentives with those of the wider community. Fans of the *Freakonomics* book series will know that the study of economics is mostly about incentives—how expected outcomes drive us to buy particular items, withhold others, or act in a variety of ways. Too often incentives are "misaligned"—as with fund manager bonuses that are tied to short-term gains when the investors they serve would be better off with a long-term growth strategy. Well, token economics is an attempt to overcome such problems, by creating a programmed value effect—essentially, a rising price—that rewards people when they act in ways that benefit everyone. In this way, it can re-align incentives.

Whereas any two consenting parties can exchange a mainstream currency such as the dollar anywhere and for any transaction, a crypto-token contains software logic that can limit and proscribe what it's used for. In Brave's case, ads within its ecosystem can only be paid for with BATs. Other models include that of the decentralized computer storage platform Storj, which allows hard-drive-starved users to access others' excess space in exchange for storj tokens. Or there's the Gamecredits token, which lets people earn money for selling virtual goods, such as pets or weapons, within online game communities, but only if those items are proven to exist as advertised via a blockchain-based record of the product's underlying software. Currently, Gamecredits says fraudulent sales are a major problem for the $15 billion market in virtual gaming goods.

Under these models, money is no longer merely a morally neutral enabler of transactions; it can now capture the common values and interests of all parties who've agreed to use it. In the case of BATs, the attention metrics captured by the browser dictate who gets tokens and how many, putting a more meaningful market value on attention than can be achieved with traditional money. The idea is that if Brave is successful, the BATs' price will rise, which will in turn encourage more and more people to join the community and abide by its good-behavior-inducing rules. It aims for a network effect, one that feeds a virtuous circle of better-aligned incentives and rewards within the online content market.

Network effects like these are a critical source of market power for many companies in the digital economy. Amazon, Alibaba, Uber, and other digital behemoths all depend on them—on how widely an idea is adopted and reinforced in a positive feedback loop. The more people use Uber, the more drivers are drawn to the system, and the easier it is to find a ride, which attracts even more people to the service, and so forth.

Issuers of tokens are arguing that they will incentivize these kinds of network effects and positive feedback loops. So far that's an unproven contention. Success will likely hinge on the liquidity of each respective token, on how frequently it is traded back and forth. In Brave's case, the risk might be that the billion tokens it issued are treated like long-term investments, hoarded by investors who withhold them from circulation. In that case, the BATs' value won't accurately reflect the market for user attention. A critical mass of *use*, not holding, is needed.

Brave's model included a token-issuance strategy for dealing with that challenge. It set aside a 300 million–strong "user growth pool" to attract new users. There's a plan, for example, to deliver a small amount of BATs to the integrated Brave wallet whenever there's a unique new download of the browser. In this way, the token is designed as a tool to bootstrap adoption, to foster network effects.

"Early on we saw this as something that would allow us to stake users with initial grants," says Brave CEO Brendan Eich. The strategy was shaped by Eich's decades in Silicon Valley, where the veteran engineer created the ubiquitous Web programming language JavaScript in the nineties and later went on to co-found browser developer Mozilla. Over time, he realized that venture capitalists were reluctant to fund the marketing cost of acquiring users and that tapping new equity or debt to do so was dilutive to the founders' and early investors' ownership stakes. "But with a token, it can be disbursed to users without credit consequences," he adds, arguing that by contrast to a dollar's worth of equity or debt, "the BAT is a *social* credit currency; it doesn't have this inflationary property."

Let's break that last comment down. The cost, for what it's worth, of distributing the token to new users is borne by existing token holders, who will see their proportional stakes in the total supply diluted. But if, as Brave intends, this distribution successfully encourages network effects of expanding usage, a more-than-offsetting rise in token value may also occur. The point is that it's all on the community—the *society* of BATs users—not on external investors, to bear the risk of that happening. That's what Eich means by a social credit.

Still, there are other concerns about Brave's "flash" ICO. One problem: bigger investors dominated the sale by offering high fees to Ethereum miners. Much as Bitcoin miners who were confined by 1MB block sizes prioritized high-paying transactions, these big bidders' fees fast-tracked them to the front of the queue when Brave's smart contract began processing orders. Once the 1 billion tokens had sold out in twenty-four seconds, it was revealed that only 130 accounts got them and that the biggest twenty holdings covered more than two-thirds of the total. Those distortions left many investors angry.

Some argue that the pre-set fund-raising cap of $35 million was the problem, as it left too few tokens available and forced an aggressive strategy from unidentifiable bidders who could game the system in their favor. But others say Brave, which decided to limit how much it took in, treated investors more fairly than the approach taken by, say, the new blockchain project Tezos, whose $232 million haul left the developers with far more money than they needed and investors with a diluted stake. As for Eich, he complained to CoinDesk that he was having a hard time hiring "Ethereum talent," in part because of the nine-figure intakes, which let startups like Tezos outbid Brave and others for coders in the tight market for engineering talent.

The most important test of these differing token sale strategies will be whether they aid or hinder the token's evolution into what it is supposed to be: not a financing vehicle but a utility token. That is, whether it will help develop the network and ensure that the particular decentralized application does what it is supposed to do. Both to avoid falling afoul of securities laws and to ensure the platform grows into the future, ICO issuers must prove that their tokens aren't just speculative instruments, that they can truly be described as "products," as software with a function. The question has intrigued lawyers and regulators, who are addressing whether these new, ambiguous methods of value exchange can be distinguished from securities and so should be exempt from the onerous laws and restrictions that apply to the latter. How things pan out will determine whether investors and users lose or make money, and what their legal response might be.

Gold Rush

The sudden ICO mania is intrinsically associated with the success of Ethereum. In 2016 and 2017, Ethereum became the go-to platform on which to run hundreds of smart contract–based Dapps and on which to issue the tokens associated with them. All of this frenetic development created a powerful, positive feedback loop that drove Ethereum's valuation ever higher through the first eight months of 2017.

On July 30, 2017, Ethereum celebrated its second birthday with a swanky bash at a rooftop bar in Manhattan. It had come a long way in the four years since a nineteen-year-old geek had dared to dream it was possible to create a global world computing system that no one controlled. Many thought that Vitalik Buterin's idea was far-fetched at the time. And even after world-class developers like the Englishman Gavin Wood signed on, Ethereum had a series of mishaps—at one stage nearly burning through all its ICO-earned bitcoin as the latter's price went through a major slump. But by 2017, much had changed. Ethereum was discussed in Fortune 500 company boardrooms and government offices. Buterin's angular face and goofy smile graced the cover of numerous magazines. People talked breathlessly, often without much knowledge, of Ethereum's possibilities and limitations, of it being a world changer.

In many respects, the driver of Ethereum's success, much like that of Bitcoin, was the community that gathered around it and poured its faith and enthusiasm into its decentralizing vision for the global economy. In particular, the phenomenon of the Ethereum Meetup was important. It was the New York meetup chapter that organized the party on this particular evening.

The group sold 300 tickets for the party, and then sold 40 more because there was so much demand. The bar, which had been told to expect fifty people tops, struggled to keep up with the crowd. What brought so many people? Well, the price of ether, the native currency of the Ethereum network, had skyrocketed in the first half of 2017, going from $8 to about $400 by mid-June. It tumbled down to about $200 after that, but it was still making people who'd bought just seven months earlier considerably wealthier—and attracting others who hoped to get in on the action.

It was a picture-perfect day, warm but not sweltering, and there was a crystal blue, cloudless sky. The revelers posed for pictures with New York's skyline all around them; to the east, the gilded dome of the New York Life Building. Just south, the Metropolitan Life Tower. To the north, looming impressively above everything else, the Empire State Building. The party drew an energetic crowd, from crypto veterans like Joseph Lubin, who helped launch Ethereum with Buterin and now runs the influential Ethereum development lab ConsenSys, to newbies. As in most tech scenes, there were more men than women, but there were still plenty of women, and a healthy contingent of Gen Xers and even Baby Boomers, all dressed very casually. They talked about the various dramas of Ethereum and Bitcoin, and the challenges ahead, but also about the price and the swirling ICO phenomenon. Business cards were handed out liberally. People networked, and socialized, and dreamed up products on the spot that they suspected would make them rich.

We met one young woman who'd quit her job a few months earlier to incorporate her business. We met a man in his sixties who'd been a wealth manager for twenty-seven years and was now selling his advisory business to build his own blockchain-based service. One millennial, a staffer at Morgan Stanley, waited patiently to talk with Lubin—he hoped to make the jump into Ethereum, to build his own decentralized application, to find his own riches. We asked if he knew others who were interested, friends or co-workers. "They all are," he said.

As financial journalists, we've witnessed and covered a few investment manias in our time. We watched Bitcoin's first big wave of interest in 2013, but we're also old enough to have reported on the far bigger dot-com boom and bust of the 1990s, the ultimate in new-money riches. This party on that Sunday in July in New York City felt like those other eras. The energy of the crowd was palpable. The expectations of instant wealth were unmistakable. Like most other tech breakthroughs, this one contained a mixture of utopianism and capitalism. Some people wanted to change the world. Some wanted to get rich. Many imagined they could do both. The massive upward price swings were partially responsible for this frenzy. Bitcoin's price had tripled in 2017. Ether's price was up by 5,000 percent. Those moves, though, weren't the whole story. The thing that really changed in 2017 was contained in the letters ICO.

ICO, as noted above, stands for initial coin offering, a pre-sale of a cryptocurrency or blockchain-based tokens. They distributed funds quite differently from the model used in bitcoin, which from day one has been "earned" by miners using computing power to fulfill the proof-of-work requirement and has been issued according to a schedule set by a software system no one controls. By contrast, it's the ICO itself, the sale by the founders of the platform, that brings into existence these particular tokens, which unlike Bitcoin's general-use status are used only in association with the narrow demands of the Dapp with which they are associated. In other words, the ICO issuers flow directly to an entity set up and controlled by the founders of the Dapp—ostensibly to cover the cost of developing it, but also to reward them and their backers for the entrepreneurial risk of building it.

The idea has been around for a while. The Ethereum Foundation's $18.4 million fund-raise was handled this way; other early blockchain projects did the same. But it took a new tool, developed by a team of Ethereum developers led by Berlin-based Fabian Vogelsteller, to make the concept take off in the second half of 2016: an easy-to-follow smart contract system for tokens known as ERC20.

This standardized set of smart contract instructions meant that tokens could retain a common, consistent format for both the ICO and post-ICO trading. The tokens did not need their own blockchain and mining community to maintain them. Instead, ERC20 tokens traded *on top* of Ethereum. They were generated by an Ethereum-validated smart contract that kept track of the issuance and exchanges by token holders. These tokens, like bitcoin and all cryptocurrencies, still needed the immutable ledger of a blockchain truth machine to maintain their provable status as non-replicable digital assets. But because of the ERC-20 solution, they didn't need to develop their *own* blockchain with all the independent computing power that would require. Instead, Ethereum's existing computing network would do the validation for them.

This low-cost solution to the double-spending challenge launched a factory of ICOs as issuers found an easy way to tap a global investing community. No painful negotiations with venture capitalists over dilution and control of the board. No wining and dining of Wall Street investment banks to get them to put their clients on the order book. No wait for SEC approval. Just go straight to the general public: *here are my tokens; they're cool, buy them.* It was a simple, low-cost formula and it lowered the barrier to entry for some brilliant innovators to bring potentially world-changing ideas to market. Unfortunately, it was also a magnet for scammers.

The example that shone a light on what was possible with the ERC20 was a notorious one: The DAO, which, as we discussed in the previous chapter, fell prey to a massive token theft in 2016. When Stephan Tual, the founder of Slock.it, the startup that created The DAO, planned an ICO with ERC20 DAO tokens, he figured they'd raise $20 million, maybe, enough money to experiment with this unorthodox new investing model. In the end, The DAO raised $150 million. That was part of its undoing, of course, because it meant that when the attack happened, there was more than just experimental money at stake, which made people demand retribution. But at the same time it showed other would-be ICOers that there was a big appetite for investment in outside-the-box ideas for decentralized applications.

Ironically, it was The DAO copycat phenomenon that rescued Ethereum from the fallout from The DAO attack. Ether, which was trading at around $20 when the attack began in mid-June, sank as low as $8 during the monthlong aftermath and Ethereum hard fork. But because the ERC20 tokens are exclusively written on top of the Ethereum platform, such that the smart contracts that control them require payments in ether, the post-DAO enthusiasm for these tokens ended up more than rescuing the ether price. The ERC20 standard put ether in the sweet spot. Before then, bitcoin was really the only currency in which you could receive funds in a token sale. That was the case for Ethereum's 2014 crowdsale and for other ICO trailblazers such as the decentralized storage provider Maidsafe. Now, the ICO currency of choice was ether. People had to buy ether to invest in the new wave of tokens, which created an upward spiral that benefited all the developers in the Ethereum ecosystem. Not only were their new ERC20 tokens escalating in value, but they also owned ether—a stash they'd either obtained as a reward for Ethereum mining or had acquired as an investment or to keep as a store of "fuel" to manage the execution of their smart contracts. And ether was skyrocketing. This positive feedback loop in turn inspired other Ethereum-based developers to come up with their own new token-based Dapps and go to market with an ICO, which further spurred demand for ether and accelerated the carousel of surging prices.

The sense that something extraordinary had been unleashed was cemented in November 2016, when a site called Golem, which offered a platform for trading idle computer power (it billed itself as the "Airbnb for computers"), raised $8.6 million in half an hour. After that, money seemed to open up for anyone with a white paper and a token to sell. An initial high-water mark came in April 2017 when Gnosis, whose platform allows users to create prediction markets for betting on just about anything, sold 5 percent of the tokens created by the company to raise $12.5 million in twelve minutes. With the other 95 percent controlled by the founders, those prices meant that the implied valuation of the entire enterprise stood at $300 million—a figure that soon rose above $1 billion as the Gnosis token promptly quadrupled in price in the secondary market. By Silicon Valley standards, it meant we had the first ICO "unicorn." But unlike other highly profitable $1 billion–plus unicorns—like Uber and Airbnb—Gnosis hadn't sold a thing.

Meanwhile, the ICO ideas kept coming—some brilliant, some way outside the box, some highly dubious, many that just seemed born of sheer opportunism. Comparisons to Pets.com, that iconic IPO of the dot-com bubble, were increasingly heard as a wild array of ICO press releases flowed into Paul's inbox at *The Wall Street Journal*. REAL was a cryptocurrency-based real estate investment firm. Prospectors was an online multiplayer game set in the gold rush days; the game's token was called, predictably, gold. Paquiarium was a group that was looking to raise tens of millions to build what it was billing as the world's largest aquarium. Investors would get to vote on the site, share in the profits, and get a lifetime admission ticket. There was a "gentlemen's club" in Las Vegas, and another called kencoin that promised anonymity for the adult-services industry. Ahoolee wanted to build a search engine for online shopping. Each made the case, albeit sometimes weakly, that the token would reward a community of users, encouraging positive feedback loops and network effects as that community grew.

Every day brought new e-mails from people who wanted to "do an ICO." One wanted to fund a new rugby league. One wanted to fund a portable, personal air conditioner. One was trying to start a new budget airline. One day, Paul received a call from a businessman who'd read one of his stories in *The Wall Street Journal* and wanted more information about how to get started and where to get legal advice. The man said he'd tried to reach the lawyer Marco Santori, a partner at the law firm Cooley who'd been quoted in the story, but couldn't get through. Santori later told us that he was getting so many calls about ICOs, he simply couldn't answer them all.

The reason all those people were jumping on this bandwagon was made clear by the findings of CoinDesk's new Cointracker service. In the first seven and a half months of 2017, ICOs raised more than $1.5 billion, far exceeding the money raised by blockchain companies through traditional venture capital funding strategies. And if anything, with four offerings—Bancor, Tezos, EOS, and Filecoin—raising $830 million among them in the two months to August 12, it seemed that the tidal wave of offerings and money was only increasing. As ether and bitcoin prices soared again in August, nothing looked capable of putting a damper on the mood, not even a July warning from the Securities and Exchange Commission, which said some of these offerings could be considered securities and subject to regulation.

When *will* this trend stop? When the market turns, that's when. When investors realize that, for many of the coins they've bought, there's no *there* there. That's when we may well recognize that a massive bubble existed.

"Most of these will fail," said Olaf Carlson-Wee, the CEO of Polychain Capital, citing poorly conceived ideas and a lack of coding development. "Most of these are bad ideas from the beginning." That said, Polychain is an investment firm that Carlson-Wee founded expressly to invest in these new projects. In fact, most of the people investing seemed to be taking a very VC-like approach to it. They understood that most of the projects would fail. They just hoped to have a few chips down on the one winner.

There's a strong case to be made, in fact, that ICOs are a democratizing phenomenon. So long as developers are being up front about the risks and investors know they are taking a highly speculative bet, ICOs could be viewed as a quicker way to offer high-risk/high-return investment opportunities to a wider group of people without venture capitalists getting in first on the ground floor. Why should VCs get all the action in early-stage investing? In fact, says Cornell cryptographer and cryptocurrency expert Emin Gün Sirer, "VCs see this as a real potential threat. You can see it in their body language." When it comes to traditional equity investing, venture capital funds, private equity funds, hedge funds, and so forth always had an advantage on smaller investors, because they're exempt from regulations designed to protect the little guy. VCs are big enough to be designated as "accredited investors" by the SEC, so they're allowed to invest in securities that haven't gone through a public offering process, which would involve a prospectus and a host of other disclosures. That privilege has gotten the venture capitalists in at the ground floor of all the big bets of the past two decades: the Facebooks, the Googles, the Ubers.

Now, says Gün Sirer, Joe Public wants a piece of the action, and the tokens craze gives him a way in. Why is he demanding it? "Because the public currently has no good places to park its money. They need returns. The banks are giving them one, two percent at most. They realized that VCs get far more in these new business models and they are eager to take on similar risks." Gün Sirer is not fazed by the money that some are likely to lose, either. It's just the risk of investing. "They might find sometimes when they really regret the decisions they've made, but this community also seems quite independent and at home with the consequences of its actions. You don't see people organizing against so and so and saying 'let's create a regulatory push.' That's very exciting on its own."

It was striking to see the closed world of Silicon Valley venture capital, a male-dominated industry beset by sexual discrimination and abuse scandals, under pressure. The West Coast moneymen who'd preached the gospel of "disrupt or be disrupted" to nervous East Coast businessmen and government officials were suddenly finding themselves in the disruption crosshairs. There was even a sniff of a southern challenge to northern California's dominance of early-stage investing, as a number of token-focused investing funds took up shop in Los Angeles. These included Erick Miller's L.A.-based CoinCircle and the

Crypto Company. The latter, run by world-champion poker player Raif Furst, employs a token-investing approach that's partly modeled on Furst's prior venture, Crowdfunder, which channels retail investors' money into diversified holdings of startups to give them a piece of the VC action. It's early days, of course, but it's fun to imagine that "Silicon Beach" might one day give Silicon Valley a run for its money.

Not surprisingly, many VCs are going for the tried and tested strategy of "if you can't beat them, join them." Big-name firms such as Andreessen Horowitz, Sequoia Capital, Union Square Ventures, and Bessemer Venture Partners announced that they would be investing in tokens via a hedge fund called Metastable Capital, which was founded in 2014 by AngelList CEO Naval Ravikant, among others. Separately, specialized blockchain investment outfits such as Dan Morehead's Pantera Capital and Blockchain Capital, backed by brothers Bart and Brad Stephens, set up funds dedicated to tokens. Meanwhile, major law firms, such as Cooley, Perkins Coie, BakerHostetler, Debevoise Plimpton, MME, and Sullivan Worcester, all got in the game, advising ICO clients on how to stay above the law. There was a real sense that the professionals of the finance world were grabbing real estate in the cryptoassets industry. For all the mania in the token markets, these players brought heft, and a veneer of legitimacy, to the industry.

It's worth noting, too, that for all the David v. Goliath talk, when the big gun VCs put their money in, it significantly boosted results. That was the case with legendary investor Tim Draper, of Draper Fisher Jurvetson, whose grandfather, William H. Draper, and father, Bill Draper, essentially created the Valley's venture capital industry and whose son, Adam Draper, was one of the earliest VC investors in Bitcoin and blockchain startups. When it became known that Draper bought into the June 2017 token sale of Bancor, a platform for other blockchain platforms to launch and manage token sales, it soon became the biggest ICO on record, topping $153 million. That record didn't last long, though, because when investors heard Draper was also backing husband-and-wife team Arthur and Kathleen Breitman's Tezos, investors threw a stunning $232 million at their new blockchain project the following month. "In December, I had a dream that we raised $30 million," recalls Kathleen Breitman, "and I thought, 'that's impossible.'"

Kathleen Breitman may now wish the actual number had been closer to that of her dream. The giant $232 million fund-raising haul thrust her and her husband into a glaring spotlight. It put extra attention on some troubling delays in software development that were exacerbated by an internal dispute between the Breitmans and Johann Gevers, the chair of the ostensibly independent Tezos Foundation that was responsible for distributing the funds. That spat attracted a lot of press coverage and fueled rumors that the SEC had formally launched an investigation, rumors the Breitmans sought to quell by stating publicly that the agency had not contacted them.

The Breitmans and other such founders are running the equivalent of startups at the inception phase, when they would normally be looking for seed capital from angel investors and friends and family. Yet here they are raising massive amounts from the broader public, something that doesn't usually happen until after years of proven business with rising revenues and steady growth. To traditional startups who've gone through the bootcamps and door-knocked multiple firms in Palo Alto and Mountain View just to secure measly early rounds of $500,000, this must seem profoundly unfair. The same goes for more established firms that have battled with lawyers and Wall Street firms to get an "exit" via the traditional initial product offering, or IPO.

Consider what online meal-kit maker Blue Apron had to do to raise $300 million in its IPO in June 2017. Initially, the company wanted to sell shares at $15 to $17 but wasn't finding any takers. So it lowered the price, then lowered it again. It finally went public at $10. Blue Apron had been around for about eight years. It had posted about $800 million in revenue the year before. It had a product and a history. The following month, a startup called block.one, which had not existed twelve months prior, raised $185 million in its ICO. Its product was the unlaunched EOS blockchain designed for enterprises to build their own decentralized solutions. Block.one has some impressive ideas and claims its blockchain will eventually run millions of transactions a second. But no one can be sure it will work.

Still, it's not accurate to compare these decentralized platforms to traditional companies like Blue Apron. In theory, everyone who owns their tokens benefits from the expansion of the service, the network effects, and rising value. Tokens don't have the same structure as traditional companies, which have clearly delineated managers and shareholders—with the latter holding a clear per-dollar vote—and a definable source of revenue. The "revenue," if you can call it that, that block.one will generate can be identified as the rising value of its tokens, the gains of which will in turn be earned and traded by EOS miners, developers, and users, allowing all of them to share in that revenue. In these networked enterprises, the lines are blurred between company, owner, investor, manager, employee, and customer. So, you could argue that comparisons to traditional equity-based fund-raising exercises aren't appropriate. In fact, these hard-to-compare definitions are at the heart of a fraught and contentious legal debate.

A Warning or Green Light from the SEC?

The big worry in the ICO space is that regulators will crack down on token issuers for having sold something to the public that should have been registered as a security. That could be the trigger that bursts the bubble. In September 2017, the market got a taste of what could come when, after Chinese regulators took the drastic step of banning ICOs altogether, prices for all coins, including even bitcoin and ether, took a dive. The move forced many popular cryptocurrency exchanges in China to delist dozens of tokens.

As for the SEC, in its no-action opinion about The DAO it made it clear that tokens involving investment promises can be viewed as securities and so can be subject to disclosure, registration, and a host of other requirements that very few ICOs have undertaken. Which tokens meet The DAO's status is the big question. The SEC did not say that *all* ICOs will be judged as unregistered securities, merely that it "will depend on the facts and circumstances."

Some lawyers representing token-issuing startups optimistically observed that the SEC had implicitly signaled that tokens need not be automatically defined as securities and explicitly expressed support for capital market innovation. Still, the opinion did have a damping effect on the industry. Hong Kong–based exchange Bitfinex chose to bar U.S. investors from trading in certain assets, including the EOS token, taking a cautionary response to the SEC's warning that token exchanges could also be penalized if they let unregistered securities trade on their platforms.

One reason for the legal ambiguity is that tokens don't fit into a neat definitional bucket. Many, such as ether, can be quite convincingly described as "products" that are necessary if developers want to build new applications on whatever decentralized platform the token is associated with. On the other hand, there's a clear fund-raising intent behind most ICOs, and, to judge from how day traders talk on crypto trading sites, many retail investors view these as purely speculative investments that they hope will turn a profit. They're not interested in how they work as tools. It remains to be seen whether the prevalence of that mind-set skews the SEC toward concluding that many token offerings meet the so-called Howey Test for being a security. That test, established in a landmark case of 1946, holds that if a sales offering entails an *investment of money* in a *common enterprise* from which there is *an expectation of profit* stemming from the *efforts of a third party*, it is a security.

Whatever regulators do, the industry is crying out for a more sophisticated investment infrastructure. Coinlist, established by AngelList's Ravikant, is creating standardized approaches to token sales that are designed to give investors clarity and legal certainty and a kind of branded stamp of approval. Advisory firms like Coinfund are helping investors and issuers understand how tokens work. The Token Report offers the first of what will likely be a variety of investor newsletters in this arena, and ICORatings.com conducts what it says are independent audits of ICOs to assign them ratings of "Positive," "Stable," "Risky," "Negative," "Default," or "Scam."

Innovation is also happening in the legal space, with Cooley coming up with a new legal vehicle called a Special Agreement for Future Tokens, or SAFT, to give greater legal certainty and assure that start-ups are incentivized to use the incoming funds to properly develop their services. Modeled on a contract known as a SAFE (Special Agreement for Future Equity), which professional investors sometimes enter into with companies yet to issue equity, SAFTs would be sold to accredited investors—which must have at least $1 million in liquid net worth and more than $200 million in income—assuring the process is legally kosher from day one. "The issuers then use the funds they raise to develop the platform's network," said Cooley's Santori. "Only then, once the network is functional, and tokens are functioning as a real product, can they be sold to the public." The SAFT gets around the risk that the SEC will judge many ICOs to be securities if their tokens aren't yet part of a functioning, decentralized platform. Many investors are clearly buying into ICOs in the expectation of profit and are relying on the development team's platform-building work to achieve that, two qualities the SAFT designers say mean they will meet the Howey Test criteria and be treated as securities. The problem is that in limiting access to accredited investors, SAFTs are a step away from the democratization of finance that people like Gün Sirer, cited above, celebrate about the ICO phenomenon.

It appears that limiting access to accredited investors won't too heavily constrain access to funds for clever developers. In its first-ever application, a SAFT offering brought in a record $252 million for the Filecoin crowdsale in early August 2017, breaking Tezos's one-month-old record. Filecoins are being sold as an incentive system for people to contribute their computers' hard drives to something called the Interplanetary File System, or IPFS, a distributed Web-hosting system that might just re-decentralize the World Wide Web.

There's another way to spread tokens, build a network, and fund the development of a platform without attracting SEC action—and, in the eyes of many cryptocurrency advocates, maintain your integrity. And that's to do things the old-fashioned crypto way: by introducing tokens into the ecosystem through the ongoing mining process. There's no pre-sale mechanism to reward founders and fund their operations. The developers must instead compete with all other miners to gain access to tokens when they are periodically released, just as Satoshi Nakamoto had to with every new Bitcoin block, right from day one.

In this model, developers are always the earliest adopters, and so typically gain a head start in accumulating coins. But the question of fair distribution still comes up, especially with the proof-of-work algorithm. That's because those who gain the most tokens are those with the most powerful computers. Yet not every mining-based cryptocurrency needs to end up as Bitcoin has, where only the biggest, most powerful computing operations—now managed on an industrial scale—can effectively compete for coins. Some new altcoins are designed to be "ASIC-resistant." This means that the protocol's in-built consensus algorithm—the puzzle miners must solve to win coins—compels their computers to carry out various functions that can't easily be performed by existing versions of the super-fast Application-Specific Integrated Chips now uniformly embedded into the equipment of the biggest bitcoin miners. The idea is to give no special advantage to those who own these expensive, single-purpose raw computation machines. This means that people running computers with relatively inexpensive graphic processing units, or GPUs, can successfully compete for a decent supply of coins and that a wider distribution of those tokens is possible.

Eventually, chip designers tend to figure out how to make ASICs that overcome this resistance, as was the case with ASIC mining equipment that was specially designed to handle Litecoin's s-crypt algorithm. But developers of Vertcoin have shown that it's also possible to create a permanent commitment to ASIC-resistance by introducing something from the real, non-digital world of social organizations: a pact. If the platform's governing principles include a pre-existing commitment from all users of the coin to accept a fork—a change to the code—that would add new, ASIC-resistant elements as soon as someone develops such a chip, the coin's community can protect the distributed, democratic structure of a GPU-led mining network.

Yet ICOs or token sales—call them what you want—can and will play a powerful role in reforming our capital markets. So, it's encouraging to see that the investment community is starting to grow up around this provocative concept, developing higher standards. More and more professional investors are entering into the market and purportedly applying longer-term buy-and-hold strategies. They will hopefully foster fiduciary standards that hold issuers to account for objective assessments and for making disclosures and putting trusteeship control over the money they receive.

If all this happens, the industry should start to look less like the Wild West. It may have to take some painful losses first, but that, too, could be cathartic. It's worth remembering that it took the bursting of the dot-com bubble and the disappearance of Pets.com and friends to bring focus onto the real innovative breakthroughs of the Internet. Those failures paved the way for Google, Facebook, and Amazon.

The Golden Age of Open Protocols

While the flood of money into ICOs gets the attention, it's the potential for a new economic paradigm, for new ways to value the preservation of public goods, that's most compelling about the emerging token economy. Union Square Ventures partner Fred Wilson compellingly explained one facet of this in a blog post in which he argued that tokens would usher in a "golden age of open protocols." Whereas developers couldn't make money building the open protocols on which the Internet was first constructed—the core protocol pair of TCP/IP, the Web's HTTP, and e-mail's SMTP, for example—those building the protocols of these new decentralized applications can now get rich doing so, even though their products are similarly open for anyone to use. That could incentivize a wave of powerful innovation within the foundational infrastructure of the digital economy, Wilson argued.

Builders of open platforms, Wilson wrote, need no longer be limited to universities, government institutes, or other non-profit entities that don't need to keep shareholders happy. So, whereas those entities always struggled to compete for engineering talent with for-profit creators of the Internet's commercial applications, platforms like Ethereum can now attract the best of the best. They can quickly tap into a "hive mind" of creative power across a global network of open-source coder communities. This speaks to our broader notion that tokens, by incentivizing the preservation of public goods, might help humanity solve the Tragedy of the Commons, a centuries-in-the-making shift in economic reality.

Though it is still tiny in comparison to traditional capital markets and will no doubt look quite different if and when the bubble bursts, this ecosystem of tokens and open platforms is starting to look like the map of a new, decentralized economic future. Startups are promising that everything from computer storage platforms and ride-sharing applications to solar power generation and online advertising contracts will be decentralized and managed with tokens. In fact, these digital assets might even become the primary means by which human beings generate and exchange value.

Digital Barter?

It took a leap of cognition for people to accept that an entry on a digital ledger that's controlled by no one could function as a currency. One lesson to take from blockchain-based digital tokens is that they will help us further redefine what money is. Whereas a "Bitcoin maximalist" view holds that every payment or expression of value will eventually gravitate to Bitcoin (so long as its network can securely scale), the token economy vision is one of fragmentation in our instruments of value. In fact, if we take it to its logical conclusion, and software-driven systems can be developed to allow liquid exchanges across digital tokens, we may not need to hold a common currency at all to make exchanges with each other.

For this to happen, we would need a powerful computer program

pollution and carbon emission targets have occurred. That act of destroying tokens, through a cryptographic function, will increase the surviving tokens' scarcity and thus their value. The point: holders are motivated to act in the interests of improving the planet now, not tomorrow.

Who knows whether Miller's big idea will work. But the refreshing nature of it is that it challenges, head-on, the real problem behind our failure to tackle climate change: the divisive politics of clashing economic interests. It's this raw power struggle that has made it nearly impossible for coal industry–captured governments like the Trump administration to do the right thing for the world. So why not bypass government altogether and address the politics via the software-driven governance of the money we use?

The current design of global capitalism, in which money is not just a means of exchange but a fetishized marker of value that we're incentivized to accumulate in a demonstration of our power, is responsible for the mess that this planet is in. Surely we owe it to future generations to redesign that system in a bid to save life on earth. The opportunity to do that may come from programmable money—money that is not itself an end-goal commodity but rather what it was always meant to be, merely a tool for exchanging and collaboratively generating value.

Of course, it's not just in the toxic poisoning of our planet that global capitalism and the political model that supports it are failing us. We have serious misalignments between the incentives for politicians to make laws that favor their corporate donors and the interests of the voters they are supposed to represent. The mass-marketed idea of retirement as some aspirational endpoint has created an industry of fund managers who peel off short-term profits every quarter while no one is properly incentivized to address the threats to those same assets that will come once our aging societies start driving economic productivity ever lower. These kinds of tensions are fueling terrorism, violence, insecurity, and a real risk that, one day, this toxic mix of protectionism, nationalism, and xenophobia will put us on a path to serious armed conflict.

To be cynical about the prospect of change, though, is to give up. So, it's in that spirit that we encourage people to reflect on these alternative visions for a post-capitalist society, to imagine these technologies as the platform for a future that is neither mired in the failed, collectivist ideas of socialism nor trapped by the centralized, exclusionary political economy of state-protected, big-business monopolies. These ideas offer a way out, but a way that requires a change in thinking about how value is created. Rather than framing the exchanges that define our life—of labor, assets, and ideas—as a means to acquire a particular form of money that's defined by a symbolic banknote, we should explore new value models, whether with tokens or something else, that incentivize collaboration for the betterment of all.

The accumulation of wealth has never been a zero-sum game. When we engage in behavior that fosters a self-reinforcing feedback loop of inclusion, efficiency, and innovation, it's possible to build wealth by creating it rather than taking it. Designed right, these new economic systems could marshal the forces of the market not to incentivize overpaid CEOs to build coal-powered generation plants but to make the most efficient use of our resources and those of the planet so that we all prosper. In the next chapter, we'll dig more deeply into how blockchain technology offers new ways to reimagine this system.

Five

ENABLING THE FOURTH INDUSTRIAL REVOLUTION

You might think, as you binge through the latest episodes of *The Walking Dead* on Netflix, beamed through your 65-inch Smart TV, that you're just somebody who likes a good zombie story. What you don't realize is, you're a futurist, too. Because that Smart TV of yours is not just projecting a program beamed over the airwaves. It is one of more than 8 billion devices around the world that are plugged into the so-called Internet of Things, a vast network of devices like TVs, cars, electric meters, and security cameras that are programmed to exchange information, to "talk" to each other, in essence. You've probably been hearing about the IoT for a few years now. You may not have realized that it's already here.

Progress has been swift since the first machines that could be called computers were produced in the years after World War II. Even twenty years ago, undergraduate students were able to make single semiconductor chips that had as much raw computing power as those room-sized computers. Today, everyday gadgets contain minuscule microprocessors with thousands of multitudes more power than the gargantuan, room-sized early computers. Information processing is no longer confined to single computers, and computation increasingly happens at the *interconnection* of computers. This is why the Internet of Things matters: it's not that we've empowered billions of new devices to do computation per se; it's that they are being connected with each other to create a computing colossus that's infinitely larger than the sum of its parts. We've reached the point of truth for Sun Microsystems veteran John Gage's famous quip that "the network is the computer." As we discover ever more ways to harness the power of these systems, the processing capacity of that "everywhere computer" just keeps building upon itself with every new device plugged into the network. This is no small moment for society. Whether this power will be leveraged for the good of the people, or to their detriment, has yet to be determined. A rugged, well-constructed, distributed truth machine meshed into these new networks would go a long way toward making sure these magnificent new virtual machines work to people's advantage.

Pushing processing power to the network was initially enabled by the wired Internet, and then by mobile computing, with the great variety of wireless connections now tying it all together. But just as importantly, growth in network capacity has also been driven by software programs that unlock networks' vast informational potential. Data analytics is becoming increasingly sophisticated, as computers mine the vast, complex information generated by massive networks to draw inferences about group behavior. Think of how accurately traffic apps like Waze now give us fastest-route estimates of our driving plans, or how vital Twitter analysis is to political campaigns. Machine learning takes this to another level, as individual computers adjust themselves to the data they receive from the network and become ever more powerful in an ongoing feedback loop.

In our opinion, though, the new software concepts that will most enhance our knowledge of social phenomena will be founded on or inspired by the blockchain. Without the principle of a distributed trust protocol, the applications of virtual machines are limited; data controlled by centralized, trusted third parties, which monopolize the analytics through secret algorithms, is inherently limited. Not only is the data inaccessible to the wider community unless fees are paid, but mistrust of the monopoly can lead data providers to withhold information. A "global brain" can't really come into existence in an economy dominated by the centralized trust model. Blockchain-based network designs probably won't get the same attention in homeware magazines as smart doorknobs and self-driving cars, but they will be a fundamental backbone of the network computational capacity of an Internet of Things economy in which tens of billions of devices like doorknobs and cars are autonomously "talking" to and trading with each other.

World Economic Forum founder Klaus Schwab says we're moving into a "fourth industrial revolution," not because one particular new line of products is coming but because a variety of technologies are combining to create whole new systems: mobile devices, sensors, nanotech processors, renewable energy, brain research, virtual reality, artificial intelligence, and so forth.

Linking billions of data-gathering and processing nodes to a global, ubiquitous networked computer architecture will have a profound impact on how we interact with our world. It means that our *material* existence, both within the worlds of natural resources and of human-made manufactured objects, will be far more comprehensively measured, analyzed, and explained, creating an omnipresent, *dematerialized* understanding of that existence.

New, interconnected computing and sensor systems will soon give us a far deeper understanding of how that material world functions—how fast, hot, or cold our devices are; how accurately, efficiently, or reliably they are running; or how long a particular resource, be it a store of electricity, a water source, or a supply of oxygen, will last. This expanded, more up-to-date, and more accurate information could have a huge impact on how we manage the planet's desperately stretched resources and on how we might improve our economic processes to produce more, or at least better, things—such as food and tools—to widen the net of comfort and prosperity for all humanity.

Imagine a world where a network of sensors on the ground, combined with advanced data analytics, can identify problems with a bridge well before it collapses. Imagine a world where pandemics never happen because health professionals see viruses spreading in real time and cut them off at the moment of contagion. Well, this revolution can't arise—the information simply won't be optimized—unless we enable a distributed architecture for addressing the problem of trust. If we build a centralized IoT world, massive stores of device-driven information will be monopolized by overly powerful companies. Their giant honey-pots will be irresistible to thieves, prompting security and privacy breaches far bigger than those we experience now. And the threats from such attacks are arguably more serious. It's bad enough when a stolen password grants a hacker access to your e-mail. Imagine if it granted access to your thermostat, or car, or to a city's traffic management system. Security is a big issue now, without a global network of connected devices. It could be a dystopian nightmare if our current level of cybersecurity is not improved.

So, looking first at the structure of IoT itself, let's examine the various ways in which we can incorporate the distributed trust concepts of blockchain thinking into this new approach for managing the material world.

Saving the Internet of Things from Itself

Not that long into the IoT mania, cybersecurity experts began to take stock of the dangers of rushing headlong into a technology over which there is so little control. Worst-case scenarios were easy to dream up: hackers gaining access to your house, your car, your phone, your television, your medical records, your criminal records, your voting habits. State-sponsored attackers remotely taking control of airplanes, toll roads, voting booths, or the electricity grid. Terrorists killing thousands by turning off their pacemakers. Security expert Bruce Schneier laid it all bare in a 2016 article in Motherboard: "It's one thing if your smart lock can be eavesdropped upon to know who is home. It's another thing entirely if it can be hacked to allow a burglar to open the door—or prevent you from opening your door. A hacker who can deny you control of your car, or take over control, is much more dangerous than one who can eavesdrop on your conversation or track your car's location."

With the Internet of Things and other such "cyber-physical systems," Schneier said, "we've given the Internet hands and feet: the ability to directly affect the physical world. What used to be attacks against data and information have become attacks against flesh, steel, and concrete." Making matters worse is the challenge people face in upgrading software to their devices; we have a hard enough time keeping up with Microsoft's and our app providers' security patch updates on laptops and smartphones, let alone having to update the software on our Internet-connected fridge. (This particular problem was laid bare by the attack on domain name service provider Dyn, which was executed by taking control of poorly maintained devices, as discussed in chapter two.) If the IoT is going to be a tool that helps people rather than oppresses them, we're going to need to rethink the design principles that make it secure.

Between its analytics, cloud-computing, and other enterprise software businesses, IBM has become a major player in IoT infrastructure and is now embracing blockchains. In a widely read paper titled "Device Democracy: Saving the Future of the Internet of Things," a pair of the company's scientists homed in on the core ethical quandary: how to ensure trust. Who is capable of and can be trusted to run a global network of billions of devices that will tap into virtually every single thing we do on a daily basis? It's one thing for a private company like, say, Comcast, to offer a relatively simple service such as cable for millions of people. But trusting a monopoly gatekeeper with all the sensitive personal data that's broadcast by your devices is much more problematic. If you are already uncomfortable with what Google, Amazon, Facebook, and Apple know about you, think about it in the context of a centralized IoT. Having transactions pass through a small number of behemoth companies would not only be an inefficient way to route data and require regulatory constraints to the system, but it could also create an Orwellian level of control. Do we really want

Amazon Web Services or any other big cloud service provider controlling all that valuable data? Not only would that company gain an unprecedented, privileged window onto the entire world of material things and human activity, but it would, in effect, put those centrally controlled companies in charge of what will be billions of machine-to-machine transactions of tokens and digital currencies. That would give a new meaning to the phrase "too big to fail."

One alternative is for governments to act as gatekeepers—but if you think Edward Snowden's NSA snooping allegations were bad, just imagine the Feds intermediating all the personally revealing data flowing from your gadgets. No thanks. "The Internet was originally built on trust," write the authors of the IBM paper, Veena Pureswaran and Paul Brody. "In the post-Snowden era, it is evident that trust in the Internet is over. The notion of IoT solutions built as centralized systems with trusted partners is now something of a fantasy."

Pureswaran and Brody argue that the blockchain offers the only way to build the Internet of Things to scale while ensuring that no one entity has control over it. A blockchain-based system becomes the Internet of Things' immutable seal. In an environment where so many machine-to-machine exchanges become transactions of value, we will need a blockchain in order for each device's owner to trust the others. Once this decentralized trust structure is in place, it opens up a world of new possibilities.

Consider this futuristic example: Imagine you drive your electric Tesla car to a small rural town to take a hike in the mountains for the day. When you return you realize you don't have enough juice in your car and the nearest Tesla Supercharger station is too far away. Well, in a sharing economy enabled by blockchains, you would have nothing to fear. You could just drive up to any house that advertises that it lets drivers plug into an outlet and buy power from it. You could pay for it all with cryptocurrency over a high-volume payments system, such as the Lightning Network, and the tokens would be deducted from your car's own digital wallet and transferred to the wallet of the house's electric meter. You have no idea who owns this house, whether they can be trusted not to rip you off, or whether they're the sort of people who might install some kind of malware into your car's computer to rob its digital-currency wallet. The homeowner has similar reasons to be concerned about you, in addition to the fact that he or she cannot know whether you're truly good for the money you're sending. But here's the thing: if there's a distributed trust system such as a blockchain in place, so that the integrity of the devices and of the transactions can be assured by a tamper-proof record that both parties can trust, this mutual lack of knowledge about each other doesn't matter. A distributed trust system lets complete strangers—and most importantly, complete strangers' machines—transact with each other.

The kind of system that Pureswaran and Brody proposed should give credibility to the billions of transactions running across a single network of globally connected devices. Under their model, the data shared would be limited to that needed to assure trust in each device, not a fire hose of identifiable information for prying eyes to see. So that when your car swaps cryptocurrency with the house's electric meter, neither of you, nor anyone in the broader network of users and validators of the blockchain, gets access to any personal information about either party initiating the transaction.

"In our vision of a decentralized IoT, the blockchain is the framework facilitating transaction processing and coordination among interacting devices," Pureswaran and Brody wrote. They explained how the distributed trust system lets people do more with devices than they currently can because they can trust that whatever other device they are engaging with isn't acting maliciously. "Each [device] manages its own roles and behavior, resulting in an 'Internet of Decentralized, Autonomous Things'—and thus the democratization of the digital world." Think of it as a machine society building its own version of social capital.

"Trusted" Computing

There's still a problem here: we need to know that the device itself hasn't been compromised at some point, that the machine's own "identity," going back to its origins as a pile of unassembled parts in the factory, can be trusted. It's a hard nut to crack. Device manufacturers use the phrase "trusted computing" to describe their efforts to resolve it. It's a concept that chipmakers AMD and Intel Corp. have worked on in concert with IBM, Microsoft, Cisco, and others within a consortium known as the Trusted Computing Group.

As it is currently designed, trusted computing is intended to confirm that a computer will act as intended—for example, that it will communicate the very string of text that the user types in, and nothing else, when certain keystrokes are hit—that is, that it has not been compromised by malicious code. To achieve this first requires watertight security within both computerized design labs and semiconductor fabrication centers. Demonstrating the extent of this challenge, researchers at the University of Michigan recently showed how a rogue actor could insert a microscopic "backdoor" into a semiconductor chip by tweaking just one transistor—in theory, we could be using smartphones with in-built listening devices that someone has installed without either our or the manufacturer's knowledge. Preventing such incursions is vital.

Once assurances of site security are given, the next step in a trusted computer module is to load the device with cryptographic tools that allow it to communicate securely with its software.

The current approach to trusted computing involves a device's installed hardware and software components sharing cryptographically signed messages to prove that each one has not been corrupted. This system is not without controversy among privacy advocates. That's because, in order to assure a foolproof environment free of human error, these systems do not let device owners control or even read the inter-component messages that are occurring right inside their gadgets. It forces users to trust the companies that built these devices and installed these secure messaging systems—big players like Intel—which effectively insert their authority into the system's security equation. Once again, we are back to the trusted third-party problem—and in this case, the intermediaries are controlling what's going on the devices that *we* own. For now, though, this trusted computing model is what we have and, for the most part, it works.

Trusted computing is only one part of the larger challenge of securing the Internet of Things. The record of a device's activities is also important: its history of transactions; the different password-activated authorizations it has received to perform various tasks; who and what has handled it throughout its life cycle from the moment it was built, to when it was shipped, to its time of active service, and then to its ultimate retirement. Just as maintaining accounts of humans' actions helps prevent fraud, good record-keeping is also vital for knowing a particular device is safe to engage with and whether it's not counterfeiting the digital currency it is sending to another device. And if there's a case to be made that blockchains are superior to centralized ledgers for tracking and managing human transactions, then there's an arguably stronger case for doing so with IoT devices. For one, machines are not legal entities; they can't have bank accounts or use Paypal, Venmo, or any other regulated digital wallet.

The envisioned scenarios in which IoT gadgets would pay for short-term access to services controlled by other devices—to use a nearby person's iPhone Wifi hotspot to send one vital e-mail, for example—assumes an economy of multi-party, rapid-fire micropayments. And this environment simply couldn't be managed by the convoluted payments system of the existing centralized financial model, with its three-day settlement periods and high transaction costs. If IoT devices are to trade value with each other they need a more decentralized system of record-keeping and transacting—like a blockchain. Lots of companies are trying to build one.

One early mover into this field is Intel. The chip-making giant has developed a blockchain technology it calls Sawtooth Lake that builds on top of its pre-existing trusted computing module, known as Software Guard Extensions (SGX). The system is designed to be "blockchain agnostic," meaning that it can be run on either a private, permissioned blockchain set up by a company or on a public, permissionless network of devices. A purist might argue, however, that Sawtooth's dependence on Intel's proprietary SGX trusted computing model diminishes the decentralization advantages of a permissionless system, since users must now trust Intel's software. Nonetheless the capacity to incorporate IoT-specific protections into a permissionless blockchain is important because it opens up a much broader vision of an IoT future than one that is controlled by select IT companies.

Consider one scenario that some envisage in an IoT world, where a self-driving car that needs to get somewhere in a hurry can make a small payment to another self-driving car to let it pass. As discussed, you'll need a distributed trust system to verify the integrity of the transaction, which may involve a lot more information than just that of the money transfer before it can be processed—for example, you may need to know whether the overtaking car is certified as safe to drive at the faster speed, or whether one car's software can be trusted not to infect the other with malware. These kinds of verifications, as well as that of the fund balance in the paying car's wallet, could be run through a blockchain log to check the validity of each side's claims, giving each the assurances they need without having to rely on some certifying central authority. The question, though, is: would this transaction be easily processed if it were based on a private blockchain? What are the chances, in a country of more than 230 million cars, that both vehicles would belong to the same closed network run by a group of permissioned validating computers? If they weren't part of the same network, the payment couldn't go through as the respective software would not be interoperable. Other car manufacturers might not want to use a permissioned verification system for which, say, GM, or Ford, is the gatekeeper. And if they instead formed a consortium of carmakers to run the system, would their collective control over this all-important data network create a barrier to entry for newer, startup carmakers? Would it effectively become a competition-killing oligopoly?

A truly decentralized, permissionless system could be a way around this "walled-garden" problem of siloed technology.

A decentralized, permissionless system means any device can participate in the network yet still give everyone confidence in the integrity of the data, of the devices, and of the value being transacted. A permissionless system would create a much more fluid, expansive Internet of Things network that's not beholden to the say-so and fees of powerful gatekeepers.

The problem is that the currently available decentralized, permissionless blockchains face limitations. Based on its block-size data limit and "on-chain" processing capability, Bitcoin can't currently handle more than a few transactions a second—though the "off-chain" Lightning solution may advance that significantly—and Ethereum, though faster at processing blocks, will also often fail to process transactions when the network gets busy. Those limits, if they remain, are deal-breakers for the Internet of Things, which is projected to handle a massive amount of microtransaction traffic over billions of devices.

Here too, though, there are companies attacking the challenge. A startup called IOTA is using an unorthodox consensus algorithm that is intended to be less taxing on the computing network than a traditional blockchain. Within its so-called tangle system, each transacting device is also a validating node—unlike the contemporary Bitcoin dichotomy, which distinguishes users from miners. The way IOTA works is that in order for one device to make a transaction with another one—to send it money in the form of IOTA tokens or other forms of valuable information—it must itself confirm the validity of two randomly assigned transactions from elsewhere in the network. Two transactions out of millions is obviously a significantly lesser computing load than is faced by miners in Bitcoin and Ethereum, who must process all of those within a given block. It's on this basis that IOTA makes its claim to scalability. But its success—and, in fact, the security of the entire IOTA network—depends on network effects. If there are only a few devices on the network, then a rogue actor in charge of one machine would sooner or later get assigned by the random process to validate one of his or her own past transactions, creating an opportunity to approve a double-spending or otherwise fraudulent transaction. On the other hand, as the network becomes much bigger, the chances of that happening become exponentially less likely, providing strong assurances of integrity. IOTA says it gets stronger and more scalable the bigger it gets—the opposite of Bitcoin.

IOTA gathered an enthusiastic band of supporters around it, many of whom invested in its IOTA token, which became one of the best performing tokens on the market. But things became rocky after cryptographers at MIT's Digital Currency Initiative discovered easily exploited flaws in the algorithm IOTA created to generate transaction hashes. Rather than use a standardized hashing tool like the SHA-256 algorithm used by Bitcoin and many other cryptocurrencies, the IOTA team had opted for a customized version, and it turned out to be seriously flawed. The revelation prompted a sharp drop in the value of IOTA's token and required every user to upgrade to a new version of its software or be locked out of the IOTA economy—a hard fork, in other words. After the MIT group reported on its findings and cited the case as an example of why better security audits are needed, IOTA's token plunged in price. Investors in IOTA—clearly unhappy about the fall in their tokens' value—went into damage control on social media, accusing the MIT team of deliberately spreading "FUD" (fear, uncertainty, and doubt) to further their interests and attacking the integrity of a *Forbes* journalist who'd written up the MIT findings. Co-founder Sergey Ivancheglo took to an IOTA-linked blog to argue, unconventionally, that the flaw in the code had been deliberately inserted as "copy protection," so that anyone who made a copy of the open-source software to compete with IOTA would confront problems. This prompted a barrage of criticism from many in the cryptography community, for whom there is a long tradition of openly critiquing each other's work to fix bugs and make code more secure.

But if IOTA lost the confidence of some of the most respected cryptographers in the blockchain community, it continued to generate enthusiasm among a variety of big-name enterprises. That's perhaps because, quite apart from how badly or otherwise it developed and managed its cryptography, the IOTA team's economic model is enticing. If its cryptographic flaws can be fixed, the tangle idea could in theory be far less taxing and expensive in terms of computing power than Bitcoin and Ethereum's methods, which require every computer in their massive networks of validators to process and confirm the entire list of new transactions in each new block. German engineering and electronics giant Bosch has been running a range of experiments with IOTA, including one involving payments between self-driving trucks arranged in an energy-saving linear "platoon." The idea is that the trucks at the back that are enjoying the benefits of the slipstream would pay IOTA tokens to those at the front to compensate them for bearing the bulk of energy costs in creating that slipstream. Meanwhile, IOTA and Bosch are both part of a consortium called the Trusted IoT Alliance that's committed to building and securing a blockchain infrastructure for the industry. Other members include Foxconn, Cisco, BNY Mellon, and a slew of blockchain-based startups, such as supply-chain provider Skuchain and Ethereum research lab ConsenSys. The group's Web site touts "Blockchain IoT for Business" with the promise of "Powering the Fourth Industrial Revolution together." IOTA's controversial approach may be the wrong one, but there's a lot of interest in developing the kinds of scalable solutions on which it is focused.

Even the U.S. government has shown its interest in this field, with the Department of Homeland Security awarding blockchain infrastructure builder Factom a $199,000 grant to develop an IoT security solution. It's a small number by ICO fund-raising standards but a noteworthy vote of confidence in blockchain technology from a government agency. Factom's model would create an identity log of data emitted by a device, including its unique identifier, its manufacturer, its update history, its known security issues, and its granted authorities. The idea is that if a device's history of performance, permissions, and certification is recorded in an immutable ledger, hackers can't alter the record to disguise a flaw they've exploited. It's not clear how much oversight the U.S. government would have over the system.

Context Labs in Cambridge, Massachusetts, is doing similar work to achieve what it calls "data veracity." In various industries, it is pulling together consortia of interested parties to agree on open-data standards for APIs (application processing interfaces) that would allow parties to share data stamped with unique cryptographic hashes that provably identify the device and its owner. By processing the information it gathers through a blockchain, Context Labs hopes to foster greater trust in data generated by IoT devices such as climate change–measuring sensors. CEO Dan Harple argues that if agreement to use a standardized open API can be forged by a consortium of varied stakeholders that reflect a wide enough cross-section of a particular industry, concerns about permissioned blockchains being coopted by oligopolistic players should be diminished. In theory, that would make it easier to build scalable solutions for the massive IoT universe.

But such claims, like pretty much everything in the nascent blockchain industry, are yet to be proven. What we currently have are some core ideas that point to a big opportunity. What's exciting is that those core ideas, those that let us imagine a world of decentralized trust, also signal the potential for some very big changes in how our economy works. Get IoT security right, and we may well unleash a wave of innovation like none we've ever seen, one that will not only make the Internet run more efficiently but will also improve how businesses and consumers use all other resources in the economy. The result: significantly lower costs and environmental impacts for everybody. We'll look now at what this means for production of the most important resource in the universe: energy.

Blockchain Energy

In October 2015, at the UN's "COP 21" conference on climate change in Paris, India's prime minister Narendra Modi announced a bold goal for his country: 175 GW of renewable capacity would be installed by the year 2022. Based on total grid capacity of around 280 GW at that time, that figure is equivalent to the current power consumption of 600 million Indians. The effort was geared toward another bold goal, too: bringing electricity to 300 million people currently living without access to reliable electricity. This vitally important mission speaks to a pair of goals humanity must achieve if it is to avoid destroying itself and its planet: a massive reduction in carbon emissions and a steady increase in the development and well-being of the world's 4 billion low-income-earning people.

We'll make another bold statement here, one that isn't (yet) resonating in the halls of government in Delhi: this massive rollout simply won't be possible if the government doesn't simultaneously decentralize the grid, pushing generation control and ownership out to the village level. It needs what some of us call "energy democracy."

The planet's climate-change problems aren't solely due to power generation plants' reliance on dirty, carbon-heavy fuels like coal; it's that the entire centralized grid model—from the geographical layout, to the security risks, to the giant, multi-year, politically driven financing models—is fundamentally inefficient. The goal of delivering as much energy as possible at the lowest cost and with the most efficient use of renewable resources *must* involve bringing the source of generation as close as possible to the source of consumption. Rapid improvements in photovoltaic generation have begun to make this look possible, pushing solar energy into such a Moore's Law–like trend of plunging costs that a Chinese-Japanese consortium was in 2016 able to place a stunningly low 2.42-cents-per-Kwh winning bid to build a solar generation plant in Abu Dhabi. That's about half of the typical cost in the United States, a difference that, importantly, makes solar competitive with fossil fuels. And while the plant in Abu Dhabi was itself a centralized solution, with a big solar panel farm designed to contribute to the emirate's overall daily load capacity, it underscores what's also possible with locally based solar microgrids.

The community benefits of decentralized power are staggering. If communities can take charge of their own energy sources—by perhaps building microgrids that share the generation capacity of panels on each person's home—they can eliminate a significant amount of power loss due to long-distance transmission, which can be as high as 30 percent in some cases. Decentralized microgrids are less vulnerable to cyber-attacks because it's so much more costly for hackers to go after multiple distributed centers of activity than it is to just try to take out a single

server in a region's centralized grid. Decentralized grids also create redundancies—or backups—to limit the impact of natural disasters. (Check
out nighttime photos of Manhattan after the Sandy superstorm, when
most of the downtown area below 34th Street is blacked out because
of damage to the centralized grid, except for a pocket of light around
Washington Square Park, where New York University and surrounding
buildings were part of a common decentralized microgrid.) Meanwhile, although it's hard to stamp out all forms of corruption, small,
localized deals aren't the same magnets for crooked political operatives
and shady bankers that giant power plant projects have long been in
the developing world. And without the thirty-year bond deals backed
by international investment banks and political risk insurance, there's
potential for far less financial waste along the way, which should put
more energy per dollar in citizens' homes.

More important is the fact that decentralized approaches to grid design allow for a much more nuanced, controlled management of power
consumption. Handled properly, with computer-driven modeling, this
should result in far greater resource efficiency. With the aid of sophisticated software monitoring, automated smart meters, and optimized,
price-driven timing for individual device use, localized in-home
"nanogrids" can receive a high-tech level of micromanagement that puts
public utilities' region-wide load-management strategies to shame. The
revolution that started with smart thermostats like Nest and Ecobee
is poised to go a lot further. But this low-cost, low-carbon-footprint
future depends on two things: decentralized control of the energy system (of power generation, distribution, and consumption) and the capacity to design and run an intelligent system of interconnected smart
meters and Internet-connected appliances and devices that respond to
price signals. It's a big IoT play, in other words.

This also means we need to think about the organizational structure.
Who's managing the bills? You can't put a big public utility—essentially
a trusted third party, a kind of bank that runs a ledger to keep track of
everyone's meters, invoices, and accounts—inside a multitude of localized, microtransaction deals among neighbors' on-roof solar cells and

each other's IoT-connected air conditioners. It would not only be a pro-hibitively inefficient management problem for the utility, but it would be in conflict with the interests of the overall community, which wants to use as little power as possible. Still, if utilities can't manage these microgrids, you'll still have a trust problem. Given that the profit inter-ests of those selling power won't align with the cost-saving interests of those buying it, neighbors can't just blindly trust each other—the big-ger the community, the more this is true. How do you prove people aren't meddling with their meters or overcharging for power delivery?

Also, if you want to do this properly, you need all those payments and receipts to be settled in a special, internally traded currency, a to-ken whose floating value is pegged to kilowatt hours and that the user can convert into dollars, to help optimize local grid management. That way, you will have a market pricing mechanism to carry out similar load-management strategies as those used by traditional grid managers in much wider energy regions. A floating KwH token represents a local price for power, and like all market prices it functions as a signal to us-ers within the microgrid. But because it's a digital signal, people can finely tune their devices' response to it. They can choose to charge their Teslas only when power is abundant and cheap, for example, or they can create priority lists of different devices, some of which can automati-cally turn off (for example, the TV), while others will be programmed to stay on (the refrigerator). These same pricing signals, which will re-flect the balance of demand and supply for power, can guide the soft-ware running the microgrid to divert excess electricity to battery storage when it is abundant or tap that same backup when the system is in defi-cit. The question is: who or what is going to manage this internal power market and payments system? For reasons we've outlined elsewhere—high intermediary fees, the inefficiencies of post-trade account recon-ciliation, and the risk of interference by a ledger-keeper, such as a public utility, whose interests misalign with users'—decentralized groups such as these really need decentralized trust solutions.

This is where LO3 Energy ended up when it developed its Transac-tive Grid in Brooklyn, a prototype of interconnected households and businesses that share locally generated solar power. The community was motivated by a desire to give environmentally conscious consumers and users the capacity to know they are buying clean, locally generated power as opposed to just helping pay their utility buy renewable credits that fund green energy production elsewhere in the United States.

In the Transactive Grid, building owners install solar panels that are then linked together with those of their neighbors in a distribution network, using affordable smart meters and storage units, as well as inverters that allow the grid's owners to sell power back to the public grid. The magic sauce, though, comes from a private blockchain that regulates the sharing of power among the smart meters, whose data is logged into that distributed ledger. And in the summer of 2017, LO3 took the process a step further by developing an "exergy token" to drive market mechanisms within and among decentralized microgrids such as Brooklyn's. (Exergy is a vital concept for measuring energy efficiency and containing wasteful practices; it doesn't just measure the amount of energy generated but also the amount of useful work produced per each given amount of energy produced.)

Note that LO3's microgrid is based on a private blockchain. Microgrids offer one of those cases when this model is likely sufficient, since the community is founded on a fixed group of users who will all agree to the terms of use. That means that some of the large-scale processing challenges of Bitcoin and Ethereum can be avoided and thus that the high transaction power of a blockchain could be harnessed without requiring the implementation of the Lightning Network and other "off-chain" scaling solutions currently under development. A private blockchain can process microtransactions, run smart contracts that allow, say, prepaid electricity access to be administered based on whether a user has made a digital currency payment or not, and enable efficient peer-to-peer exchanges of energy in return for KwH tokens. It's the blockchain, then, that enables the decentralized marketplace and pricing signals that the microgrid needs in order to optimize efficiency. It means the system can run without some centralized company or authority deciding who gets power and at what price. It also means the grid's capacity can grow organically as each member of the community will add new revenue-earning panels and other equipment as it becomes profitable to do so, knowing that the same system will incorporate it efficiently.

LO3 is far from the only player in this space. Another important driver of blockchain ideas for energy is Berlin-based Grid Singularity, which has formed an alliance with the Rocky Mountain Institute, a non-profit renewable energy advocate, to accelerate the commercial deployment of blockchain technology in the energy sector. Grid Singularity focuses on how it can be used to securely read and interpret massive amounts of data from thousands of independent devices to give power system managers granular knowledge of how power is being used so they can best manage local and public grids. Such initiatives are part of a big push to use blockchains to improve and authenticate the all-important data that will be needed for governments, businesses, and other special interest groups to monitor and address the challenges of climate change. As the problem grows worse, this kind of micromanagement of efficiency—of exergy, really—will be essential to calibrate the world's response.

These ideas were given urgency by hurricanes Irma and Maria, which devastated electricity grids across much of the Caribbean. Two months later, the concepts were showcased during a hackathon on the sidelines of the COP 23 annual UN conference on climate change in Bonn.

One of the challenges of developing microgrids has been how to finance them—because although battery costs are falling, those systems are not cheap to install across communities. And there's the question of how best to let the owners of the solar cells monetize their investment. For now, that challenge has meant that for-profit solar initiatives are mostly going up in well-established, developed markets, where owners of the equipment can use net-metering kits to sell some of the power they generate back to the public grid. Not only does that require high-tech equipment and reliable transmission facilities, it also needs non-corrupted regulators to compel grid managers to set reasonable buy-back tariffs, even if it's against the utility's immediate profit interests. The utility has all the bargaining power, so solar system owners are beholden to the policy positions of local government.

This could all change, however, with the coming revolution in storage capacity. Partly spurred by the massive R&D that companies like Tesla are investing in battery technology, fuel cells, and thermal storage models, the mobility and effectiveness of storage capacity are improving rapidly while costs are steadily falling. This could eventually allow full energy independence. One can imagine an off-grid community that collectively owns a blockchain-managed decentralized solar generation plant, creating a system for storing, transporting—via self-driving electric cars—and exchanging batteries with other off-grid communities.

This spells opportunity for all sorts of communities: those off-grid Indian villages with their 300 million electricity-poor residents; sovereign indigenous communities such as Native Americans in the United States or Aboriginals in Australia who seek energy independence; or farmers and other users in low-density rural areas who are cursed by their low level of community demand and for whom the cost of installing transmission lines and relay stations can be extremely burdensome. In many of these cases, power delivery has been subsidized by governments, in effect by taxing urban users with higher tariffs than they would otherwise pay.

Yet we still have to deal with another challenge here, and that is financing the up-front costs of these decentralized, blockchain-based microgrids in places that don't have a reliable credit infrastructure. It so happens that blockchain tech might help there, too. We'll go into it in chapter seven, where we look at asset registries, alternative collateral, and innovative finance for the developing world.

Energy resource management is not the only part of the material economy where blockchain and IoT solutions hold promise. There's also rapidly growing interest in blockchain management of supply chains, those sequentially organized, interlinked sets of business relationships that determine how the goods we consume are derived from raw materials, pass through intermediate processes of production, and finally are distributed to retail outlets from which we consumers acquire them. Managed properly, the improvement in transparency across these chains has the potential for smaller producers to better compete, for financing and insurance to be more efficiently priced, for resources to be used less wastefully, and for customers to gain greater confidence in how safely or ethically their products are being made.

Tracking the Stuff We Make

An E. coli outbreak at Chipotle Mexican Grill outlets in October 2015 left fifty-five customers ill and shattered the restaurant chain's reputation. Sales plummeted, and Chipotle's share price dropped 42 percent to a three-year low, where it languished through the summer of 2017. At the heart of the Denver-based company's crisis was the ever-present problem faced by companies that depend on multiple outside suppliers to deliver parts and ingredients: a lack of transparency and accountability across complex supply chains. Many Chipotle patrons probably assumed the outbreak stemmed from poor practices at one of the chain's restaurants or facilities. But, as painful as that would be for the company's reputation, the reality was actually worse: Chipotle had no way to pinpoint where the dangerous virus got into its food offerings; it only knew that it came from one of its many third-party beef suppliers. Five months later, the best management could come up with was that it "most likely" came from contaminated Australian beef. At the heart of the problem was the lack of visibility that Chipotle—like any food provider—has over the global supply chain of ingredients that flow into its operations. That lack of knowledge meant that Chipotle could neither prevent the contamination before it happened, nor contain it in a targeted way after it was discovered.

Supply chains are composed of distinct, inherently independent businesses. Their interests align around the goal of maximizing the sale of an end product—the makers of transistors, chips, capacitors, screens, and other components of a Samsung smartphone will, for example, gain if Samsung experiences rising demand. But since they are also engaged in price-sensitive purchasing contracts with each other, there's also an inherent misalignment of interests between different upstream and downstream members of the chain. It's that latter part that makes it difficult to share information with each other, with the standard arrangement being that each party maintains their own data records on internal work processes and inventory movements. Each company can inquire with the others, but just as banks in a sequence of payment processors maintain separate ledgers that are closed to everyone else, there is no visibility across these different silos of information. That means that a company like Chipotle has no way to check whether the work records at the Australian slaughterhouse show the staff fulfilling compliance requirements and carrying out mandated procedures. Barcodes and RFID chips have in some respect improved traceability of goods across the world, but the real problem in visibility lies behind the closed doors of each supplier. End-producers, and just as importantly, consumers, are flying blind.

Blockchain technology, with its capacity to get groups of potentially mistrusting people to coordinate around a common interest, offers a potential solution to this problem. Companies that wouldn't otherwise share information can now use a cryptographic hash of information to verify that key procedures have taken place without revealing vital secret information. Those hashes can then be recorded into a blockchain to which all chain members have access, creating an easily traceable, immutable record to which all have consented, one that naturally enhances trust in the data. A growing number of startups, bankers, and even large-scale manufacturers have begun to explore this idea, seeing it as a potential solution to problems of disclosure and accountability that were previously too hard for these far-flung communities of suppliers to resolve. Once mutually important data is updated in real time— in anonymized or encrypted form if necessary—it removes the need for laborious, error-prone reconciliation with each other's internal records. It gives each member of the network far greater and timelier visibility of the total activity. It could allow Chipotle at any time to more reasonably verify that its supplier butchers are appropriately handling the meat that will later be served to the restaurant's chains. While it's still possible, of course, that a supplier could falsely record work that has not actually been performed, the very existence of an all-knowing ledger of activity could compel better behavior.

Extrapolating this blockchain model of shared transparency and real-time tracking to the entire network of international commerce, we see the potential for a worldwide system of supply chains that uses resources way more efficiently and that could radically change the trading terms of the global economy. By unlocking information and attaching unique, digital asset–like tokens to each part of a production process, the technology could unlock value for exchange at intermediate stages of multi-party manufacturing and shipping processes. This could give businesses far greater flexibility to find markets and price risk at any point along the chain and to respond quickly to orders from consumers, who will demand to know where the things they buy came from. What we end up with are dynamic *demand* chains in place of rigid *supply* chains, resulting in more efficient resource use for all.

Provenance, a UK-based startup, advertises that it is using blockchain technology to "[b]ring to life the information and stories behind your business and products" so as to "[t]rack unique batches of products with verified claims from origin to consumer." Walmart is working with IBM and Tsinghua University in Beijing to follow the movement of pork in China via a blockchain. Mining giant BHP Billiton is using the technology to track minerals analysis done by outside vendors. The startup Everledger has uploaded unique identifying data on a million individual diamonds to a blockchain ledger system to build quality assurances and help jewelers comply with regulations barring "blood diamond" products.

These solutions are also IoT blockchain plays because they are intrinsically linked to the sensors, barcodes, and RFID chips that are increasingly used in manufacturing and shipping to trace goods, trigger actions, and prompt payment. Once again, there will be a need for "know-your-machine" systems that can "identify" these devices and assure they are operating in a trustworthy way. Once smart contracts are added in, signals from these devices can automatically execute pre-established rights and obligations for payment and delivery that all signatories have agreed to. These models also envisage customs officers, port authorities, trade finance providers, and other interested parties plugging into these networks to manage their own processes.

The benefits of traceability and automation don't just pertain to things; blockchains could also keep human beings in check along supply chains. Staff and supervisors from different vendors could be assigned special, cryptographic permissions, which, when placed into a blockchain environment, would appear as unique, traceable identifiers. (Here we would want to use the kind of strong encryption techniques being explored for digital identities, so as to protect the employee's personal information.) This would allow all members of a supply-chain community to monitor the activity of each other's credentialed staff. Chipotle, for example, could see in real time whether a properly credentialed person in a beef facility is carrying out appropriate sterilization and disinfection procedures.

This kind of provable, transparent credentialing will be especially important for what's called additive manufacturing. That technology, the industrial version of 3D printing, is central to the dynamic, on-demand production model of the so-called Industry 4.0 movement, a phrase that describes a manufacturing sector that can respond in rapid time to changing consumer and other demands. 3D printers are already producing parts that are lighter than traditionally built parts, are much stronger in design, and are more readily produced on demand for machines as sophisticated as NASA rockets and Air Force fighters. But for mission-critical products like these, there's also a risk, one that's put into context by James Regenor, director of the additive manufacturing and innovation unit at precision parts manufacturer Moog, Inc.: "How can the maintenance crew on a U.S. aircraft carrier have absolute confidence that the software file they downloaded to 3D-print a new part for a fighter jet hasn't been hacked by a foreign adversary?" To tackle this problem, Regenor's team at Moog has launched a service it calls

Veripart, which uses blockchain technology to, among other things, verify the software design and upgrading work performed by different providers of 3D-printed products along a supply chain. It plans to incorporate a host of features that, among other things, will protect intellectual property and make it more flexible and dynamic as an asset. The team at Moog plans to invite all members of its far-flung global supply chain to participate. Meanwhile, defense contractor Lockheed Martin, one of Moog's biggest customers, has also seen the light with regard to blockchain's value in secure work processes within this highly sensitive industry. The company announced that it has entered into a joint venture with Virginia-based GuardTime Federal to integrate blockchain technology into its supply-chain risk management.

If we view supply chains in this way—as an interactive sequence of agreed-to-work functions—the kinds of industries that can benefit from this new approach to information become quite broad. In the construction industry, for example, Nashville-based startup Keyturn wants to use blockchain technology to help general building contractors manage the supply chain of work and materials for particular jobs, collectively monitoring hours and materials used to save resources and money for the end-customer. It's also looking to ensure that undocumented construction workers get fairly paid, challenging the often Dickensian treatment of a group of workers who make up 7 percent of the global workforce in an industry that McKinsey Global Institute says accounts for 13 percent of world GDP.

Account reconciliation can benefit greatly from a distributed supply-chain solution. Using a permissioned distributed ledger to track and manage the more than 25,000 vendor disputes it handles annually, IBM said in 2016 that it had cut the resolution time of those disputes down from forty-four days to ten days. Essentially, record-keeping of payments and deliveries that all can view and verify in real time allows common agreements to be reached more quickly. This isn't a chump-change problem, either. Those disputes currently tie up $100 million in capital every year, IBM says.

So there's a great deal of potential for saving and efficiency that can

accrue to everyone along the chain, from raw mineral miner to consumer. The question is: how will it be monetized, and who will benefit?
One key opportunity lies with finance and insurance.

Around the world, small and medium-size enterprises, known as
SMEs, have woeful access to letters of credit and other trade-finance
facilities used to cover the period in which an exporter's goods are being shipped overseas to the buyer. A major reason: lending institutions
can't sufficiently trust the documents, such as port-issued bills of lad-
ings, that SMEs furnish as collateral for loans. As of now, even the slight-
est amount of suspicion that, say, an exporter in possession of a bill of
lading has already pledged that shipment to some other lender is the
kiss of death for a loan application. If evidence of those documents and
their attached liens can be securely recorded in a blockchain, proving
they haven't been duplicated, perhaps SMEs can finally assert their
creditworthiness, bringing even more competition to global markets.
Standard Chartered in Singapore has already developed such a proof of
concept.

Alternatively, this technology could allow the dominant players
within a supply chain to become de facto banks or insurers to their suppliers. Exploiting enhanced, blockchain-proven information about
suppliers' inventory, they can fine-tune payment terms—shifting from,
say, ninety days to thirty days. That would help upstream providers
unlock capital that's otherwise tied up in stock. Foxconn, the giant
China-based electronics manufacturer that services major producers
such as Apple, is leading the charge in this area. Foxconn rolled out a
prototype for the thousands of suppliers in its various value chains,
and not long after the company said that the prototype's use had generated $6.5 million in loans for them.

A more radical way to extract value from blockchain solutions in
supply chains would involve the issuance of unique tokens of the kind
discussed in the previous chapter, special digital assets that represent
goods and services moving along a supply chain. This has the potential
to bring flexibility to business dealings in the export-import field and
innovate new business processes. Tokenization, when combined with

GPS data and other information recorded in a blockchain, would let the owner of goods in transit transfer rights to any buyer anywhere at any time, without the shipment having to be recorded by a port. Companies whose products were among the $14 billion worth of cargo trapped at sea when South Korea's Hanjin Shipping Co. declared bankruptcy in 2016 might have welcomed this option. One can imagine markets for wholesale or intermediate goods developing similar pricing dynamism and liquidity as securities markets, greatly enhancing businesses' risk management.

Blockchain-proven digital tokens point to what blockchain consultant and entrepreneur Pindar Wong calls the "packetization of risk." This radical idea introduces a negotiable structure to different phases of the chain. Intermediate goods that would otherwise be encumbered by a pre-established chain of unsettled commitments can instead be put out to bid to see if other buyers want to take on the rights and obligations associated with them. This would attract alternative sources of impromptu demand, which could have a market-clearing effect on resource management. Enhanced visibility on business processes, when coupled with the ability to find liquid markets for goods-linked digital assets, means that industrial actors could be incentivized, like never before, to be both environmentally responsible and profitable. It's similar to the principle, explored above, of using price signals to optimize a solar microgrid. If tokens allow us to set prices for goods and services for which there was previously no alternative source of demand, producers might be able to make much better resource decisions. This is why many people believe that the concept of a "circular economy"— where there is as much recycling as possible of the energy sources and materials in production—will hinge on the transparency and information flows that blockchain systems allow.

The principal challenge remains scaling. Open-to-all, permissionless blockchains such as Bitcoin's and Ethereum's simply aren't ready for the prime time of global trade. If all of the world's supply chains were to pass their transactions through a permissionless blockchain, there would need to be a gargantuan increase in scalability, either off-chain or on-chain. Solutions may come from innovations such as the Lightning Network, discussed in chapter three, but they are far from ready at this stage. Instead, companies are looking at *permissioned* blockchains, which we'll discuss in more detail in chapter six. That makes sense because many big manufacturers think of their supply chains as *static* concepts, with defined members who have been certified to supply this or that component to a finished product. But in the rapidly changing world of the Fourth Industrial Revolution, this might not be the most competitive option. Emerging technologies such as additive manufacturing, where production can be called up anywhere and delivered by anyone with access to the right software files and a sufficiently configured 3D printer, are pointing to a much more fluid, dynamic supply-chain world, where suppliers come and go more easily. In that environment, a permissionless system would seem necessary. Once scaling challenges are resolved, and with robust encryption and reliable monitoring systems for proving the quality of suppliers' work, permissionless blockchain-based supply chains could end up being a big leveler of the playing field for global manufacturing.

Legal matters also pose a challenge. A complex array of regulations, maritime law, and commercial codes governs rights of ownership and possession along the world's shipping routes and their multiple jurisdictions. It will be difficult to marry that old-world body of law, and the human-led institutions that manage it, with the digital, dematerialized, automated, and de-nationalized nature of blockchains and smart contracts. What standards will port officials use to confirm that an importer has taken ownership of goods delivered by a shipper when a blockchain's notion of ownership depends not on possession of physical things but on control over a private cryptographic key associated with a digital record of those goods?

Developing blockchain applications for supply chains that improve commercial opportunities for all, increase small businesses' access to finance, reduce waste, and give consumers more insight into where the products they buy come from will also require some level of standardization. Competition is good, of course, but standards allow a wider array of users to connect with technology, creating network effects. It has been the same for all technologies, be it measurement models such as the metric system or railroad track gauges. The Internet couldn't grow as it did until a large enough group began using the core protocols for transmitting data, sending e-mail, sharing files, and securing information. At this stage, there is no single, global body seeking to develop such standards, but in various industries—in transportation, in the trusted IoT device industry, and in food—various alliances and consortia are emerging to explore common technologies.

Again, the decentralized nature of the technology makes coordination somewhat difficult. But here, too, the Internet's precedent is useful. In Hong Kong, a diverse group of companies and other stakeholders called the Belt and Road Blockchain Consortium has been developing an Internet governance approach pioneered and tested by ICANN, the private sector–led body that administers and adjudicates the Internet's global system of domain names and other unique identifiers. California-based ICANN, which stands for the Internet Corporation for Assigned Names and Numbers, is one of a number of important pillars of how the Internet is governed. Its authority over the assignment and management of domain names—the Internet's all-important URL real estate—is not bound by the rules of any one government but rather by multiple stakeholders with diverse interests that are designed to protect the public-good qualities of the Internet.

The Belt and Road Blockchain Consortium is also important for the scope that it seeks to cover. The group, which includes firms like KPMG and HSBC and has engaged shipping and logistics firms like Hong Kong behemoth Li & Fung, takes its name from a massive Chinese global investment program. Beijing's Belt and Road Initiative—also known as the "One Belt, One Road" project—contains a plan to invest $3 trillion in collaboratively developing high-tech manufacturing within sixty-five different countries along three separate trade routes tying Asia to Europe and Africa. Some have described it as a Beijing-led Marshall Plan, but as McKinsey partner Kevin Sneader notes, the ambitious program is twelve times the size of General George C. Marshall's 1948 project to reconstruct Europe with American investment. The way Pindar Wong, founder of the Belt and Road Blockchain Consortium, sees it, "such a complex set of supply relationships across 65 different jurisdictions with varying degrees of trust will need a distributed information-sharing paradigm if it is to work." Hence the opportunity for blockchain technologies to function as an international governance system. Hong Kong's role will be important: the territory's British legal traditions and reputation for respecting property rights have made it a respected safehouse for managing intellectual property and other contractual obligations within international trade. If the blockchain is to be inserted into global trade flows, the region's bridging function may offer the fastest and most impactful route. For Hong Kong residents who want the territory to retain its British legal traditions, that role could be a vital protection against Beijing undermining them.

These sweeping new ideas for the twenty-first-century global economy, with its high-tech devices and dynamic supply chains, are both a big opportunity and a major threat for the kinds of companies that have dominated commerce since the previous century. Those companies cannot afford to lie still. But can they afford to embrace Bitcoin's sweeping, disruptive model for managing economic relationships? In the next chapter we'll survey the different ways in which both financial and non-financial enterprises are exploring blockchain technology and are trying to discover their place in the decentralized economy of the future.

Six

THE OLD GUARD'S NEW MAKEOVER

On August 5, 2015, Bitcoin came to Wall Street. Or, to be more precise, a new, more buttoned-down version of Bitcoin came to Wall Street.

In its early days, bankers who'd heard of Bitcoin viewed it as a mere curiosity. Its wildly volatile price might make for a fun speculative investment, but the instability ruled Bitcoin out as an alternative currency. As far as bankers were concerned, Bitcoin had no role to play in the existing financial system. Banking institutions thrive on a system of opacity in which our inability to trust each other leaves us dependent on *their* intermediation of our transactions. Bankers might give lip service to reforming the inner workings of their system, but the thought of turning it over to something as uncontrollable as Bitcoin was beyond heresy. It wasn't even conceivable.

At the same time, committed Bitcoin fans weren't much interested in Wall Street, either. Bitcoin, after all, was designed as an alternative to the existing banking system. An improvement. Truth be told, despite an impressive movement that had coalesced around this upstart cryptocurrency in the almost seven years before the August 2015 event, and despite the innovations and the myriad other cryptocurrencies and networks and possibilities it had spawned, Bitcoin really hadn't made much of a dent in reshaping the old order. Wall Street's money machine remained firmly at the center of the global economy—and still does. For now, if you want to use technology to improve the world of finance—to reduce systemic risk in bond markets, for example, or make it easier for the poor to send and receive money—you still need to talk to Wall Street.

That's what a group of technologists from the startup Symbiont set out to do on that sunny August day in 2015. They took their new, less subversive version of Bitcoin downtown, and while their model was better described as "inspired" by Bitcoin than as a close copy of it, they still promised a revolution, if a more controlled one. Among the Bitcoin-like features their model contained were the vital elements of a distributed ledger, a capacity to transfer digitized assets peer-to-peer, and low-cost and near-instantaneous transactions. But Symbiont had jettisoned other Bitcoin features, including those that obviate the need for banks as payment intermediaries. Most notably, this system did not include its own native cryptocurrency for rewarding miners and for maintaining a permissionless system of validation. In essence, Symbiont was promising "blockchain without bitcoin"—it would maintain the fast, secure, and cheap distributed network model, and a truth machine at its center that validated transactions, but it was not leaderless, permissionless, and open to all. It was a blockchain that Wall Street could control.

Whether it's possible to separate bitcoin, ether, or any cryptocurrency from a blockchain is yet to be long-term tested. Some digital currency aficionados argue that stripping out the internal cryptocurrency would destroy the integrity of a blockchain. Without a native digital currency with which to reward and incentivize transaction validation, a permissionless network won't arise, which falls short of what many see as the prerequisite for a truly decentralized system of value exchange. Cryptocurrency-less systems necessarily end up as permissioned, or private, blockchains, in which the computers that run the network are approved by the company or groups of companies that run the ledger. That has its advantages—these networks' identifiable members are more easily corralled and governed than Bitcoin's unruly global mob, which means the processing capacity can be scaled more readily. But these permissioned systems are less open to experiments by computer engineers, and access rights to the data and software are subject to the whim of the official gatekeeper. That inherently constrains innovation. A *private* blockchain, some say, is an oxymoron. The whole point of this technology is to build a system that is open, accessible, and public. Many describe them with the generic phrase "distributed ledger technology" instead of "blockchain."

But the bankers in the room that day didn't care much about such nuances. For the most part, they liked what they heard. They knew their own system for trading among each other was also constrained by the fundamental problem of *centralized trust*. The mutual mistrust among their institutions forced them to keep information from each other, to keep data in closed, inaccessible corporate siloes. That added time, cost, inefficiencies, and risk to their back-office procedures.

Making matters worse was the convoluted, multi-party machine of modern finance, a sequence that included an originating bank, a correspondent bank, a clearinghouse, a broker, a settlement agency, a payment processor, etc. Knowing full well how friction-filled and costly that system was, the bankers tacitly recognized some of what Bitcoin creator Satoshi Nakamoto was trying to resolve. They might not have envisaged regular Joes sending money from the West to the East Coast without any intermediaries, but they knew there were lots of pointless processes that slowed down the finance system, added costs, and left customers unsatisfied.

As Nakamoto wrote in 2009:

The root problem with conventional currency is all the trust that's required to make it work. The central bank must be trusted not to debase the currency, but the history of fiat currencies is full of breaches of that trust. Banks must be trusted to hold our money and transfer it electronically, but they lend it out in waves of credit bubbles with barely a fraction in reserve. We

have to trust them with our privacy, trust them not to let identity thieves drain our accounts. Their massive overhead costs
make micropayments impossible.

Nakamoto was writing in the middle of the financial crisis. The
global banking system had become so opaque, so dense, that nobody
could trust what it was telling them anymore. Asset values became impossible to determine. In one fantastic conflagration, it all blew up.
Bitcoin may have been designed to get around all that, but it wasn't
inconceivable that the core aspects of what made it possible—its system
for verifying the truth in a way that was resistant to manipulation by
insiders—could also be leveraged by Wall Street.

The August 2015 event was the unveiling of Symbiont's new "Smart
Securities" trading platform, and it was held, ironically, at the top of a
skyscraper overlooking Zuccotti Park, the tree-lined block where the
Occupy Wall Street movement was born four years earlier. Using a distributed ledger that functioned similarly to Bitcoin's blockchain—
with the vital omission of an independent cryptocurrency—Symbiont's
platform aimed to reorganize the core functions of a global financial
market system that managed more than $200 trillion in assets. It prom-
ised to streamline the issuance, buying, selling, and transfer of stocks,
bonds, and other financial contracts—activities that sustain the tribes
of investment bankers, brokers, and asset managers who inhabit New
York, London, and Hong Kong. Could we call this co-optation? A technology with which a community of cyber-anarchists wanted to bypass
the giant toll collectors of our international monetary highway system
had been repackaged as something to sell to those same institutions.

Half a decade earlier, the park below had teemed with grime-covered
tents, drum circles, and dreadlock-wearing lecturers on soapboxes who
wanted Wall Streeters thrown in jail. Many within that spontaneous
movement, certainly those who embraced a libertarian, anti-corporatist
critique of Wall Street's privileged position, would come to embrace
Bitcoin. The digital currency had been first floated in October 2008,
right in the middle of the worst moment of the financial crisis, as a kind

of answer to those problems. That financial meltdown became Exhibit A for Nakamoto's point about the risks of investing trust in less-than-trustworthy institutions such as Lehman Brothers. Yet here was Symbiont CEO Mark Smith pitching some of those Bitcoin principles to institutions that would have followed Lehman Brothers into the graveyard if it weren't for a taxpayer bailout whose real cost Bloomberg News estimated at $12.8 trillion.

Smith's audience included officials from UBS, Morgan Stanley, and the Depository Trust & Clearing Corp. (DTCC)—the bank-owned institution that's responsible for clearing and settling virtually all equity and bond trades in the United States. Duncan Niederauer, the former CEO of the New York Stock Exchange, was there, though not as a representative of the old guard but rather as an investor in the new startup.

Smith began with a simple promise—he could save the bankers time and money—a lot of money. He unveiled a product that could compress the entire convoluted sequence of trading and delivering securities, steps that can take days or even weeks to complete, down to a few clicks of a mouse and a matter of minutes. He pulled up the Smart Securities platform, which looked somewhat like the "checkout" page on Amazon. It contained fields for all the variables for a debt instrument—the name of the issuer, the amount, the yield (the effective interest rate), the maturity date on which the issuer's bonds fall due, and so on. In this case, he was trading a bond issued by SenaHill Partners, an investment firm that had a stake in Symbiont. He filled in the various fields, hit the execute button, and then went on with his presentation. A few minutes later, he announced that the confirmation had come in. The bond had been sold, bought, and the transaction settled, all in a matter of minutes—a dramatic improvement from the two-day settlement timeframe that was standard in U.S. capital markets.

This meant the dangers of a counterparty or middleman not holding up their end of the deal, of losing or failing to deliver money or securities owed, were dramatically reduced. It's a real problem: the DTCC says such "fails" run to more than $50 billion daily in U.S. Treasury bond markets alone, often because investors use the two-day window to make short-term loans out of the money or securities owed but then can't retrieve them when called to deliver. It might turn out that the third-party recipient to whom they lent the security has sold it in what's known as a short-sale—a bet that its price will fall—and is struggling to find someone who wants to sell it back to them at its lower price target. All of that feeds back into balance sheet losses for the bondholder. Solving this issue could thus unlock trillions of dollars that investment institutions hold in reserve to cover for such risks.

That day Symbiont showed the first inklings of a possible future, and in the years since, there has been a lot of activity around trying to build a blockchain-based system for the traditional financial industry. Wall Street had gone from mocking Bitcoin to trying to build its own version of it.

Wall Street Goes for an Alternative: Private Blockchains

Though Bitcoin fans frowned upon permissioned blockchains, Wall Street continued to build them. These tweaked versions of Bitcoin shared various elements of the cryptocurrency's powerful cryptography and network rules. However, instead of its electricity-hungry "proof-of-work" consensus model, they drew upon older, pre-Bitcoin protocols that were more efficient but which couldn't achieve the same level of security without putting a centralized entity in charge of identifying and authorizing participants.

Predominantly, the bankers' models used a consensus algorithm known as practical byzantine fault tolerance, or PBFT, a cryptographic solution invented in 1999. It gave all approved ledger-keepers in the network confidence that each other's actions weren't undermining the shared record even when there was no way of knowing whether one or more had malicious intent to defraud the others. With these consensus-building systems, the computers adopted each updated version of the ledger once certain thresholds of acceptance were demonstrated across the network.

These private, closed, permissioned blockchains didn't attract the same enthusiasm among developers as all those wild Ethereum ideas to disintermediate the world or as the token issuers whose ICOs were drawing in eight- or nine-figure fund-raisers. Helping a bank save money on its securities settlement procedures wasn't quite as sexy. But Wall Street had deep pockets, which did help in recruitment. In particular, the funders of these projects attracted some key developers and early cryptocurrency adopters during the worst moments of Bitcoin's block-size civil war. At that time, people were frustrated by the lack of progress in Satoshi Nakamoto's experiment and here was something that they could go ahead and build without having to get a sprawling, divided community on board.

The biggest winner in this hiring spree was the research and development company R3 CEV, which focused on the financial industry. It sought to build a distributed ledger that could, on the one hand, reap the benefits of real-time securities settlement and cross-industry ledger harmonization but, on the other, would comply with a vast array of banking regulations and meet its members' proprietary interest in keeping their books private. By the spring of 2017, R3 CEV had grown its membership to more than one hundred. Each member firm paid annual dues of $250,000 in return for access to the insights being developed inside the R3 lab. Its founders also raised $107 million in venture funding in 2017, mostly from financial institutions. Some of that money went to hire people like Mike Hearn, a once prominent Bitcoin developer who dramatically turned his back on the cryptocurrency community with an "I quit" blog post complaining about the bitter infighting. R3 also hired Ian Grigg—who later left to join EOS—another prominent onetime rebel from the cryptocurrency space. Leading its research team was the ever-thoughtful and well-regarded full-time IBM blockchain guru Richard Gendal-Brown. These were serious engineering hires.

Before their arrival, R3 had also signed on Tim Swanson as research director. Swanson was a distributed ledger/blockchain analyst who was briefly enthused by Bitcoin but who later became disillusioned with the cryptocurrency's ideologues. He became a vocal, anti-Bitcoin gadfly who seemed to delight in mocking its travails. Of a similar breed was Preston Byrne, the general counsel of Eris Ltd., later called Monax, which designed private blockchains for banks and a variety of other companies. When Byrne's Twitter feed wasn't conveying his eclectic mix of political positions—pro-Trump, anti-Brexit, pro–Second Amendment, pro-encryption, anti–software utopianism—or constant references to marmots (the Eris brand's mascot), it poured scorn on Bitcoin's fanatic followers. For guys like Swanson and Byrne, Bitcoin's dysfunctional governance was a godsend.

But poking fun at Bitcoin's weak points cuts both ways. Although R3 may have bought itself some tech cred with the hires of Hearn, Gendal-Brown, and Grigg, the ownership structure of R3 lent itself to caricature. It screamed "Wall Street old boys' club." The nine founding members were Barclays, BBVA, Commonwealth Bank of Australia, Credit Suisse, Goldman Sachs, J.P. Morgan, Royal Bank of Scotland, State Street, and UBS. All but two—BBVA and Commonwealth—were listed in the Financial Stability Board's 2016 list of G-SIBs, global systemically important banks. They weren't just plain-vanilla, "too-big-to-fail" banks whose gargantuan balance sheets posed problems for their domestic markets; they were part of a special category whose loan books were so large they could pose a danger to the global economy. And many were on the receiving end of billions of dollars in fines.

To followers of trends in financial technology, this looked familiar. Wall Street's banks have a long history of co-opting technologies to neutralize disruptive threats. In the late 1990s, when a wave of electronic trading systems for foreign exchange, bonds, and other opaque areas of the capital markets promised peer-to-peer investing that cut out the investment bank middlemen, the biggest banks banded together to launch their own online exchange service. This ensured that the banks' inventories of stocks, bonds, and commodities contracts remained at the center of all investment exchanges and that they retained their privileged positions as price setters.

Regulators with fresh memories of the 2008 meltdown also had reason to be wary of Wall Street's bid to build private, permissioned blockchains. At hearings organized by the Financial Stability Board, the international body of regulators founded by the Group of Twenty nations, staff from central banks and national securities commissions explored whether the market structure of future blockchains might foster systemic risks and financial instability. On the one hand, regulators were comfortable with the familiar membership of R3's consortium; they were more accustomed to working with bankers than with T-shirt-and-jeans-wearing crypto-inventors. But on the other, the idea of a consortium of the world's biggest banks having say-so over who and what gets included within the financial system's single and only distributed ledger conjured up fears of excessive banking power and of the politically unpopular bailouts that happened after the crisis. Might Wall Street be building a "too-big-to-fail" blockchain?

A Fix for Financial Crises?

Let's face it: even though it would be great to see the unnecessary layers of financial intermediation stripped away from the old boys' club, regulatory and economic barriers make such revolutionary change almost impossible to achieve from within. None of this is to say, however, that the big brains at R3, as well as those of its member banks' in-house blockchain labs and of distributed ledger startups such as Digital Asset Holdings and Symbiont, aren't producing phenomenally powerful reforms to improve a bottlenecked financial system.

In the current system, to manage the laborious process of cross-firm reconciliation, middlemen ledger-keepers have been created—clearinghouses, settlement agencies, and correspondent banks, custodial banks, and others. Those intermediaries solve some of the trust problems but they also add cost, time, and risk. In the United States, the final settlement of a trade takes two days for U.S. Treasury bonds and up to thirty days for instruments such as syndicated loans. Not only do massive errors and omissions still occur, but the time lag paralyzes literally trillions of dollars of potentially useful capital, which must wait in escrow accounts or collateral agreements until all parties have cleared their books and the trade is settled. A more efficient, real-time system would unlock those funds, sending a wall of money into the world's markets—yes, to make bankers richer, but also to provide more credit to businesses and households. In theory, R3's distributed ledger could achieve all that. It could unleash a tidal wave of money.

The settlement time is also a factor in a financial crisis, and it contributed to the global panic of 2008. Uncertainty over whether counterparty institutions will make good on their promise to deliver either money or securities always gives investors pause. But when the market turns bearish, when fear outruns greed, that nervousness can prompt a cascade of risk-averting actions that evolve into a self-perpetuating process of wanton wealth destruction.

This systemic risk problem is what drew Blythe Masters, one of the key figures behind blockchain innovation on Wall Street, into digital ledger technology; she joined Digital Asset Holdings, a blockchain service provider for the financial system's back-office processing tasks, as CEO in 2014. Masters is best known for one of the most contentious financial innovations of our time, the credit default swap (CDS), a financial derivative contract in which one institution agrees to pay another if a particular bond or loan goes into default. At the age of just twenty-five, and as part of a crack team at J.P. Morgan, she conceived of CDSs as a way for investors to buy insurance against the risk they bear on their balance sheets—and thus to unlock capital hitherto tied up against that risk—as well as for other investors, the banks, and other institutions that issue the CDS to place a bet on the underlying asset without actually owning it. The contracts were tradable, so the parties to a CDS could on-sell them to other, third-party institutions.

This system added convenience and liquidity to credit markets and the CDS market grew to a staggeringly large proportion, with an estimated nominal value of $600 trillion around the time of the crisis. The problem, as described in more detail in Michael Lewis's *The Big Short*, among other places, was that no one had a clear picture of how risks associated with the obligations owed to one institution might influence *that* institution's capacity to repay another one, and so on. CDS deals were "over-the-counter" trades, unlisted on public exchanges and almost entirely unregulated. There was no way to keep track of them. As the crisis worsened, this giant, opaque pool of contingent obligations became one of the biggest sources of worry—vindicating Warren Buffett, who in 2002 labeled derivatives "weapons of financial mass destruction." The CDS meltdown became a self-fulfilling event as it fueled doubts around the solvency of a growing list of banks, so that markets were not only worried about the risk of borrowers defaulting on the shaky mortgage loans underlying the CDS instruments but also about the insidious problem of counterparty and settlement risk. Worried banks, wondering whether their counterparty banks could deliver on their promises, began to pull credit out of the market. A toxic bundle of interlocking panic arose, one that required tens of trillions of dollars of public guarantees, bailouts, and fresh currency issuance by the world's central banks to bring it under control.

None of this was envisioned by the CDS pioneers—because it didn't reflect flaws in credit default contracts per se but in the market's lack of transparency. That's where Masters eventually saw the sweeping potential of blockchain tech, with its capacity to give everyone the same universal view of every transaction in the market. If this transparency-promoting technology had been in place in 2008, Masters wondered, would the crisis have even happened? That thought "was like being hit on the head by an apple," Masters says. She suddenly realized that "the concept of a shared, secure and immutable ledger doesn't just reduce inefficiency, risk and cost, but can provide a real-time window into systemically important information."

"In the post-crisis world," Masters says, "addressing these issues has reached existential consequences for the financial services industry. After spending the best part of three decades working in financial markets and thinking about regulation, plumbing and risks, the transformative power of distributed ledger technology led me to make the leap from a giant investment bank to a tiny technology startup in pursuit of a new way to change the world I knew."

That people like Masters and the R3 team are now tackling these failures of our financial system is undeniably important. As we've said, blockchains, both the permissioned and permissionless kind, attack the problem of social trust. And guess what? That's the very same problem at the heart of systemic market breakdowns, in this case as they pertain to interbank and inter-institutional relationships. It's just that to address such breakdowns, this new wave of distributed ledger system designers have cherry-picked the features of Nakamoto's invention that are least threatening to the players in the banking system, such as its cryptographic integrity, and left aside its more radical, and arguably more powerful, features, especially the decentralized, permissionless consensus system.

The explicit mission of these bank-employed developers is to serve the legacy financial system. So, we can't fault them for turning their noses up at Bitcoin's disruptive version of decentralization. Bitcoin's scaling challenges pose real reasons for concern, too. The DTCC, which settles and clears the vast majority of U.S. stock and bond trades, handles 10,000 transactions per second; Bitcoin, at the time of this writing, could process just seven. And as strong as Bitcoin's value- and incentive-based security model has proven to be, it's not at all clear that a few hundred million dollars in bitcoin mining costs would deter rogue traders in New York or London when government bond markets offer billion-dollar fraud opportunities. Maybe the market would drive up the prices of bitcoin and mining infrastructure to set a new, higher bar for security. Maybe not. Either way, for the firms that R3 and Digital Asset serve—managers of the world's retirement funds, corporate payrolls, government bond issuances, and so forth—these are not security risks they can afford. For now—at least until solutions such as Lightning provide large-scale transaction capabilities—Bitcoin isn't anywhere near ready to service Wall Street's back-office needs.

There are also legal concerns. R3's Swanson has argued that the mere possibility of a 51 percent attack—that scenario in which a miner gains majority control of a cryptocurrency network's computing power and fraudulently changes transactions—means there can never be "settlement finality" in a cryptocurrency transaction. That state of perpetual limbo is a scenario that Wall Street lawyers can't live with, he said. We might retort that the bailouts and various other deals with which banks reversed their losses during the crisis make a mockery of "finality," and that Bitcoin's track record of irreversibility is many magnitudes better than Wall Street's. Nonetheless, Swanson's catchy critique caught on among bankers. After all, he was preaching to the choir.

Using such logic—that is, by ignoring the very problem of concentrated gatekeeping that got our global financial system into its mess in the first place—bankers could now embrace permissioned ledgers as if they were a perfect alternative to the development challenges faced by Bitcoin and other permissionless systems. In a permissioned system, the member institutions are incentivized to validate and maintain the shared ledger because it serves their common interest. They're not racing each other to win currency rewards, which also means they're not constantly building a wasteful computing infrastructure à la Bitcoin. Neither does a permissioned system need to resolve the tough political and economic problems that permissionless ledgers face in their efforts to scale. There's no need to find consensus among a global, leaderless community of thousands of unidentified users; proposals for changes are simply processed by a relatively small committee of known members.

The problem, of course, is captured in that very image: a club of members deciding what goes and what doesn't. A bank-led permissioned system would hinge entirely on the interests of the very same big institutions that already control the financial system, those responsible for the systemic risks, gatekeeping restrictions, and political crises that cryptocurrencies seek to overcome. You could argue that permissioned ledgers in the banking system will just take us back to 2008, the moment of systemic and societal breakdown that triggered the backlash and the motivation for cryptocurrencies to take off.

That's why we argue that individuals, businesses, and governments really need to support the various hard-core technical solutions that developers are pursuing to help permissionless ledgers like Bitcoin and Ethereum overcome their scaling, security, and political challenges.

We discussed these in chapter three: off-chain ideas like the Lightning Network and Ethereum's new Plasma concept, and on-chain solutions like SegWit and "sharding," which compress data and make it possible for a decentralized network to securely manage, store, and agree on the integrity of a massive database while using far less computing resources. Regulators should avoid the temptation to curb these developers' experiments so they can freely work on these exciting solutions, and investors should help fund them. We can't, and shouldn't, stop banks from pursuing clever solutions to their very real back-office inefficiencies. But with the scars from the financial crisis still present, we all have an interest in designing blockchain systems, permissioned or otherwise, in which the capacity of large incumbent institutions to garner excessive market power is curtailed. It's in society's interests to encourage open-access platforms in which permissionless innovation can transform a broken financial system and expand the universe of participants with access to it.

The Other Model: Central Bank Fiat Digital Currency

There's a wild card in all this that complicates the outlook for financial institutions. They may have a giant institutional competitor to contend with in addition to open, interoperable permissionless networks: central banks. If central banks follow through on their growing interest in adopting digital currency technology, the industry facing the biggest disruption will eventually be the banking system.

In the last chapter of *The Age of Cryptocurrency*, we speculated that governments and central banks might explore issuing their own digital currencies. Well, as of January 2017, twenty-six different central banks were running projects to explore blockchain technology, including the Bank of England, the Bank of Japan, and the Bank of Canada, the financial technology news service Finextra reported. Many more, smaller central banks are doing preliminary research. Nobody knows what will come of these efforts, but the ramifications could be profound.

At the MIT Digital Currency Initiative, an international project to develop a prototype digital fiat currency that central banks and governments might deploy is also under way. The starting point is a blockchain toolkit called Cryptokernel, created by DCI researcher James Lovejoy, that makes it easier to experiment with the technology. CK, as it is known, is open-source software—anyone can experiment with it. That's vital, says Robleh Ali, a research scientist who joined MIT after leading the Bank of England's groundbreaking digital currency project, because it means "the design of our future financial system is open to the imagination of anyone anywhere. Broadening the number of people working on this gives us a better chance of developing a truly decentralized financial system in the hands of people, not banks."

The first application of CK is an experimental digital currency called K320 that differs from Bitcoin in a critical way. Whereas Bitcoin's issuance schedule is hardwired to max out at 21 million coins by the year 2140, K320's is not rigidly fixed. The hope is that reducing the scarcity factor will dissuade people from hoarding the cryptocurrency, an instinct that's rampant with bitcoin and leaves many to conclude that bitcoin's most important role in society will be as a store of value— a digital version of gold, perhaps—rather than as a regular currency for day-to-day transactions. Societies need people to spend a currency, not save it; the instinct to do the latter is part of a long history of economic problems, the most extreme of which were seen during the Great Depression. To avoid this fate, K320's issuance is designed to go on in perpetuity with a mild inflationary bias. That means that, after an initial ramped-up release over eight years, the supply of coins will eventually slot into a steady increase of 3.2 percent per year. This is deliberately just above the 2 percent rate of increase that most central banks target for their countries' consumer price indexes. The K320 team is aiming for a balance that's not too deflationary (which can result in hoarding crises like the Great Depression) and not too inflationary (when no one wants to hold the currency, as occurred during Germany's Weimar Republic in the 1920s).

While the thinking behind K320's monetary issuance schedule

reflects that of central banks, it's unlikely that many in the developed-world central banks would adopt a digital currency whose issuance schedule they cannot control. Their first digital currency rollouts will likely borrow much more from the current system than K320 does. There's a stronger case to be made that the first central bank experiments in algorithmic monetary issuance and digital currencies might happen in the developing world, where the payoffs of having political control over the currency are put into question by a long history of financial crises. Either way, the fact that central banks of all stripes are exploring digital currencies at all opens the door to a very different fiat-currency financial system in the future.

If government- or central bank–issued digital currencies existed, people and companies looking for a safe place to store funds purely for transactional or custodial purposes could now do so with the institution that creates that money. It would be cheaper and safer than leaving your money exposed to the solvency of a private institution and the fees it would charge to maintain a profit. In other words, central banks would become disruptive new competitors to commercial banks whenever households and corporate treasurers have to choose where to hold short-term funds for payment purposes, whether that money is for groceries or for the monthly staff payroll. Think of Apple. It had a staggering $246 billion in cash on its books at the end of December 2016. Most of that was invested in short-term "cash-like" instruments such as Treasury bills, but the small percentage that sat in bank deposits was still a very large amount of money. It's reasonable to assume that companies like that would move a significant part of their holdings into central bank custody, given the choice. This is one reason why researchers at the BOE speculated that differential interest rates would be needed—lower for central bank digital currencies but higher for bank deposits, perhaps—to discourage a destructive exodus of funds and smoothly manage the transition to digital currency.

Nonetheless, many central bankers concur that gradually getting banks out of the payment business would be a positive thing. In theory, it reduces costs and inefficiencies, since profit-seeking banks (some might call them rent-seeking) are no longer acting as a tollgate to the economy's commercial activity. Just as importantly, there would be less pressure on governments and central banks to bail out banks than there was in 2008, when it was feared that a looming collapse would cut off the economy's payments lifeline. Central banks know too well now just how that crisis, which forced them to drive interest rates to zero and left them powerless to do more, seriously curtailed their capacity to stimulate economic growth. One of the strongest arguments for central bank digital currency, then, is that it could foster financial stability.

In this way, the arrival of digital currency technology has highlighted a divergence of interests between central banks and the private institutions they oversee. For years, a kind of symbiotic relationship existed as banks enjoyed exclusive, regulated access to official monetary facilities in return for being agents of central bank policy objectives. That has long encouraged conspiracy theorists to trot out centuries-old, and often anti-Semitic, myths about secretive cabals and the world order. The reality has always been far more complicated than that, of course. But now, with blockchain technology offering new models for creating, exchanging, and managing currencies, the two sides may actually find themselves in direct competition.

Hyperledger's Battle with Itself

It's not just the old guard of the financial sector that's confronting these changes. A wide array of non-financial heavy-hitter corporations are also getting their feet wet in blockchain technology and grappling with what it means for them. One project that's attracted a lot of their attention is Hyperledger. A broad corporate consortium dedicated to a mostly open-source collaborative approach, Hyperledger is seeking to develop nothing less than a common blockchain/distributed ledger infrastructure for the global economy, one that's targeted not only at finance and banking but also at the Internet of Things, supply chains, and manufacturing.

In joining Hyperledger, the founding corporate members were declaring a common interest in seeing the digital global economy evolve into something far more open and powerful. Describing the technology as "an operating system for marketplaces, data-sharing networks, micro-currencies, and decentralized digital communities," the group's Web site declared that Hyperledger "has the potential to vastly reduce the cost and complexity of getting things done in the real world." Such a sweeping vision can't afford to be too closed-minded toward the kinds of models that might win out in the future. So, it's notable that among its more than one hundred members as of the end of 2016, there were numerous Bitcoin-focused companies inserting their case for decentralized cryptocurrency systems. These included Blockstream, blockchain applications provider Bloq, and Blockchain.info, the bitcoin wallet and data-processing company. Still, the biggest players in this group were large incumbent companies. And that posed a coordination challenge. Those firms' business models were mostly built on centralized control of data and on acting as trusted intermediaries for their customers' transactions. So, inevitably, the same tensions and power battles over the permissionless versus permissioned ledger dichotomy seemed bound to arise.

Hyperledger's core founding members, including IBM, Digital Asset, Accenture, DTCC, and Intel, brought in the respected Linux Foundation to run the project. The foundation is behind the ubiquitous Linux operating system kernel, which powers 90 percent of the world's servers, is widely deployed in routers, set-top boxes, and smart TVs, among other devices, and is the bedrock of Google's Android operating system. The Linux story is a textbook case of how open-source software development can tap the widest possible talent pool to build the best, most robust, and most universally applicable technology. Hyperledger also picked an executive director with strong bona fides in the development of *open* platforms: Brian Behlendorf, who spearheaded the open-source Apache Web server software and was a board member of the Mozilla Foundation and the Electronic Frontier Foundation.

These were important signals. With a blank canvas but also the daunting task of designing a new operating system for the global digital economy, it was vital that a group like this encourage open innovation, so that potentially disruptive new ideas weren't constrained by threatened gatekeepers. As MIT Media Lab's Joi Ito puts it, the online economy was not won by the closed-loop "intranets" of the early networking business—not by France Telecom's Minitel system, or by the internal networks of AOL or Prodigy—but by the fully accessible Internet made possible by the TCP/IP pair of open protocols. The Internet's open constitution has since been protected by an alphabet soup of global, not-for-profit bodies—albeit with some concern about their excessive power. The Hyperledger project seemed to be forming around similar principles.

Still, Hyperledger's big-name membership raises challenges. Each company has its shareholders' interests to protect, which it serves by pushing to insert coding elements that meet its business priorities into the open-source project's codebase. The most well-resourced companies in the consortium are best placed to do that, simply by writing reams of code. When those interests contradict those of other contributors to the project, disputes and internal politics will arise. "Signing off on the press release was the easy part. Making the thing is what's hard," said Jim Zemlin, Linux Foundation executive director, at the inaugural gathering of the Hyperledger membership's developer community in January 2016. "We are trying to boy-band an open-source project. . . . We are artificially bringing people together who are coming up from a different place. So let's listen to everyone's perspective." He told the group about the lesson IBM learned from the Linux development process. The company initially rewarded its Linux engineers depending on how much IBM code lines they inserted into the project. Presumably the rationale was that IBM would profit if the Linux operating system's underlying code were optimized to work with the company's computers and servers and the particular brand of IT solutions it peddled to its clients—especially if dominating the Linux code also meant it didn't work so well with competitors' models, which were configured differently. But, as Zemlin described it, IBM soon realized this was an ineffective way to engage with the Linux open-source community. Instead, it started compensating its engineers for work that made the overall program function better and found that that served IBM's interests more than anything.

It was an important anecdote, given that IBM was already asserting itself as Hyperledger's 800-pound gorilla. At that same January 2016 meeting, the tech behemoth open-sourced 44,000 lines of its "chaincode" for automated smart contracts, effectively donating it to Hyperledger's common ledger software, now known as Fabric. On the one hand, this could be viewed as a generous, no-strings-attached donation of resources. But it also meant that the tech giant was setting the shape of the project from the start. And as time went on, it seemed like the system IBM had in mind was specifically designed to feed into its own, closed-loop business of providing "cloud" hosting business. Was this in the interests of the wider community?

To be sure, others contributed code and ideas—Digital Asset donated its Global Synchronization Log for financial institutions and Intel bequeathed its Sawtooth Lake program for affirming the trustworthiness of computing devices. But IBM's early move made it the major player in the Hyperledger ecosystem. This raised the likelihood that it would dominate the design of the system's underlying code and so dictate its business and economic priorities. It's no different from the concerns that people on either side of Bitcoin's "civil war" raised about which companies were paying particular developers' salaries; they knew that those developers would then argue for or against an increase in block size depending on their employers' views.

IBM's interest in the Hyperledger project was very much driven by opportunities in supply-chain applications of blockchains. As mentioned in the previous chapter, it was already using its code to improve the dispute resolution mechanism for vendor and supplier payments within its own business lines. When Jerry Cuomo, IBM vice president for blockchain technologies, gave an account of the success of that operation at that early Hyperledger meeting, it made a compelling case for private blockchains. You didn't need an open, permissionless system, it seemed, to extract value from a blockchain-like approach to sequential record-keeping. Yet, unintentionally, he was also showing how the legacy business interests of an influential member could distract an open-source consortium like Hyperledger from building a truly open, innovative system. It soon became clear that the business opportunity IBM saw was to steer clients, particularly those eager to resolve supply-chain management problems, back to its own legacy businesses. A year later, IBM launched its "Blockchain as a Service" offering—marked by the first TV ad to use the word "blockchain." The service encouraged clients to work with their supply-chain partners to create private blockchains that were structured entirely around an integration with IBM's pre-existing cloud service. Having IBM host your blockchain-relevant data—relying on a "trusted third party"—kind of goes against the whole, disruptive, self-help spirit of the blockchain.

The cynicism in part stems from the misleading imagery fostered by the term "cloud computing." When IBM, Amazon, Google, or any other cloud computing provider stores your files or runs out-sourced computing services for you, that operation runs on identifiable servers owned by those companies. They are the landlords of our rented server space. The "cloud" conjures images of an amorphous, decentralized system when it's very much a centralized solution with total dependence on a trusted third party.

The grand vision of blockchain technology lies in decentralization, in users not having to depend on any single entity to execute an operation on their behalf. (In fact, as we discuss elsewhere in this book, specific decentralized applications are already being built on blockchain architecture that are intended to provide truly decentralized file storage and off-site computer services.) IBM's blockchain model appears to be focused on burnishing a profitable, centralized business that's threatened by that decentralized vision. This is a fully understandable, rational, and smart strategy from the point of view of IBM's shareholders, but it contradicts the open-platform spirit conveyed in Hyperledger's own marketing material. It also raises legal questions—if key elements of a blockchain's data are stored on the computers of one company, do the prevailing laws about data residency give governments power to control that blockchain?

These issues also speak to the challenges of getting a consortium of corporate members, many of whom are now many decades on from their rebellious startup beginnings and reliant on entrenched businesses that are vulnerable to disruption, to truly act in the broad, cross-industry interests of the members and of future users. That matters because the best option for achieving that will be one that's led by a community that shares our interest in decentralization. Inclusion, opportunity, and the most powerful processes of idea generation will ultimately result from an open system, one that rejects the excessive influence of institutions whose interests lie in curtailing innovation that threatens their position.

The Limits of Permission

The permissioned, quasi-centralized solutions that big financial institutions and incumbent tech firms are pursuing are not inherently bad or even counterproductive. The learning and discovery that's emerging from the serious research at R3 and Hyperledger will contribute to the bigger pool of knowledge from which the world's engineers and entrepreneurs will build a better global system of trust management. But if we absorb the historical lessons, cited by MIT Media Lab director Ito above, about the ultimate victory that open Internet protocols like TCP/IP had over closed, walled-garden "intranets" such as Minitel, AOL, or Prodigy, we see the inherent limits of these permissioned blockchain proposals. Those closed intranet models eventually lost, Ito points out, because they couldn't compete with the amount of activity and application development drawn to work on the overall, global Internet ecosystem. Why would either users or developers want to work with AOL's clunky "you've got mail" system when they had access to an open network e-mail system to which new features were being added from multiple locations around the world? The same possibility for success and failure could arise in the blockchain and distributed ledger battles, Ito says.

Permissionless systems like those of Bitcoin and Ethereum inherently facilitate more creativity and innovation, because it's just understood that no authorizing company or group of companies can ever say that this or that thing cannot be built. Even if the stewards of the permissioned systems say they will make their platforms open to others, having them as gatekeepers leaves open the possibility of restrictions on outsiders. And that will give pause to open-source volunteers who might otherwise be drawn to work on such platforms. It's the guarantee of open access that fosters enthusiasm and passion for "permissionlessness" networks. That's already evident in the caliber and rapid expansion in the number of developers working on public blockchain applications. Permissioned systems will have their place, if nothing else because they can be more easily programmed at this early stage of the technology's life to handle heavier transaction loads. But the overarching objective for all of us should be to encourage the evolution of an open, interoperable permissionless network.

There's a reason we want a world of open, public blockchains and distributed trust models that gives everybody a seat at the table. Let's keep our eyes on that ball.

Seven

BLOCKCHAINS FOR GOOD

The shantytowns that surround the stadium of Pope Francis's beloved San Lorenzo football team, in the Bajo Flores area of Buenos Aires, are home to hundreds of thousands of poor Bolivian immigrants. Many live in precarious dwellings prone to being swept away when the waters of the nearby Matanza River overflow. In the middle of this community, however, there is one tiny, two-block street in which the housing is of a distinctly stronger foundation. The local school is in that neighborhood, as is a health clinic and a host of other institutions used by Argentina's Bolivian cultural community. Charrúa holds no unique geographic advantage over all the other neighborhoods in the area. So, the question is: why do the families who live in those two blocks seem comparatively blessed? Why is this place the focal point of Bolivian-Argentine cultural pride?

Two words: property title.

After a long multi-decade fight with the city, the 200 households of Charrúa were in 1991 granted something that would offer them the most important foundation for development they could get: certificates of property ownership. The Charrúa families didn't earn higher incomes than those in other parts of the neighborhood, and they weren't more educated or better connected. The difference was that they had the capacity to *prove* home ownership with the indisputable seal of a government. And that status opened the door to a whole host of other benefits. As taxpaying property owners, they now had standing in the community, which meant they could lobby the government for services. That led to the school and the clinic. And they could use the deeds as collateral to borrow money to invest in businesses, which is why Charrúa became a commercial center, lined with stores and small restaurants. A visitor from the tony neighborhoods of the city's northern corridor would still see a stark lack of amenities, but to the Bolivian locals, this two-block strip is proof that at least some of their kind have *made it.*

What does this have to do with the blockchain? Well, to answer that, let's not focus on the comparatively lucky 200 households of Charrúa but on the hundreds of thousands of Bolivians and other slum-dwellers of Buenos Aires and shantytowns all around the developing world who don't have a title to their home. Their communities will acknowledge them as the owners but there's nothing official saying so, nothing that's accepted by the government or a bank, that is. Public registry systems in low-income countries are prone to corruption and incompetence—so a poor resident of a slum in a village in Uttar Pradesh or Manila might try to get a loan with their home as collateral, but no bank would accept it. Even wealthier homeowners run into frequent problems around the world—they'll buy an apartment from a developer only to find that the businessman bribed the registrar to keep his name on the title. Proving ownership in such places is so precarious that banks are reluctant to provide mortgage loans, at least not at reasonable interest rates.

Recently, though, we've seen startups attempting to use blockchain technology to solve this registry problem. The idea is that because a blockchain is immutable, time-stamped, and publicly auditable, and because it can execute property transfers almost immediately and completely, letting both parties verify the exchange with their unique private keys, it's near impossible for one person to unilaterally make a change in their favor. The developer in the case described above would, in theory, not be able to bribe the registrar to reverse the title transfer because neither could provide the cryptographic proofs needed to do so.

We say "in theory," because we're dealing with an untested idea within the extremely complicated and politically fraught realm of land rights. You could still have many cases of bribes resulting in bad information being entered into blockchain ledgers. In poor countries where registries need to be built from scratch, there's a risk that corrupt government officials charged with attesting to people's ownership would embed harmful falsehoods into the blockchain-based registry from the outset. Below we'll discuss ways in which this risk might be mitigated. Still, when a ledger is assumed to be an unquestioned truth, the issue of what information gets into it is a serious one.

Nonetheless, if we take a macro view and assume that in the vast majority of cases blockchains will be used honestly, the wider benefits of a cryptographically secure asset registry are pretty enticing. Peruvian economist and anti-poverty campaigner Hernando de Soto estimates that the amount of "dead capital," the pool of untitled property around the world, is worth about $20 trillion. If poor people could use that capital as collateral, he says, the multiplier effect from all that credit flowing through the global economy could create growth rates in excess of 10 percent in developing countries, which account for more than half of world GDP.

And it's not just land. This technology has kindled interest in how to help the poor prove ownership of a much wider array of assets, such as small business equipment and vehicles, as well as reliably show their personal good standing on questions such as creditworthiness and make sure their votes are counted. There's hope that the blockchain could give people the power to prove claims about themselves so they can become active citizens in a global economy from which they have, until now, been excluded.

The Proofs

Human society has devised a system of proofs or tests that people must pass before they can participate in many aspects of commercial exchange and social interaction. Until they can prove that they are who they say they are, and until that identity is tied to a record of on-time payments, property ownership, and other forms of trustworthy behavior, they are often excluded—from getting bank accounts, from accessing credit, from being able to vote, from anything other than prepaid telephone or electricity. It's why one of the biggest opportunities for this technology to address the problem of global financial inclusion is that it might help people come up with these proofs. In a nutshell, the goal can be defined as proving *who I am*, *what I do*, and *what I own*. Companies and institutions habitually ask questions—about identity, about reputation, and about assets—before engaging with someone as an employee or business partner.

A business that's unable to develop a reliable picture of a person's identity, reputation, and assets faces uncertainty. Would you hire or loan money to a person about whom you knew nothing? It is riskier to deal with such people, which in turn means they must pay marked-up prices to access all sorts of financial services. They pay higher rates on a loan or are forced by a pawnshop to accept a steep discount on their pawned belongings in return for credit. Unable to get bank accounts or credit cards, they cash checks at a steep discount from the face value, pay high fees on money orders, and pay cash for everything while the rest of us enjoy twenty-five days interest free on our credit cards. It's expensive to be poor, which means it's a self-perpetuating state of being.

Sometimes the service providers' caution is dictated by regulation or compliance rules more than the unwillingness of the banker or trader to enter a deal—in the United States and other developed countries, banks are required to hold more capital against loans deemed to be of poor quality, for example. But many other times the driving factor is just fear of the unknown. Either way, anything that adds transparency to the multi-faceted picture of people's lives should help institutions lower the cost of financing and insuring them.

It's not just a developing world problem. In the United States, 7.7 percent of the population is "unbanked," meaning they don't have bank accounts, and 17.9 percent are considered "underbanked," meaning they rely upon payday, rent-to-own services, and the like. In Baltimore, 14 percent of residents are unbanked. In Memphis, it's nearly 17 percent. In Detroit and Miami, it's 20 percent. There are plenty of middle-class people who are penalized by the inability to prove their good standing, too. Various types of loan repayments are not captured in the all-important FICO score, for example. Still, most of us in the advanced economies of the West simply take for granted things like reliable birth certificates, driver's licenses, bank accounts, and credit ratings—the proofs with which we access services. The real opportunity for change, not surprisingly, exists in the developing world.

For the more than 2 billion adults worldwide that the World Bank describes as "unbanked," the good news is that a combination of humanitarian and financial motivations has produced a global movement to move the unbanked into the world of modern finance. That's also good news for people looking for the next market: if we crack this nut, there's potential for an economic boom the likes of which nobody has ever seen. It lies on the other side of incorporating the new markets, new customers, new products, and trillions of dollars of untapped capital that these people would bring with them.

The term "unbanked," widely used by the development community, is misleading. While it accurately describes the fact that these people don't have access to standard banking services, making it harder for them to engage in economic exchange, it suggests that the answer lies only in providing them with bank accounts. But as Bitcoin and the blockchain have shown, the peer-to-peer system of digital exchange, which avoids the cumbersome, expensive, and inherently exclusionary banking system, may offer a better way.

For now, though, banks are still part of the official discourse around "financial inclusion." Among the key goals in the UN's plan to eradicate global poverty by 2030 is "to encourage and expand access to banking, insurance and financial services for all." And the World Bank has a specific initiative called "Universal Financial Access by 2020," or UFA2020. A variety of groups—financial institutions, foundations, donors, and investors—committed a combined $31 billion in 2013 toward increasing financial inclusion, according to the advocacy group

Consultative Group to Assist the Poor, and that figure is expected to grow about 7 percent annually.

How can blockchains help? Let's step back again and remind ourselves what this technology purports to create: a better, universal information and record-keeping system, one that could stand, immutable and open for all, for all time. This concept shifts the bargain between institutions, such as governments and corporations, and the people they are supposed to serve. Having control over our own information allows us to assert our rights as citizens. It gives us a rock-solid basis upon which to interact and negotiate with others. By contrast, if we can't control that information, if it's fleeting and unstable—whether it's the data around the property we own or the history of our on-time payments to our landlord or utility provider—we're immediately placed into a weaker bargaining position than those who have established that control. This imbalance, to borrow the subtitle from de Soto's influential book *The Mystery of Capital*, is "why capitalism succeeds in the West and fails everywhere else." That we might now have a chance to address that imbalance is a tantalizingly powerful thought.

The Digital Stamp

What blockchains bring to the table can be boiled down to the value of a time-stamped record. In the West, when you buy a piece of property, a house, or a car, when you register a business, when you have a child, there is an official notice that comes with each of those developments: a document from the hospital, a "pink slip" from the auto dealer or the previous owner, a title deed. Each is stamped by a notary, an official recognition of ownership. That stamp is symbolic but powerful. Essentially, it's a stand-in for "the truth."

It would probably never occur to you that you might be challenged on the ownership of your home or car, or that foundation of your business, or your child's birth, but if you were, you would produce this signed, notarized document. With your notarized document, you are codified, you are legalized, you are bona fide. The time stamp makes this all possible, because it inserts a declaration that a milestone event has occurred—a birth, a graduation, a property transfer, a marriage— into a commonly accepted record of history to which all can refer.

Stamps date as far back as 7600 BCE. The first carved-stone cylin- der seals were made during the Neolithic Period in modern-day Syria. They were small enough to be carried on a necklace or bracelet, or even pinned on a shirt. They were used as a personal seal, and everybody from kings to slaves had them. Later the tool for these seals became a stamp rather than a cylinder, but the point was the same: the stamp, in clay or wax, was an official seal of authenticity. This tradition lives on today, though again, we in rich countries take it for granted. In fact, if you think about this stamp at all, you're likely to focus on the mundane annoyance of finding a notary public. The stamp, though, is incredibly powerful. And that, essentially, is the service that blockchains provide to people. This public, recognizable open ledger, which can be checked at any time by anybody, acts in much the same way as the notary stamp: it codifies that a certain action took place at a certain time, with certain particulars attached to it, and it does this in a way that the record of that transaction cannot be altered by private parties, whether they be individuals or governments.

It is quite possible that the blockchain will come to replace the no- tary stamp, in some incarnation, whether by an individual govern- ment's blockchain-based platform or a universal platform that is beyond the reach of any individual government. It should be no surprise that some of the earliest non-currency applications of the blockchain focused on providing immutable notarization. One of the first to figure out that documents could be recorded and proven this way was Factom, an Austin, Texas, company that created an audit trail of financial docu- ments' changes, creating a model that, if it's widely adopted, will even- tually replace the whole industry of quarterly and annual accounting and auditing with something that happens in real time. Another player in this space is called, appropriately, Stampery. Stampery was founded by Luis Iván Cuende, a remarkable young Spanish entrepreneur who founded his first major software project at the age of twelve and at the age of twenty-one had amassed a reputation as one of the world's most innovative hackers and developers. Stampery takes hashes of documents and records the trail of changes to them to the blockchain, providing valuable proof of status for companies involved in negotiations or litigation. It can help, for example, to keep track of multiple iterations and red-line changes that different lawyers and signatories might make to a contract through the evolution of a business deal.

But we can think of this time-stamped certification process in a more expansive way than merely the authentication of documents and we can certainly take it beyond the stuffy world of lawyers and business deals. Consider the field of credit-scoring, where the cost—as bankers call it—of "acquiring" a customer, which essentially amounts to doing due diligence to ensure they are creditworthy, has been prohibitively high across the developing world. The huge amount of time that's needed to learn about someone who doesn't have a paper trail of records and isn't easily accessible, or doesn't have an official ID, is too often more than it's worth to issue a loan. Microfinance institutions—which provide small loans to the poor—have strived to solve the problem by sending dedicated volunteer credit officers out into the field to get to know people, vouch for them, and physically pick up and deliver cash for loan disbursement and repayment collection. But the personnel costs in this model just don't scale. It perhaps shouldn't have been a surprise that, sometime after Grameen Bank founder Muhammad Yunis won the Nobel Peace Prize for pioneering the microfinance industry, increasing default rates and a host of scandals shed light on the limits of this industry. Billions of people remain underserved by credit, precisely because of the poor state of information.

And that's essentially the problem that blockchain technology has the potential to solve: it can improve the state of information. The more expansive version of this idea goes back to some folks who, with a leap of imagination, transformed the Bitcoin blockchain from a platform solely for recording and exchanging bitcoin currency into one that could do the same for other assets. That led to all sorts of sweeping, related ideas that have gripped innovators across multiple industries and that populate the pages of this book.

It goes back to a team of developers, led by Alex Mizrahi, who launched a "Bitcoin 2.0" implementation called Colored Coins in 2013 based on a 2012 white paper by Meni Rosenfeld. The idea was to take unique trusted, certified metadata about a real-world asset—perhaps the serial number on the chassis of a car or the geospatial coordinates of a piece of land—and associate it with a rightful owner who would have private key control over a bitcoin address. Bitcoin transactions include information fields, so that when the deed to a car is transferred from one person to another, the hash of that document can be inserted into a bitcoin transaction that's validated by the mining network. (Here, the hashing process is similar to that which Bitcoin miners themselves do, as explained in chapter three, except that it is done by whoever holds the title to the asset, or is otherwise authorized to update information about it. Essentially, the text of a title document showing any changes to the assignment of rights and obligation, including the owner's name as well as liens on the property, is run through a hashing algorithm that produces an alphanumeric string. That hash is then inserted into a blockchain transaction.)

In these cases, the amount of bitcoin used is irrelevant—a few cents perhaps, though there may well need to be more compensation paid in fees if miners are going to incorporate the transaction into a block. The transaction merely becomes a vessel within which information about some right or claim is conveyed to the world. This is possible because, as we've discussed, cryptocurrency on a blockchain gives money a capacity that it doesn't have in the traditional monetary system—it becomes programmable, able to communicate information and instructions. Note as well that the owner of such an asset need not only use this tool to send an asset to someone else; they could also make the transaction between two bitcoin addresses that they control, doing so solely to indelibly record the fact that they have a claim on a house, car, or other asset.

In reality, Bitcoin proved to be a somewhat clunky way to perform such transactions, because its programming language is quite limiting, which is why the more versatile Ethereum and other Bitcoin successors have attracted much of the work in this field. But conceptually, Colored Coins—whose founders have since formed a blockchain startup called Chromaway that has a contract to register land titles in Sweden—was a significant breakthrough. It raised the prospect of tamper-proof asset registries, bringing this powerful new concept of decentralized trust and immutability to the centuries-old practice of tracking property—who owns it, who holds liens against it, and the dates on which title is transferred.

If you've bought a house, you're likely familiar with the idea of a title search, though you may well be unclear why it's necessary. An entire industry exists around the mundane task of determining the provenance of a property. (The last thing you want to do is plunk down $300,000—or, more likely, borrow $300,000—on a property you can't actually buy because there's an unreported lien against it.) What happens after you've put down your money for this part of the process? A title company searches through the property title's history to make sure it is free from defects, that there wasn't, say, a forged document somewhere along the chain of ownership. If changes in title information were hashed and recorded to a blockchain, this search would take seconds, cost nothing, and significantly cut down on any fraudulent claims of ownership.

Even in developed countries with relatively well-functioning land recording systems, there's a chicken-and-egg problem. Depending on which U.S. state you live in, you're subject to a standard title system, or Torrens system, in which the state essentially creates the registry and stands behind it. The first entry takes a lot of time to record, because each new entry requires a full record of all pertinent details. The second is simpler to administer, but it is harder to search for historical details such as liens and transfers. In some respects, a blockchain represents the automation of the abstract system, so as to arrive at a more searchable model of the Torrens system. But building a distributed ledger that way requires the accumulation of sales events to build up the record, which could take generations before it's meaningful. The easier thing to do, then, for a reform-minded government, is to hire a startup that's willing to go through the process of converting all of an existing registry, if one exists, into a digital format that can be recorded in a blockchain. Either way, obviously, there's a lot of legwork involved. The impact of a distributed ledger for ownership records would be immense. The title insurance business, by which firms provide guarantees to homeowners that they'll cover their losses if something faulty is later found with their property rights, would wither and die. Real estate investors forced to tie up large amounts of money in escrow for months on end would be able to deploy this capital. The positive impact on both housing and stock and bond markets could be profound.

The Great Promise: Unlocking Dead Capital

Disrupting the developed world's titling and insurance business is appealing. But, as we've suggested, we're most inspired by the potential impact on the developing world. That's because it's not just the act of recording information that's powerful, but the prospect of changing a whole way of life, of creating newfound trust in a community's system of information-keeping, a vital tool for building social capital and expanding the frequency and scope of economic exchanges.

De Soto, who has come to see blockchain technology as a tool to achieve his lifelong ambition to give the poor of the world property title, describes the potential behavioral impact this way: "The reason people don't go around recording themselves, besides the fact that record-keeping systems in former Soviet and developing world countries are shabby, is because when they give over that information, they don't trust who they are giving it to. . . . They don't want to be vulnerable to something that can be used against them. And that's what's interesting about the tamper-proof blockchain—if you can get the right message about it out there, [people will see] that it's worthwhile recording yourself."

Now, in concert with BitFury, the Peruvian economist has infused energy into his life mission. He is working on a pilot in the Republic of Georgia to transfer that country's property records to a blockchain setting. Other pilots are being conducted elsewhere—Chromaway's Sweden project, another by a startup called BitLand in Ghana. Even in the United States, things are happening, as blockchain startup Ubitquity is partnering with Priority Title & Escrow, a Virginia Beach title company, to "simplify the process of tracking and recording to enable a long-term chain of custody of title," according to CEO Nathan Wosnak.

While these projects offer hope, there are challenges in applying them to the world's poorest countries, challenges that remind us of the dangers of treating blockchain technology as a silver bullet for fixing poverty. There's still an enormous amount of "off-chain" institution-building that needs to be done if these countries are to build the social capital needed to foster functioning, inclusive economies. Here, we are sobered by the experience of the impoverished West African nation of Sierra Leone, where a dozen state agencies have been working since 1999 to reform a poorly managed land title system. As it is now, Sierra Leone's land titling system discriminates against most citizens in favor of a minority of landholders whose rights were first established under the property registry of the old British colonial system. The postcolonial hybrid system that was set up after that is fraught with multiple, competing, and contested claims. They got so bad that the Ministry of Lands had a moratorium on all land transactions in western areas from 2008 to 2011. A new national land policy was implemented in 2015 to address these concerns. The problem is no one really knows where to start. Will the government have the will to see the reforms through? Will parties that stand to lose accept the reforms? And this is just one country.

You'll note that, perhaps with the exception of Ghana, all the pilots we mention above involve taking existing, relatively reliable registries and proving them to an immutable blockchain. They are not, as of now, bringing title to places where people don't have it at all or where poorly maintained paper records are kept in a sometimes rotting, disintegrating state. The key reason for that is the "garbage-in/garbage-out" conundrum: when beginning records are unreliable, there's a risk of creating an indisputable permanence to information that enshrines some abuse of a person's property rights. This problem was highlighted in a critical study of blockchain startup Factom's since-abandoned property registration pilot in Honduras by University of British Columbia professor Victoria L. Lemieux, who warned of the dangers of overly relying on the technology. Lemieux argued that blockchain property registries, while useful for tracking transactions, "may negatively affect the authenticity of information as well." It boils down to a problem of attestation, which brings us back to the trusted third-party problem, one that in this case cannot be entirely avoided. Whom do we trust to assert this or that piece of property belongs to him or her? It's another "off-chain" problem, one that stems from weaknesses in the original source of the information, not in the act of hashing the data to a blockchain.

Considering the messy records that date back centuries in many developing countries, one fear is that rushing to enter them into a permanent, immutable blockchain record would enshrine and legitimize the claims of the powerful and corrupt, to the detriment of others. The battle to reach this definitive, final accepted state could bring out conflict—and violence and intimidation. Then there's the problem of just letting the criminals win. In slums, rights to property are often defined by the local drug gangs. Do we want their view of the world to be validated by this system?

Still, superior accounting and auditing systems, which are what this technology represents, can themselves be powerful drivers of positive behavior. A blockchain won't capture the off-chain payment of a cash bribe, but it can reveal irrefutable patterns of activity that, in the event of a dispute, can be used as evidence against corrupt officials. Every step of the titling process—the land survey, the interviews with neighborhood members, the inscribing of the deed, and so forth—can be logged and recorded into the blockchain. That audit trail offers a powerful tool for challenging the official record, one that doesn't exist with mutable registries, since they can be amended to remove the trail of wrongdoing. People tend to behave more circumspectly when they know they are being watched.

De Soto insists that we shouldn't be cowed by the social challenges associated with recording people's titles to their assets. The social and economic benefits of creating reliable titles far outweigh the costs of perpetuating the old injustices. He also swears by his experience that it's often possible to draw on deeply embedded cultural knowledge of who owns what and convert it into reliable digital data.

In Cameroon and Senegal, Julius Akinyemi, another MIT Media Lab researcher, has found a way to use established cultural practices to resolve the challenges of attestation. He's asking village elders to decide who owns what in the village so that he can record the data in a digital registry—one that's managed by his system, not a blockchain. The trick, though, is that he's attached to their record a reputational scoring system designed to keep the elders honest. If they sign a piece of land over to their brother, or some livestock that's not rightfully his, there's a way for aggrieved parties to register their concerns through the scoring system. Akinyemi says he's found a positive feedback loop where elders are now seeking recognition through positive reputation scores.

Beyond Land

Since we've mentioned Akinyemi, it's worth highlighting another idea of his that gets at a wider concept of property rights beyond land. He's working to build a blockchain-based registry of the intellectual property of developing countries rich in biodiversity, starting with a project in concert with the government of Mauritius. The idea is that by pre-registering natural assets in rainforests and other biochemistry-rich places and then recording them in a blockchain as a property claim on behalf of local communities, those communities can better assert their rights. That way, they can't be as easily exploited by foreign pharmaceutical and cosmetic companies, which have lodged countless patents based on the extraction of materials in such places over the years. The concept is only loosely formed at this stage but we raise it here to point out that the assets a blockchain can register go far beyond land. In fact, other assets may be much easier to quantify, with less politics and less ambiguity over ownership.

People are talking about blockchain registries of *movable* assets such as cars, potentially with signals from embedded RFID chips that record unique serial numbers into a blockchain. Blockchain registries could be built up at the point of sale, with loans collateralized right there and then against the asset, a process that would not need the same level of intervention as an official registry.

In yet another project from MIT Media Lab, this one led by Michael Casey's Digital Currency Initiative colleague Mark Weber, a team is working with Inter-American Development Bank to lay a blockchain-based technical foundation for an open-source public asset registry that could support claims on a variety of assets. These could include commodities, accounts receivable, equipment, as well as land. The team's first test application is aimed at providing poor farmers in developing countries with an immutable receipt for crops deposited at a warehouse. Warehouse receipts are an integral part of any country's management of trade in agriculture. But in developing countries, banks have long been unwilling to accept them as collateral as the banks can't be sure that the receipts, often issued on flimsy, easily duplicated paper in poorly monitored facilities, haven't been pledged to other lenders to create competing liens. The blockchain can assure that only one receipt has been generated for each deposit of crops and can keep an immutable record of how much of the deposit has been pledged and to whom. It's yet another way that blockchains prevent double-spending.

And in the field of solar energy, a team that Michael's leading is exploring a model that would capture usage rights to energy generated in a communally owned microgrid as a way to funnel collateralized financing to off-grid communities that don't have well-established legal and property title systems. Already, a team composed of IoT startup Filament, Nasdaq, and a team from IDEO Colab has found a way to integrate signals from a smart meter device with a blockchain so as to prove that a uniquely identified photovoltaic panel has produced and delivered a verifiable, measurable amount of solar power. In effect, that proven flow of power could be registered as a kind of certified claim to solar energy, which can then be traded or collateralized. Then, if we were to connect a device such as Filament's with a digital payments and smart-contract system, along with an on/off "kill" switch to regulate access to that power, a form of remotely executable "smart property" is created. If the system detects that digital currency payments have ceased, the smart contract would deactivate access to the power until payments are resumed, or could divert it into storage or to another part of the system in which payments *are* being made. This has potentially far-reaching implications in the world of finance.

Clearly, the terms of such an agreement must be fair to all parties. (Already, ethical and safety questions are being raised about similar kill-switch solutions to secure auto loans in the United States.) It might sound unwise to submit control over your energy grid to a decentralized algorithm. But once all parties agree to the contract and acknowledge that the blockchain's neutrality assures that its terms and conditions will be carried out as agreed, this model could help supplement an otherwise flawed legal system, and so proactively lower the cost of financing in such places.

Imagine a small investor, say a green energy–conscious retiree in Portland, Oregon, partly investing their savings in a blockchain-backed loan to partly fund a microgrid in Uttar Pradesh, India. That claim could be sold to other investors who would retain the same smart-contract-backed protections for their investments. Now imagine that that secured loan could be bundled with other loans to microgrids— some from microfinance institutions, some from credit unions, others from local banks—into pools of securitized "crypto-solar" financial assets that could be sold to investment houses and bigger institutions. A blockchain is vital in this because it can allow a level of granularity and micromanagement of the investment and energy flows that's simply not possible in a non-digital world, where the lack of transparency and high transaction costs of the legacy financial system couldn't sustain such tiny transactions. But with a network of computers regulated by a blockchain able to act as a decentralized, automated portfolio manager, keeping finely tuned track of the performance each divisible portion of each microgrid's financing package, a more complex aggregation of micro-investments is at least conceivable.

It's a lofty goal: turning tiny little pieces of developing world assets into pools of wealth that Wall Street investment banks might wish to buy and sell. It's like a more down-market but arguably more reliable and safer version of the mortgage-backed securities market through which Wall Street's financial engineers created investment-grade bonds out of large pools of home loans. Might we one day unlock the same kind of financing revolution to fund the rollout of this vital, decentralized energy infrastructure around the world? Energy is the most important resource that any community has. If we can get fair-priced financing for marginalized people to build access to that resource in renewable form, might this be a way to both save the planet and give poor communities an economic development platform from which to build dynamic local businesses?

Money Everyone Can Use

Much of the hope that the development community has recently invested in the prospect for financial inclusion stems from the rapid expansion of mobile phone usage in the developing world and—with that—of mobile money systems. Following the trailblazing launch of M-Pesa in Kenya in 2007, there are now ninety-three countries with some form of mobile-money services, with 271 "live" deployments, and 101 more planned. But many are still only scratching the surface of the potential market. In fact, the statistics belie a deeper problem. "Between 60 percent and 90 percent of [mobile] accounts opened by new banking customers fall dormant almost immediately without a single transaction," writes mobile payments expert Carol Realini. Why? Most of these systems are still based on an underlying banking infrastructure, and the banks that run them don't have a good handle on the needs of "unbanked" customers, many of whom are confused by the demands placed upon them. Once again, the obsession with being "banked" and the divide between those who strive to be allowed into this hallowed space and those who deny them that opportunity stand as a barrier. Banks, too often, are actually the problem—or at least the regulatory and risk-management model in which they operate is the problem. Maybe getting people into them shouldn't be the goal at all.

Mobile credit, in particular, has been hard to expand. And here too the banking paradigm is a hindrance. Once credit is involved, mobile money platforms like M-Pesa, which must be backed in aggregate by each country's financial system, fall back on the classic loan approval models of the traditional banking world. As such, inferior proofs of identity and subjective, poorly defined measures of creditworthiness become barriers to entry, especially once the dominant telecom providers use their privileged position as gatekeepers of these new e-monetary systems to charge exorbitant fees. The mobile providers, including Kenya's Safaricom, are reluctant to make their systems interoperable with other providers, ensuring that cross-telecom and cross-border exchanges must go through the African banking system, which is inefficient, cumbersome, and expensive. These localized mobile money solutions are nothing like the open, permissionless innovation platforms that blockchain and Bitcoin purists dream of. It means that while the unbanked poor can now more easily send payments to each other, at least within the closed loops of their local telecom, the problems of the banking system's exclusionary model still affect them—especially when they need credit, which they often do in times of emergency. Unable to prove who they are, what they do, and what they own, the poor continue to be at the mercy of loan sharks, who do as much as anyone to keep them in a cycle of poverty.

If a borderless cryptocurrency were widely used, like bitcoin, which makes no demands for such personal proofs, it could help the poor break out of the banks' and telecoms' closed-loop fiefdoms. It might also entice innovators to develop innovative new blockchain services, including credit, to further help marginalized communities.

The tech sector has spent a lot of time discussing its promise to help the financially excluded (including those excluded from the tech sector itself). Nine years on, though, adoption of the digital currency by people outside of the tech sector remains low. Part of the problem is that cryptocurrencies continue to sustain a reputation among the general public for criminality. This was intensified by the massive "WannaCry" ransomware attacks of 2017 in which attackers broke into hospitals' and other institutions' databases, encrypted their vital files, and then extorted payments in bitcoin to have the data decrypted. (In response to the calls to ban bitcoin that inevitably arose in the wake of this episode, we like to point out that far more illegal activity and money laundering occurs in dollar notes, which are much harder to trace than bitcoin transactions. Still, when it comes to perception, that's beside the point—none of these incidents helps Bitcoin's reputation.)

The other big detracting factor, though, is one that innovation could help solve: bitcoin's price volatility. Since people, for now, tend to *think* in their national currencies, the digital currency's wild swings against the dollar make it hard for Regular Joes to consider it as a medium of exchange. Who wants to shop with something whose value can make your grocery bill swing by 30 percent week to week? This is a massive barrier to Bitcoin achieving its great promise as a tool to achieve financial inclusion. A Jamaican immigrant in Miami might find the near-zero fees on a bitcoin transaction more appealing than the 9 percent it costs to use a Western Union agent to send money home to his mother. But if there's nowhere convenient for his mom to quickly exchange the funds into Jamaican dollars, exchange rate swings could soon wipe out those savings.

Innovations bubbling up within Bitcoin's vibrant ecosystem of innovation are starting to resolve this problem, however. Startup remittance providers such as small business–focused Veem, formerly Align Commerce, are using Bitcoin and blockchain technology as the "rails" over which to transfer between currencies, bypassing the costly banking system. With smart hedging strategies that take advantage of blockchain technology's transparency and low transaction costs, they've figured out how to minimize their own risk in briefly holding bitcoin, which lets them pass on affordable rates to their customers, who only deal in their local currencies. The approach is paying dividends, as evident in the recent success of BitPesa, which was established in 2013 and was profiled in *The Age of Cryptocurrency*. The company, which offers cross-border payments and foreign-exchange transactions in and out of Kenya, Nigeria, Tanzania, and Uganda, reported 25 percent month-on-month growth, taking its transaction volume to $10 million midway through 2017, up from $1 million in 2016. Separately, there were reports that 20 percent of the remittances that Filipino immigrants in South Korea send back home were handled in bitcoin.

An especially innovative solution to bitcoin's price volatility comes from Abra, which lets someone in one country send money via their smartphone directly to the smartphone of another person in a different country—with no intermediary involved. With Abra, the user buys bitcoin but the app removes the volatility risk by deploying a high-tech hedging system that takes advantage of the transparency and low transaction costs of blockchain transactions. Without the user needing to even think about it, the app uses a blockchain-managed smart contract system to commit their account to automatically pay a third party if the value of their bitcoin rises above the original purchase price and to receive money if it falls below it. This so-called contract-for-difference, which is a bit like a foreign exchange option, has the effect of locking in the value of the underlying bitcoin. All the customer sees on their screen is the fiat-currency value—say, in dollars—that they initially transferred into their Abra account. When a San Francisco–based Filipino immigrant sends money to a family member in Manila, the same process will begin with the Philippines-based person's smartphone, albeit in a contract involving bitcoin and Philippine pesos. This system is only possible because the use of the blockchain and smart contracts removes banks, lawyers, escrow agents, and other middlemen that manage the traditional business of derivatives trading. It creates a much cheaper way of hedging exchange rate risk.

There's another massive problem, though: money-servicing regulations. These were given more relevance after the New York Department of Financial Services established its precedent-setting BitLicense regulation for digital currency service providers in 2015. The BitLicense encapsulated an evolving mind-set among regulators that they were responsible for exchanges between fiat currency and digital currencies, even as they vowed to allow innovation to blossom within the development of software for commerce that stayed in a bitcoin-to-bitcoin universe. The result was a set of compliance rules that added costly burdens to acquiring and using digital currency. Startups that provide "on-ramps" from dollars into bitcoin said the regulations hindered their ability to provide cheap services for end-users. Many are choosing not to operate in New York. But, this being New York, the BitLicense matters. Not only must money often flow through the New York jurisdiction, but New York's global relevance as a world financial capital means the model has become something of a template for other regulators around the world. (Though many have elected to take a less draconian posture.)

The biggest challenge is the compliance requirements for licensees to show they can identify people. This regulation is in keeping with the ongoing demand to "know your customer" (KYC) that's imposed on financial service providers. KYC is supposed to protect financial institutions from money laundering, terrorism financing, and other illicit activities. Before a firm in the money-servicing business signs on a new customer, they are supposed to "know" and be comfortable with the risks that customer poses—as defined, rather ambiguously, by *who they are*. It hinges on that old state-centric notion of ID, against which potential red flags, such as no-fly-list citations, would supposedly be attached. If you don't have a reliable state ID, then you have a problem. If Bitcoin providers face the same demands, they are no easier to go to than banks.

As the regulations have become stricter in the wake of the financial crisis, rising terrorism fears, and narco-trafficking, the KYC burden has become increasingly onerous and costly for banks to comply with. It's further complicated by the fact that for international money flows, institutions and other players are expected to know that their counterpart banks and/or money transmitter firms in other countries are doing correct due diligence of *their* customers. There have also been some big fines—a $1.9 billion payment to the U.S. government by HSBC to settle charges that the bank helped Mexican drug dealers launder money was especially sobering—and which, when combined with all the compliance work, has left many financial professionals simply saying "it's not worth it." The result is a phenomenon known as "de-risking": a worldwide reduction in the provision of credit and money transmission services to people and places that banks believe are too risky for their business. It works directly against the UN's and World Bank's goals on financial inclusion.

Consider the Somalia dilemma. It's near impossible to establish identity in line with formal KYC standards in that failed state, which is a haven for terrorists, pirates, and warlords, and where very few people have sufficiently secure ID documents. So, the U.S. banks, under guidance from the U.S. Treasury Department, have essentially shut down the U.S.-Somalia remittance corridor. The result: an entire country, already extremely poor, is further starved of funds and forced to use expensive and shady black-market methods to move funds in and out of the country. If there is a more ripe recruiting scenario for al-Shabaab, East Africa's dominant Al Qaeda–linked militant Islamic group, we can't think of one. We'd call this result a major #KYCFail.

So, how might blockchains help? Well, the public transaction data can be analyzed to gain a risk profile of particular nodes or Bitcoin addresses, without having to know the names of the users. Blockchain startups like Chainalysis, Elliptic, and Skry are already working on projects with law enforcement agencies to deploy big data analysis, network science, and artificial intelligence to assess the Bitcoin network's financial flows in this way. Much as, say, Netflix uses big data analytics of its user base's watching habits to figure out what movies you might want to see, analytics of transaction flows across the Bitcoin network can reveal all sorts of insights into the behavior, and even probable intent, of its users. New encrypted cryptocurrencies such as Zcash and Monero, designed as part of a pro-privacy backlash against the efforts of Chainalysis and others, could of course give criminals a more effective way to hide their tracks. But the Bitcoin use case we're focused on here is not one of how to catch criminals per se but how to let honest users of the system *prove* that they are not criminals. It means that when ID-less people who've got nothing to hide use bitcoin to move money, their behavior can be analyzed and shown to be of good standing.

Leveraging Community Connections

Communities have a long history of building their own monetary and banking systems that match borrowers with savers, and these systems become scalable once you can solve the trust problem. Now, some blockchain developers are coming up with strategies to harness these longstanding systems in ways that might one day make banks redundant.

One area that's being explored is that of community savings circles, with the most common form being rotating savings and credit associations, or ROSCAs. These local programs take on different names in different regions—chit funds (India), arisans (Indonesia), tandas (Latin America), 'susu (West Africa and the Caribbean), Game'ya (Middle East), and tanomosiko (Japan)—but share a basic approach. A group of individuals who know and trust each other commit to putting a certain amount into a savings pool periodically—say, $50 per month. Then, the pool is periodically paid out to one member of the group, as a de facto form of credit. Everyone keeps contributing after that, until another payout is delivered to the next in line, and so on. This system means that everyone, with the exception of the last individual, effectively gets an interest-free loan at some point. The only price you pay is a responsibility to keep paying in after you've been paid out.

These systems have traditionally depended on the human trust that's instilled in close friendship and kinship bonds. If everyone knows you, it's much harder for you to stop meeting your obligations to the pool after you've received your payout. But that trust model imposes a physical constraint on scalability. Consider the Dunbar number—anthropologist Robin Dunbar's theory that the highest number of stable relationships that any one person can sustain is 150. By implication it means that a savings circle has to be quite small, because every member needs to have every other member of the group within their trusted set of 150 people, the probability of which decreases consistently as the group increases in size.

Here's where a blockchain, smart contracts, and tokens might come in. A startup called WeTrust, for whom Michael is an advisor, is using those technologies to add structure, automation, and token-based incentives to ROSCAs so that participants are compelled do the right thing. In effect, it could mean that new people can be added that aren't as well known to everyone as in traditional ROSCAs. Unlike the KYC solution, which seeks smarter ways for people to prove who they are, this one lowers the barrier to entry by finding efficiencies in the system itself so that it's less important to "know your customer."

Whether WeTrust's model works or not, it may help us learn a lot about how these new systems of algorithmic, distributed trust can interface with those old, deeply embedded social webs of trust. We think it's important that solutions to the challenges faced by the poor aren't just imposed in some cookie-cutter manner by Silicon Valley venture capitalists who insist they know best. Solutions must be informed by and tailored to the underlying cultural structures of the communities in question.

And while we should be seeking solutions like WeTrust's, which focuses on reducing the identification burden to achieve financial inclusion, the reality is that every culture has an identity system at its core. Dealing with identity is unavoidable. However, when we peel back the layers of what we mean by "identity," as we will in the next chapter, we find that it is a highly contentious issue—one fraught with security risks and social tension in the Internet era. It's an area in which some of the most radical ideas for blockchain applications are now being pursued.

Eight

A SELF-SOVEREIGN IDENTITY

Until recently, the five biggest institutions charged with confirming people's identities were, by default, the governments of the five largest countries: China, India, the United States, Indonesia, and Brazil. But now some powerful new players are performing functions that these governments handled previously. And they're doing so without performing the standard, government-led "official ID" functions of issuing birth certificates, passports, national ID cards, and so forth. What's striking is that three of these newcomers now occupy spots on that top-five list: Facebook, Google, and Twitter. These companies are now in the vital business of verifying the claims we make about who we are. In creating social media accounts, we have effectively created verifiable identities that third parties can access to confirm such claims—hence the growing use of SSO (single sign-on) systems for accessing other Web sites. How many of these new "IDs" do these tech giants manage? Well, Facebook's subscribers now exceed 2 billion and Google's are at 1.2 billion (via Gmail), while Twitter's active users number around 320 million. If there were ever a measure of the influence these companies wield over our lives, surely it is that the data they hold on us quite literally defines who we are.

This kind of corporate intrusion has sparked a backlash in the West. Edward Snowden's revelations on the U.S. National Security

Agency's surveillance of personal data also entangled companies like this and thrust the issue into public debate. In James Graham's engaging play *Privacy*, which featured *Harry Potter* star Daniel Radcliffe in the lead role for its New York premier (and included a cameo video feed from Snowden himself), audience members got a disturbing view of how the data on their phones accumulates and can be used against them, as those who gave permission had their trips with ride-hailing service Uber displayed on a giant screen.

If revelations about the tracking of our digital footprints breed angst in wealthy countries, people in the developing world face the exact opposite problem: too little data is available about their activities. They can't prove "who they are." It's made more difficult by the fact that 2.4 billion people do not have an official form of ID, either, according to the World Bank. It's not just that they can't open bank accounts, apply for loans, or travel; the absence of documentation makes them vulnerable to violent criminals. According to a study of hill-tribe children in Thailand by UNESCO, a lack of formal citizenship status and ID was the *single greatest risk factor* contributing to human trafficking. These children legally don't exist and are thus hard to track; as a result they're subjected to unspeakable degradations. When the UNHCR and NGOs set up camps for refugees, they inevitably become a magnet for child traffickers taking advantage of this vulnerability.

Former banker and financial technology entrepreneur John Edge was moved to do something about this problem after watching the Lucy Liu–produced film *Meena*, about an Indian girl kidnapped from her family and forced into prostitution. When he learned about the struggle to rescue ID-less children, he considered the role blockchain technology might play as a universal proof of identity by creating a global, tamper-proof registry of people's vital information. He founded an entity called ID2020, named for its initial goal of establishing secure digital identities for all the world's children by the year 2020. (Its objectives would later shift to align with the United Nation's sustainable development goal of official identity for all people by 2030.) Edge understood the problems that would need solving before his vision of a blockchain-based, universal identity could be achieved. Who would attest to the child's identity? Who would be responsible for controlling and securing the private key that would be used to access the records before the child reached adulthood?

In May 2016, Edge partnered with the UN to bring together some fifty tech companies and an equal number of diplomats and NGOs at the inaugural ID2020 summit at the United Nations to explore how digital technology, principally blockchains, might solve the ID challenge. It soon became clear that the technologists' approach differed markedly from that of government officials. To the diplomats, employed as they are by governments, the notion of an official, government-issued ID—a driver's license, a passport, a birth certificate—was sacrosanct. They felt that the issuance and certification of a person's identity was the proper role of the state. By contrast, the technologists, wary of state power, offered an approach that would become a buzzword of the conference: "self-sovereign." This idea holds that individuals are better off establishing their own proofs of who they are based on data about their lives that *they've* accumulated and *they* control, not a government. It's a much more autonomous conception of identity than that of the diplomats.

Where there is widespread agreement is the understanding that "analog identity," the kind that depends upon the provision of paper documents like driver's licenses, birth certificates, and passports, is outdated and that we must develop standards and norms for "digital identity." Without that, people and institutions will be shut out of the efficiencies of the modern economy. The argument is that with more and more services provided electronically, we need a better digital interface so that people, companies, and machines can be more readily identified and permitted to access those services without having to check reams of unreliable paper documents.

A starting point for this emerging digital identity model is public key cryptography, that system of math-based key-pairings that, as we discussed in chapter three, allows users to authorize transactions within Bitcoin and other blockchains. (Public key cryptography, invented in

1976 by Whitfield Diffie and Martin Hellman, long preceded Bitcoin and is widely used for security purposes in other Internet applications, including e-mail.) Just as public key cryptography lets Bitcoin users "sign" a bitcoin address (essentially, their public key) with their private key to prove that they control it, an institution certifying a person's attributes can give authority to that certification with this same digital signatures model. This pairing can create an irrefutable record that, say, your university has confirmed you have a degree, your utility company has attested that you've paid your power bills, or a birth registrar has authenticated your birth certificate.

Various blockchain developers, including at big tech firms like Microsoft, are trying to augment this digital signatures system by incorporating those institutionally signed attestations into blockchain transactions. The idea is to give an added layer of security since the certifying institution would be unable to revoke an attestation after it has been written into an append-only immutable ledger—much as a bitcoin transaction cannot be reversed. But the idea of using a blockchain for this purpose is a contentious one among identity experts. It has spawned a debate that we'll return to lower down.

Regardless of what tools are used to get there, we think society must move toward a more decentralized, digital, and ultimately self-sovereign model of identity. Irrespective of whether identities themselves reside on a blockchain, making them digital and cryptographically provable will be vital for the development of many non-identity, blockchain services. And there are even bigger, and arguably more pressing, reasons to encourage a system in which individuals have greater personal control over how the proofs of their attributes are gathered, stored, and communicated. The September 2017 Equifax hack, in which 143 million people's names, social security numbers, bank accounts, and so forth were breached, exposed how, in relying on companies that run centralized siloes of all-encompassing, highly sensitive personal data, we've exposed ourselves to their failings. As we discussed in chapter two, these ever-growing honeypots have become magnets for attackers. Self-sovereignty may be the answer.

It's somewhat encouraging that governments are getting inter-ested in this trend—though they mostly talk about the "digital" part, not the "self-sovereign" part. Many governments are betting on digital IDs based on centralized systems that *they* control, with many of them favoring biometrics such as fingerprints and retina scans for the secu-rity aspect.

In the minds of many government officials in the development community, the gold star of this bright digital future is India. There, the national government has embarked on the gargantuan task of iden-tifying every one of its citizens, tying them to a digital record of their biometric details (primarily fingerprints), and attaching that informa-tion to a massive, centralized database. As of this writing, this system, known as Aadhaar, has assigned 1.1 billion unique ID numbers, with 400 million of those assigned to bank accounts.

There are undeniable advantages from this system. It should pro-vide a seamless verification process for the provision of multiple digital services, be it opening a bank account or accessing personal health rec-ords. An entire new sector of software development has sprung up in places like Hyderabad and Bangalore to build apps that work on top of Aadhaar. In early 2017, IDFC Bank launched its Aadhaar Pay service, for example, which offered merchants an Android app that would ac-cept payments from Aadhaar IDs linked to bank accounts. Citizens would no longer need a credit card or phone to make a payment; just their finger and knowledge of their Aadhaar number. This service plays right into Prime Minister Narendra Modi's effort to develop a new, cashless economy based on what he calls "JAM"—a reference to a trin-ity of new, mutually interactive technologies: the country's new "Jan Dhan" payments-only bank accounts that banks are being compelled to provide; the Aadhaar network; and mobile telephony.

Similarly further advanced along the digital identity route is the far smaller but wealthier nation of Estonia. Its national ID system still uses a physical card, but a chip embedded in the cards allows a digital interface between a vast array of public services and its ID system. The government is encouraging private sector service providers to link to

the card as well. Estonia has even extended these ID services to foreigners via its much-lauded e-residency program, by which foreigners
can easily establish themselves as e-residents in the country, even if
they don't live there, to ease doing business there. The country's digital
ID gives holders a one-stop access point for authenticating their rights
to a supermarket of offerings, everything from health care services to a
revolutionary i-voting program that lets citizens participate in national
elections from their smartphones and computers. Here, too, this base
infrastructure has spawned a hive of innovative activity, some of which
is tying Estonia's ID system into higher-up-the-stack blockchain-
powered services. Nasdaq, for example, has introduced a blockchain-
based program for shareholder voting.

As groundbreaking as India's and Estonia's programs are, these
state-run, centralized databases carry undeniable risks. For now, both
countries are run by benign regimes that appear to respect their citizens' privacy. But the fear must always be that a rogue official—or
perhaps even a future rogue regime—could gain access to personal
information and use it for nefarious purposes such as blackmail or
worse. Modi might be a moderate, but his right-wing BJP party has a
history of stirring up Hindu nationalism against the country's Muslim
minority. What's to stop a less-tolerant future BJP government from
one day using this store of biometric data to target people because of
their ethnicity or their religion? Estonia, for its part, is only a couple
decades out from the totalitarian control of the Soviets. Already, a team
of data security experts from the U.S. and UK have advised that Estonia's i-voting system is extremely vulnerable to hacking.

We can see a recent example of this danger in New York City, where
there have been legitimate concerns that the Trump administration
might subpoena the city to unlock a trove of data on immigrant residents who signed up for its New York municipal ID program. That
program was well intended. Its goal was to help undocumented people,
many of whom have lived there for decades, gain access to services and
build a credit history, as well as help the city better monitor and manage
its provision of services. But in the end, this liberal metropolis, which

has embraced the "sanctuary city" credo of resistance against Trump's anti-immigrant agenda, unwittingly created a resource for the administration to seek, find, and potentially deport those people. This case reminds us of a stern warning from Steven Sprague, CEO of the privacy and computing services company Rivest Co.: "throughout history, identity has been weaponized." The vulnerability of these centralized honeypots of personalized data also makes a strong case for decentralized control of identity information, which is where blockchains come in.

Redefining Identity

We tend to conflate identity with official records. Because the state has played a key role in *proving* our identity, it has encroached into our definitions of who we say we are. However, as identity policy expert David Birch points out, there really are three types of identity: our legal identity, which relates to the identifiability of the individual; our social identity, which is forged from our outward-facing engagement with the rest of society, the relationships we build, and the signals we send about who we are; and our personal identity, which is how we self-identify. Those latter two categories have become more fluid, especially in the age of social media and as our cultures become more open to new ways of defining what it means to be human, whether that breaks down along sexual orientation, gender, or religious, racial, or ethnic grounds. What's powerful, though, is that the technologies driving those changes now also make it possible to turn these more dynamic aspects of who we are into a means of *proof*—primarily in the realm of our social identity. Our circle of friends and interactions constitutes a web of trust that has its own powerful, informational value. If that circle incorporates a large number of essentially trustworthy people—no one among them is on the no-fly list, for example—it's possible to deduce with decent probabilities that you are also trustworthy—or at least that you should be given a positive score, to be confirmed or challenged by other measures of your trustworthiness.

To get us to the *self-sovereign* identity construct, however, we need to give individuals, not governments—nor, for that matter, companies like Facebook or Google—control over that valuable identifying data. Some companies are trying to show that a blockchain could hold the potential to achieve this. But before we review them, it's useful to rethink how we might handle our data if we had that self-sovereign control. For one, we could selectively divulge to other people only the information needed to access the particular service we are seeking.

In this age of privacy risks, protecting this data is vital. Digitalization, which lets us break up data, make it granular or specific, allows this. Analog IDs like driver's licenses and passports, on the other hand, are static—they don't allow you to strip out different pieces of information. When you show the bartender your license to prove you're old enough to drink, you end up sharing a lot more: your full name, gender, license number, address, birthday, height, even your eye color. (Beats us why that last one's listed on New York and New Jersey licenses.) This over-sharing becomes a lot more problematic with ID-scanning technologies used by nightclubs to test authenticity. Do you really want that sleazy bouncer collecting a scanned record of your name and where you live? We need to move beyond a model where access to certain services requires us to prove some all-encompassing notion of our *identity*, and move to one in which we simply prove that we have specifically required *attributes*: that our credit score surpasses a certain threshold, that we graduated from the university we claim to have graduated from, that we were born before today's date twenty-one years ago. Provable digital data that's connected to the things we've done, to the connections we keep, and to the certifications and qualifications we've accumulated could, in theory, give us the power to do that.

The World Economic Forum has contributed usefully to this emerging idea of digitally delivered attribute proofs. In a report entitled "A Blueprint for Digital Identity," the authors noted that identity as it's understood can be broken up into three types of attributes. *Inherent attributes* are intrinsic to the individual and tend to be static, including features such as age, height, fingerprints, or date of birth. *Accumu-*

lated attributes tend to change over time and can include things like health records and shopping preferences developed via online shopping activity. *Assigned attributes* are conferred on the user by an outside entity with some degree of authority and can include a passport number from a government or an e-mail address from a Webmail provider.

In selectively releasing pieces of these different attributes, people are not confirming their identity in a static, all-encompassing legal sense, but rather they are proving aspects of their different *personas*—in keeping with the parlance of this rapidly developing field. Four of Mike's colleagues at the MIT Media Lab—Alex "Sandy" Pentland, Thomas Hardjono, David Shrier, and Irving Wladawsky-Berger—expressed it best in a submission to the U.S. National Institute of Standards and Technology's Commission on Enhancing Cybersecurity:

> Robust Digital Identity. Identity, whether personal or organizational, is the key that unlocks all other data and data sharing functions. Digital Identity includes not only having unique and unforgettable credentials that work everywhere, but also the ability to access all the data linked to your identity and the ability to control the "persona" that you present in different situations. These pseudonym identities, or personas, include the "work you," the "health system you," the "government you," and many other permutations specific to particular aspects of your individual relationship with another party. Each of these pseudonym identities will have different data access associated with them, and be owned and controlled only by the core "biological you."

The most radical part of these ideas—the one that most messes with the "official identity" assumptions of those UN diplomats—is the idea that our accumulated digital and online footprints provide so much information that they far exceed the informational power of official documents like birth certificates and passports. Already, in the age of powerful big data and network analytics—now enhanced with blockchain-based distributed trust systems to assure data integrity—our digital records are far more reliable indicators of the behavior that defines who we are than are the error-prone attestations that go into easily forged passports and laminated cards. Anyone who can use the data accumulated by their phone's GPS function to prove they spend more or less eight hours of every day in a set place that is some distance from their home can effectively prove that they have a job. Their income might not come with a pay slip; they may have no bank account to show for themselves; but the job is at least one factor that contributes to eligibility for a loan or some other service.

There are two big challenges. The first is: how can I package this personal data so that it reveals a treasure trove of information about my life but doesn't compromise my privacy and independence? It's a problem that applies both to the ongoing accumulation of digital footprints in the physical or online worlds and to the assertions and certifications that third parties such as banks and universities provide about our attributes.

Over the years, cryptographers have come up with a host of neat tricks that allow someone to use a mathematical proof to show that some statement is true even when the details underlying that proof aren't revealed. These strategies fall under the category of "zero-knowledge proofs," in which Party A can use probabilities and other mathematical tools to show Party B that Party A knows some access-opening secret without revealing what that secret actually is. An oft-cited real-world example involves a color-blind person who doesn't trust his non-color-blind friend when she tells him that the two balls in front of him are distinctly different—one red, the other green. The friend is able to prove that she's right by asking the color-blind person to mix up the balls behind his back, keeping track of which one is which, and then repeatedly present one and ask her which color it is. Because she can correctly state, over and over again, that the one distinct ball is red and the other is green, he can accept the law of probability as proof.

Another zero-knowledge approach with great potential is that of homomorphic encryption, which allows computers to figure out some useful information by running computation on a combined pool of data without knowing the details of its components. One simplified example of how to understand the concept involves a group of employees who don't want to divulge their individual salaries. How can they find out the total salary pool and average pay per employee of the group? Well, the first person comes up with a random number, adds their salary to that number, then secretly shares the sum of the two to the next person, who adds their salary to that amount and secretly shares the new sum to the next person, and so on. At the end of the sequence, the total amount is communicated to the person who started the process, who then deducts the secret starting number to figure out the total salary and average per person—conducting a rudimentary, human computation. These fundamental mathematical constructs are now baked into far more complex cryptographic software programs that allow computer scientists to do all sorts of amazing things with information that needs to be kept secret. And because computers reduce all data—whether it's a piece of text, a photograph, a GPS coordinate, or a value such as a salary—to some numerical representation, these techniques could be used to provide protection to people's personal information in the digital world.

The second big challenge is: how can I maintain sole control over my personal data and yet still assure service providers that it is accurate? This is the task that blockchain innovators are setting their minds to. A key idea is that if validation of the data is conferred to a decentralized, consensus-driven network, then neither the individual nor some particular institution, be it a government or a company, is capable of altering it once it is confirmed and recorded in the required format. The other key idea is that the relevant person, company, or machine is the only entity empowered to parcel out pieces of the relevant, hopefully encrypted, data to third parties who need it. This is a complicated problem but it's one that a host of research labs, including some big names, are focused on.

Leading startups in this space include Mooti, Civic, Procivis, Tradle, and BanQu, all of which seek to take the attestations of third parties such as banks or certificate providers and turn them into portable

ID services. The first four have a universal approach to a range of markets; BanQu targets services for the poor and marginalized communities, including refugees who have lost their documents.

Work is also being done on the concept of an "identity bureau"—or KYC bureau, if we are to use the "know your customer" parlance of the financial sector's compliance officers. Like a credit bureau, the idea is that if a person has had their credentials or attributes certified by an institution that is recognized or authorized to be a trusted ID attester, then that validation can be used to get clearance with other third-party providers. It's a little bit like the Facebook single sign-on described at the top of this section, but because a blockchain offers a proof that doesn't depend on centralized institutions such as Facebook, this form of proven identity could be interoperable with other systems, meaning that for the individual it is portable—they can take it anywhere and have anyone know that it's trustworthy. A group of banks including BBVA, CIBC, ING, Société Générale, and UBS has already developed such a proof of concept in conjunction with blockchain research outfit R3 CEV.

In theory, these systems could remove vast amounts of paperwork and compliance from the identification and due diligence processes conducted by firms, lowering costs, reducing friction, and, hopefully, increasing financial access. But they could also serve a wider social good, helping to boost financial inclusion. Undocumented immigrants in the United States could get their embassy, for example, to function as a KYC bureau. The embassy could provide a provable, digital stamp of identity that remittance companies could accept without having to ask for the person's actual ID. So long as the embassy-certified identifier can be associated with a traceable bitcoin transaction, a bitcoin-enabled money transmitter could let this person carry out fully legal remittances but still have a strong way to control for money laundering and other risks.

It's not just startups that are delving into the blockchain identity space. Microsoft, IBM, and Intel are taking it very seriously. Microsoft is seeking a sweeping, global identity solution in collaboration with open-source developers worldwide and two of the leading infrastructure developers for bitcoin and Ethereum: Blockstack for the former and the think tank ConsenSys for the latter. The sweeping goal, according to Yorke Rhodes, a key blockchain strategist at Microsoft, is "an open source, self-sovereign, blockchain-based identity system that allows people, products, apps, and services to interoperate across blockchains, cloud providers, and organizations." The idea is big: if you can establish a standard, interoperable architecture for people to accumulate their data within a blockchain address that *they* control, that address could become a single foundational, distributed identity layer that opens digital doors across different ledgers and blockchain ecosystems and allows innovators to start building powerful applications that key into those identities, opening the door to a world of decentralized commerce.

This Won't Be Easy

It's important to clarify some aspects of the prevailing identity management model for blockchains. The concept under development by key players such as ConsenSys, Blockstack, and Microsoft is not to directly store the data certifying someone's or some entity's identity in transactions on a blockchain. That would overwhelm a distributed ledger's limited storage capacity very quickly—certainly that of Bitcoin. Rather, the data will reside *off-chain*, wherever the person or institution chooses to store it: locally on their own computer, smartphone, or other device; with a cloud computing service from IBM, Microsoft, or Amazon Web Service. All those options, of course, require some level of trust in the provider. So it's interesting that some of the emerging decentralized systems for storing data over the Internet, such as Maidsafe, Storj, IPFS (the Interplanetary File System), or Sia, are also being touted as personal data management tools for identity purposes. Those hosting systems aren't controlled by a company.

Still, there is some vital information that must be stored in a blockchain environment. First, there's the key-pairing information, based on the same public key cryptography that we discussed above, though in this case it determines what the individual does with his or her private key to share identifying information with others, not the signatures of the certifying institution. A person or entity signs a public key that's explicitly linked to a name or identity that holds meaning in the real world—call it "Paul Vignal," "MichaelCasey9342," "Acme Corp," or "theageofcryptocurrency.com." This way the user demonstrates to the blockchain's validating computers, and therefore to the world at large, that they, and only they, have control over that name and can therefore legitimately link it to data stored off-chain.

Using this model, let's imagine that Michael is applying for a job. He could prove to the prospective employer that he graduated from the University of Western Australia by (1) using his private key to sign his "MichaelCasey9342" public blockchain address and (2) using that same private key to sign a digital record, or hash, of his UWA degree that was itself cryptographically signed by the university and which he stores off-chain. These actions, together, create an immutable, verifiable log of the claim Michael is making to this particular attribute, his status as a graduate of an Aussie university. The point is that, with its capacity to build a time-stamped sequence of events, these blockchain transactions can affirm that the sequence of access rights to the data have been properly controlled by the rightful authority, the user.

If that sounds like a complicated process, it is. Not surprisingly, there are various doubters of blockchain tech's capacity to fix the identity problem. Identity is fraught with privacy risks and, as with the problem we addressed in the previous chapter with regards to certifying a person's property title, proof of identity hinges on the attestation of some outsider, which brings us back to the old trusted third-party problem. In many cases, we're still going to need the validation of a bank (to show we have a fraud-free bank account), for example, or a university (to show we have a degree), or a Webmail provider (to show we have a legitimate e-mail address and are not a bot).

These blockchain detractors are not necessarily from the outdated "official ID" crowd. They include influential digital ID advocates like

Steve Wilson, a strong advocate for shifting from the outdated model of static personal identity to that of cryptographically proven attributes. "The public [permissionless] blockchains deliberately and proudly shirk third parties, but in most cases, your identity is nothing without a third party who vouches for you in some way," Wilson told TechCrunch. "Blockchain is great for some things, but it's not magic, and it just wasn't designed for the IDM [identity management] problem space."

But what if we could actually end our dependence on third-party certifiers altogether? If we want a blockchain model to prove that we are worthy to do or buy something, it would be more informative to confirm all the rich digital information we passively accumulate through our online lives than to rely on the third-party certifications of our life events—birth, degree, first job, etc. If we deploy appropriate encryption methods to hide sensitive data, our rich digital footprints can, for example, reveal a profile of the social network we keep, showing whether we hang out with high-school dropouts or people with graduate degrees. It can also glean useful information from our payment history, our sleep patterns, our travel, and, of course, our online surfing. If social media companies and others that gather such data can agree to open standards on metadata, a new identity culture could be formed that would be much more informative than anything produced by, say, credit score keepers such as Equifax. This is precisely what a new breed of algorithmic credit-scoring companies and other such big data–driven startups are doing. Putting all of that into a blockchain-proven system could be a powerful way to get people to trust each other and expand their social and economic exchanges.

Or it could be oppressive. There are serious social implications in resorting to algorithmic interpretations of our behavior. Done poorly, we are almost guaranteed to create biased benchmarks of "worthiness" that discriminate against those who, for whatever cultural, circumstantial, or personal reason, don't meet the algorithm's standard. Do I have better or worse credit if I view a lot of Republican political Web sites? This is dangerous territory. As pseudonymous cryptocurrency journalist Juan Galt put it, a web of trust can become an Orwellian web of shame.

Influential cryptocurrency thinker Andreas Antonopoulos argues that the problem lies in trying to solve identity in the first place, which he says is in breach of what Bitcoin's open, permissionless architecture represents. Blockchain developers building these identity/reputation tools are promoting a "relic of traditional financial systems," he argues. Outdated financial institutions such as banks need reputation to function as "a proxy to identifying the default risk associated with a specific identity" because they're unable to safely manage that risk, he says. What we should be doing, instead of acting as judge and executioner and making assumptions "that past behavior will give me some insight into future behavior," Antonopoulos argues, is building systems that better manage default risk within lenders' portfolios. Bitcoin, he sustains, has the tools to do so. There's a lot of power in this technology to protect against risk: smart contracts, multi-signature controls that ensure that neither of two parties can run off with the funds without the other also signing a transaction, automated escrow arrangements, and, more broadly, the superior transparency and granularity of information on the public ledger. In other words, investors already have the tools to protect against the risk of loss; who cares about the identity, past behavior, and reputation of the people we are transacting with?

But Can We Afford *Not* to Tackle Identity?

Antonopoulos's take offers an appealing libertarian vision, one that treats privacy as a value to protect in order to promote economic exchange. But is it practical? Our entire economic system is built on something we might call *the identity-financial complex*, a model that's deeply ingrained in the trust architecture with which society gets stuff done. Identifying people—whether it's through the outdated analog tools of government documents, the dynamic gathering and personal management of our digital footprints, or simply asking someone their name—will continue to be a requirement to enter into exchanges with people and institutions.

So, although all these pros and cons might make your head spin, the reality is that we still have a big problem. We really need to fix our failed identity and personal security model and make it ready for the digital age. Most importantly, we need people to take charge of their data, to advance the empowering ideal of self-sovereign identity. Figuring out how to do that should be priority number one.

A key line of attack is to find ways to help people manage their private keys so that they aren't worried about losing this critical passcode for both spending money and sharing their identifying attributes. If you forget your password at work, you can ask the system administrator to create you a new one, but there's no one managing the Bitcoin blockchain who can do the same. What often seems like the obvious solution—biometrics—has its own serious issues. Even beyond the privacy issues we cited with India's Aadhaar program, the problem is that biometrics, if stolen, cannot be reset. (You can't just think up a new fingerprint or retina.) And hackers have demonstrated, for example, how easy it is to use putty to swipe a fingerprint from a wineglass and then crack into an Apple iPhone's Touch ID system or to trick facial recognition programs with photographs.

Let's be clear, too: for all the self-help philosophy and "be your own bank" mind-set of the Bitcoin community, most people will prefer entrusting a professional custodian to look after their most sensitive asset rather than having to worry about it themselves. Most people are stressed out enough by the myriad Web site passwords they have to remember, let alone having to look after the private keys to their digital identity or cryptocurrency assets. In fact, this custodian model is how many bitcoin wallet providers, including the biggest of all, Coinbase, are structured. You ask Coinbase to execute your bitcoin transactions on your behalf; you don't really do it yourself.

Lest this take us back to the bad old days of dependence on banks, the blockchain community has spent great energy developing solutions that make it hard for custodians to steal or lose your assets. Here, "multsig" (multi-signature) technology offers a good compromise. It assigns a set of matched private keys to more than one actor, both the customer and one or more custodians, so that if a transaction or data-signing action is to take place, no one person can do it unilaterally; it needs the

combination of a certain number of keyholders. The system can include one or more offline, or "cold," keys for the customer, both to protect against loss of the active, or "hot," key and to give the customer the
power to override the custodian combining all those backup keys. Mul-
tisig is a decent compromise: you're trusting a third party to efficiently
manage your assets, but you always have control over them.

And there is a philosophical rebuttal to those who say the inevitable dependence on outside attestation brings vulnerability into
blockchain-based identity solutions: We already trust these entities to
make attestations on our behalf now; if a blockchain's status as a universal machine of truth allows us to take those proofs, leverage them,
port them to other places, and expand our access to services, surely
it's an advance on the existing system. If we can make those digital
identities from proxies of digital and online footprints that provide
more data points to enhance accuracy and help confirm conclusions
while reducing the prospect of human error or fraud, it's all the more
empowering.

As we've discussed elsewhere, the future of this technology lies in
how to interface its admittedly limited function as a "trustless" time-
stamped ledger of transactions with the trust-based systems of the
non-digital world. Solutions that combine those alternative aspects of
society's record-keeping system will have a far more transformative effect than those that rely on the blockchain alone. When information
from the outside world is placed into these ledgers, they serve to *enhance* trust, not replace it.

Self-sovereignty over our identifying information is a worthy goal.
It points to a world in which people, not the centralized institutions
with which they engage, define who they are and what they want to share
about themselves to the world. But it's hard to see how we get there without a blockchain that protects all parties from manipulation of the
data. If all we have is a cryptographically signed certificate from some
institution, we may have a reliably certified document, but we're also
vulnerable to that institution's unilateral power to revoke its signature.

This is effectively what President Trump has done in reversing some of the orders of his predecessors—in revoking the rights of transgender soldiers, for example. The same risks always apply with digitally signed rights when they don't reside in an immutable record.

If an attestation of identifying information is locked into an immutable blockchain environment, it can't be revoked, not without both parties agreeing to the reversal of the transaction. That's how we get to self-sovereignty. It's why, for example, the folks at Learning Machine are developing a product to prove people's educational bona fides on Blockcerts, an MIT Media Lab–initiated open-source code for notarizing university transcripts that hashes those documents to the bitcoin blockchain. Note the deliberate choice of the most secure, permissionless blockchain, Bitcoin's. A permissioned blockchain would fall short of the ideal because there, too, the central authority controlling the network could always override the private keys of the individual and could revoke their educational certificates. A permissionless blockchain is the only way to give real control/ownership of the document to the graduate, so that he/she can disclose this particularly important attribute at will to anyone who demands it. As Learning Machine CEO Chris Jagers says, "self-sovereignty isn't automatic; it must be explicitly architected into any blockchain-based social infrastructure."

Why obsess about this control/ownership question? Here's how Chris Allen, a research scientist at bitcoin infrastructure developer Blockstream and one of the leading thinkers on blockchain-based digital identity, sees it:

> Identity is a uniquely human concept. It is that ineffable "I" of self-consciousness, something that is understood worldwide by every person living in every culture. As René Descartes said, Cogito ergo sum—I think, therefore I am. However, modern society has muddled this concept of identity. Today, nations and corporations conflate driver's licenses, social security cards, and other state-issued credentials with identity; this

is problematic because it suggests a person can lose his very identity if a state revokes his credentials or even if he just crosses state borders. I think, but I am not.

There is no silver bullet, no. The challenges are great, yes. These ideas are at this stage aspirational, we know. But this stuff matters. We're talking about the essence of the human condition. Whether it's with a blockchain truth machine or some other decentralizing, liberating technology, we owe it to humanity to try to restore human agency to the business of just being in this world.

Nine

EVERYONE'S A CREATOR

Cast your mind back to chapter one, when we talked about triple-entry bookkeeping. Let's think about what that means for a particular industry built on the existing system of *double*-entry bookkeeping: accountants. The Big Four accounting firms—Deloitte, Price Waterhouse, Ernst Young, and KPMG—seem to be taking an "if-you-can't-fight-them-join-them" approach to the onset of blockchain technology. As of mid-2017, Deloitte alone had 250 people working in distributed ledger laboratories, and the other three are being similarly aggressive. Of course, these labs occupy a tiny sliver of these firms' massive payrolls, but the dedicated R&D speaks to how seriously the companies view the technology. If immutable distributed ledgers become a reality, their audit and accounting divisions will eventually become obsolete, with a huge human impact. At just under 40 percent of their combined $127 billion in revenues, the firms' audit and assurance divisions directly employ around 300,000 people.

These firms are exploring how this disruptive technology could affect their clients. What will become clear to them is that accounting as we know it—as a quarterly exercise in which teams of people review samples of past transactions to judge the integrity of past events—will become obsolete. And the Big Four's audit divisions are just the tip of the accounting business iceberg. It's not just the big-name auditors at risk; it's every auditor—including companies' internal auditors. In fact, once account-keeping itself becomes fully automated and reconciliation functions become superfluous, both those who keep the books and those who audit them will be out of work. Machines will input the financial data, analyze the financial data, and audit the financial data— all within a few minutes, if not seconds. In the United States alone, there are 1.3 million people employed in accounting, according to the Bureau of Labor Statistics.

The labor force disruption won't stop with the accountants. The entire investment profession, which is structured around the delayed release of official, audited financial figures, is also very much at risk. The investment cycle of Wall Street stock brokerage and research is built around those data releases—analysts come up with updated projections on what they expect a company's quarterly earnings per share will look like; the market places its bets; and then, when the numbers are dumped on them every three months, investors re-calibrate the share price, either positively or negatively. Everything in equities revolves around the quarterly numbers. The same is true for asset managers at mutual funds, pension funds, and hedge funds, whose compensation is determined by how well their portfolios perform on a quarterly basis compared with the broader market. Even government bond traders march to the drum of delayed, audited releases of financial information, in their case economic indicators on estimates of inflation, unemployment, and GDP growth. What happens to this industry when all financial and economic data is being updated, automatically and indisputably in real time? What happens to the people who lose their jobs? What happens to the work culture?

If the future foreseen by this book comes to pass, we'll witness the biggest employment shakeup the world has ever seen. And this time, the most vulnerable jobs are not the usual suspects: the factory workers, the low-level clerks, or the retail store assistants. Now it's the accountants, the bankers, the portfolio managers, the insurers, the title officers, the escrow agents, and the trustees—and, yes, even the lawyers. To be sure, the common refrain that lawyers will be replaced by "smart contracts" is somewhat inaccurate since the terms of agreements, the actual contracts themselves, will still need to be negotiated by human beings. Nonetheless, the legal industry is also in for a huge shakeup. Lawyers who don't understand code are likely going to be valued far less than those who do. (One of the most employable joint degrees to have will be a law-plus–computer science degree.) In any case, you get the idea: the middle class is facing a tidal wave.

Many of our politicians seem to have no idea this is coming. In the United States, Donald Trump pushes a "Buy America First" campaign (complete with that slogan's echoes of past fascism), backed by threats to raise tariffs, tear up trade deals, boot undocumented immigrants out of the country, and "do good deals for America." None of this addresses the looming juggernaut of decentralized software systems. IoT systems and 3D printing, all connected via blockchains and smart-contract-triggered, on-demand service agreements, will render each presidential attempt to strong-arm a company into retaining a few hundred jobs in this or that factory town even more meaningless.

Society will be forced to confront this reality if we are to manage the pain of lost incomes and avoid an even worse backlash against foreign scapegoats and other marginalized groups. In the past, new technology has spurred a sufficiently healthy gain in the U.S. economy to foster new, higher-tech jobs that offset the losses of the lower-tech and typically lower-paying ones they replaced. Farmworkers became factory workers and factory workers became office workers. But this shift to decentralized trust, along with all other disruption coming from, you name it—self-driving cars, automated medicine, peer-to-peer credit, 3D printing, artificially intelligent writers—will be too big to keep up with. The idea that the office towers of New York and Chicago will be left half empty for decades is not unfeasible. "Software is eating the world," as Marc Andreessen likes to say.

It's not just the loss of jobs that's the problem. It's also the broader problem of letting algorithms decide what our world looks like. The priorities, preferences, and prejudices of software designers are baked into the code they write, whether it's the program that dictates which passengers Uber drivers pick up or the incentive model in the Bitcoin protocol. Consider how Airbnb has grappled, imperfectly, with complaints that its insistence on users being identified with a photo has enabled homeowner discrimination against renters of color. These kinds of platform technologies will become even more all-encompassing, and if we fail to address these biases they will eat away at the fabric of society. "Unless we understand better how technologies affect basic forms of social interaction, including structures of hierarchy and inequality, words like 'democracy' and 'citizenship' lose their meaning as compass points for a free society," says Sheila Jasanoff, a Harvard-based professor of science and technology studies.

The solution to these challenges certainly cannot be left to the technologists. Nor will it be enough to say, "Everyone needs to become a coder." This is where the offline institutions of society—political, legal, philanthropic—must be brought to bear. Without them, social cohesion will fall apart. And all of the great, value-creating power of this new, decentralizing software will be for naught.

One proposal gaining weight among some policymakers and certain economists is that of a universal basic income, or UBI. Under this policy, which has been proposed by the UK Labour Party and is present in some form within a number of Scandinavian countries, governments provide a basic living wage to every adult citizen. This idea, first floated by Thomas Paine in the eighteenth century, has enjoyed a resurgence on the left as people have contemplated how robotics, artificial intelligence, and other technologies would hit working-class jobs such as truck driving. But it may gain wider traction as decentralizing forces based on blockchain models start destroying middle-class jobs. In fact, even though a universal basic income would, on the surface, run against the classic economic rationalist belief that state subsidies disincentivize work, the idea has some support on the right. One reason is that a simple, universally distributed transfer of this kind could be more efficiently distributed with far less waste and bureaucracy than a means-tested welfare system. Also, what exactly does "disincentivize work" mean when there isn't any work to be had?

Others say that basic universal income could encourage inequality in status, if not also in income and wealth. Social cohesion could suffer from the stigma of state dependence. Owners of capital and assets will continue to build wealth for themselves, while the UBI-dependent masses subsist. So, as an alternative to UBI, some are instead talking about "universal basic assets": people are given an investable, ownership stake in our social and economic infrastructure. What if, for example, everyone owns shares in their local town's distributed microgrid, represented in the form of a crypto solar-security? Would they use it as a down payment on a business that requires more energy inputs? Earlier in the book, we discussed things like reputation tokens and personal branded currencies, a concept that treats a personal skill set and stored labor more as a vehicle of wealth creation than as a service to exploit, and that potentially finds a way to incentivize human beings to build public goods. This may be how we confront the future: as owners of our personal stakes in the common good.

There's a common thread in the philosophical case for finding some kind of societal base of support for those in the firing line of disruption. It hinges on the dignity of the human being, a sense that people deserve the right to be able to make something of their lives. As we increasingly find machines to do both blue- and white-collar jobs, that will spark discussion over the "purpose" of life. One potentially constructive way to think about it is that we must design a post-industrial existence that puts at its center the encouragement of human creativity, regardless of whether that creativity is monetarily rewarded. The idea is that everyone, not just big-dreaming entrepreneurs like Elon Musk or mass-marketed artists like Jeff Koons, Beyoncé, or J. K. Rowling, is defined by their capacity to create.

This is not a new idea. Some late nineteenth- and early twentieth-century socialists dreamed of a political economy in which communally owned technology freed human beings from the drudgery of work and allowed them to unleash their innate creative selves. In his 1891 essay

"The Soul of Man Under Socialism," Oscar Wilde argued that "[s]ocialism would relieve us from that sordid necessity of living for others" and that in that utopian future, technology would relieve all people of work and allow "a man to realise the perfection of what was in him, to his own incomparable gain, and to the incomparable and lasting gain of the whole world." He said he had "no doubt at all that this is the future of machinery, and just as trees grow while the country gentleman is asleep, so while Humanity will be amusing itself, or enjoying cultivated leisure . . . or making beautiful things, or reading beautiful things, or simply contemplating the world with admiration and delight, machinery will be doing all the necessary and unpleasant work."

With less florid language, we explored an element of this in *The Age of Cryptocurrency*, where we discussed former Bitcoin developer Mike Hearn's vision of a car that was not only driverless but also ownerless. It wasn't exactly socialism. But the result was similarly one of a machine acting in full service of a community. In essence, the car would be programmed via smart contracts and interactions with all sorts of other devices, online marketplaces, and systems to run at the most optimal value for all, filling itself up on gas at the best price and deciding when, based on the market, to make itself available and when not. The reason why a community would put such a thing into existence is that, as with The DAO–like cooperatives we discussed in chapter eight, there would be no profit motive to distract it from maximizing benefits for all. This is the kind of contemporary vision of public infrastructure that could be possible when the efficiencies of IoT connectivity are combined with the automated governance of distributed trust systems like blockchains. It paints a much more benign notion of technology as being designed to free human beings from work while improving the experience of life for all with the lowest drain on resources.

But what of Wilde's romantic vision that our machine-led liberation from work can unleash everyone's inner artist or poet and that, in this way, "each man will attain to his perfection"? (That he called this vision "new individualism" spoke to Wilde's unorthodox, anarchistic version of socialism.) In the essay itself, the playwright, as if to get ahead of his critics, acknowledged that this notion was "unpractical, and it goes against human nature." But that, he insisted, "is why it is worth carrying out." Well, take a look at how humans behave in the twenty-first-century era of social media. It's hard not to sense that most people with a Twitter account want a public voice. And while the "selfie" may not be high art, it's hard to argue that the perpetual pouting and preening on Instagram isn't a type of performance. There is something to the notion that we all want to release our inner creative selves. What's interesting is that this technology is turning creation into a more collaborative process. Humor is now "crowdsourced"—think of how memes and hashtag jokes evolve, with each new witty version building on the last one. Music, brands, and subculture are being blended into one by these communal creative exercises. The (forever) sixteen-year-old Japanese "vocaloid" performer Hatsune Miku (a piece of software that performs as a hologram accompanied by a band of living musicians) has a repertoire of 100,000 songs written and produced by her fans, as well as 170,000 uploaded YouTube videos and a million Miku-inspired artworks.

In case you're a little snobbish about such lowbrow art, we should also point out that a similar mind-set of collaborative creation now drives the world of science and innovation. Most prominently, this occurs within the world of open-source software development; Bitcoin and Ethereum are the most important examples of that. But as computing power becomes relevant to much more than just computers, the power of interconnected, crowdsourced creation is being spread even further. One example that was perhaps a little ahead of its time was the Pink Army Cooperative launched by biotechnologist Andrew Hessel in 2009. Hessel created an open-source community of bio-engineers whose mission was to collaboratively work on gene-editing software to devise code for a synthetic oncolytic virus to target and kill breast cancer cells. The idea was that a global community of experts would bring so much more creative power to the objective of finding a pressing medical solution than a patent-driven pharmaceutical company could ever hope for—at near-zero cost. Hessel has since incorporated a company, Human Genomics, to raise some good-old-fashioned money to fund this effort, but the open-source collaborative principles behind the idea remain intact.

It is potentially idealistic to think that our collective, self-motivated production of content and ideas can gestate ideas in service of the wider good without any difficulties. One problem is that the ownership of those ideas is very ambiguously defined and hard to establish. And that means that the ability to extract value is not always fairly distributed. This is particularly so in the realm of digital artistic or written content, where blogs, aggregator sites, and social media platforms absorb most of the ad revenues generated around that content. But it's also true for professional artists whose earnings from revenue-sharing arrangements on YouTube and other services are distributed under opaque, poorly defined terms. This too presents an opportunity for blockchain technology, where innovators are toying with new models of decentralized publishing to give content creators greater control over their output. A core idea is that, just as blockchains can create unique, digital assets out of currency tokens and hashed documents, they might also give the same quality to content, so that the "double-spend" problem that Bitcoin solved might one day also be applied to, say, digital photos. From that starting point, we may have the makings of a fairer system.

Restoring Artists' Control

Before we review some of the proposals, let's briefly look at one of the most egregious abusers of our publishing and news consumption rights: Facebook, which now has, staggeringly, 2 billion users. As legendary cybersecurity expert Bruce Schneier has said, "Don't make the mistake of thinking you're Facebook's customer, you're not—you're the product." Facebook takes the posts we upload, the media we share, the commentary we make, and, most important, the followings we build, and packages all of that as a valuable, curated audience to advertisers.

Facebook's newsfeed isn't just a sequential flow of posts, like that of Twitter; it's the product of a proprietary algorithm. With that intelligent, profit-maximizing machine making value judgments about who would want to read what, posts gets prioritized and delivered to subsets of users that Facebook's marketing folks describe worryingly as "lookalike audiences." This is how the infamous "echo chambers" of social media, those teams of like-minded users with whom we find ourselves unconsciously aligning and whose reading lists never include the other side's point of view, get actively created and reinforced. Unknowingly, we all get fed a diet of information that affirms our political views. A *Wall Street Journal* report titled "Blue Feed, Red Feed" showed just how different Facebook's politically defined feeds have become.

This is a toxic mix for politics because it precludes the possibility of engaging with the other side, of finding consensus and compromise, of moving society forward. But it's a fabulous environment for advertisers. They now get to work with a clearly defined audience and can benefit from the networking effect and reinforcing power of its members' "likes" and "shares" on a piece of content. This setup means that articles that are intended to get a rise (which manifests as "likes" or "shares") can be quite literally made up out of nothing, deposited into this echo chamber, and used to steer valuable eyeballs back to their original sites in return for native advertising or Google Ad dollars. Think of what that means for *The New York Times* or *The Wall Street Journal* or other serious news outlets that also strive to use Facebook's powerful platform to attract audiences back to their own ad-bearing sites. Those news outlets spend hundreds of millions of dollars on newsrooms, bureaus, lawyers, and all manner of infrastructure to make sure they *get the story right*. Yet here they are having to compete, with an inferior ability to build an echo-chamber audience, with fake news providers such as those teenagers in Macedonia who, during the 2016 election, successfully fed conservative "lookalike audiences" stories such as the one saying that Pope Francis had "forbidden" Catholics from voting for Hillary Clinton.

Lots of other distortions in algorithms and biases exist across other social media platforms. But the especially insidious Facebook version, which is, naturally, welcomed by its shareholders, underscores the dangers of centralization in the social media environment. Both the audience for the content that we produce as Facebook subscribers and the content that we see from others are dictated by the company's secret algorithm. And who gets compensated for our unknowing participation in all this social engineering? Not us. Not the producers of the content. All the gains go to Facebook's shareholders.

We are long past due for a decentralized system of publishing. There's no way to turn back the clock to the centralized, top-down control of traditional media, so the game is about social media as a platform. There needs to be a level playing field of news production and distribution across this network of interconnected human brains.

But how?

An important starting point is to work with the original content that people produce. Right now if you put a photo up on the Internet, or perhaps a piece of your music that's not produced by a record label, it is open season for copying and sharing. You *could* go after every single instance of its reproduction that you discover, assert your copyright, and, if you can find a real person behind the relevant site, sue them. Of course, given all the effort and legal costs involved, no one but big media companies ever takes such action, and even then they don't have the resources to go after all the many small violations that gain minimal audience reach.

Nor would cutting off the free usage of your content necessarily be in your interest. One of the magical things of the open, sharing nature of the Internet is that it has created value by building audiences and connections. This is the notion of the online "commons," an open-access space of communication that generates value for everyone. Artists don't charge people for accessing their works within this space, and yet, when the commons works, value feeds back to them in the form of more advanced profiles, reputations, or influence. And that gets monetized in different ways: musicians attract more people to their concerts, artists get commissions, writers get speaking gigs. Or, as average users of Facebook or Twitter, we simply enjoy the social capital from having people follow us or like our posts. Still, given that so much of the advertising revenue on such platforms is siphoned off to those that control them, it's hard to argue that the commons' value-generation process has been equitable. And in large part that's because artists have struggled to definitively associate themselves with the art they create. They might have some visibility over how their works are generating social value within a particular platform—by viewing how many likes they get on Facebook, for example—but once it is copied and shared across platforms, the connection is broken.

The ingenious Creative Commons license is helping bring some fairness to the reuse of art and photos, creating a legal structure that explicitly licenses various forms of free use so long as there is compliance with certain conditions. Based on a series of categories of the license, these conditions specify what kind of attribution is required, for example, or whether the work is to be used for commercial purposes. Today, there are well over a billion works licensed under the Creative Commons system, most residing on publishing platforms such as Flickr and Wikimedia. Yet so much more could be done to empower artists and enrich their relationships with consumers. In all creative industries, but especially music, this lack of empowerment results in continued exploitation by the intermediaries that monopolize distribution and marketing of artistic material and that, in return for their services, claim contractual "rights" over it. The commons is still far from the utopian world of an open, creativity-inspiring system of sharing envisaged by Harvard professor Lawrence Lessig and other leaders of the "free culture" movement.

How might blockchain technology and related cryptographic systems of distributed information help address this imbalance?

We've already discussed in chapter four how Brave's Basic Attention token is aimed at rebalancing the advertising industry by compensating consumers of creative content for the attention they provide and by helping advertisers better measure the effectiveness of that attention. Judging by the lineup of competitors to Brave, there seems to be a meeting of minds around how this tech could fix *that* aspect of the creative content industry. An Ethereum-based service called adChain is creating a blockchain-based audit trail of data used in the ad industry while a consortium of media heavyweights that includes Comcast, Disney, NBCUniversal, Cox Communications, Mediaset Italia, Channel 4, and TF1 has launched a "Blockchain Insights Platform" to shift ad-buying to such a system. But a much bigger challenge lies in figuring how blockchains could be better used to measure and compensate the production of creative content—especially given that in the age of social media, we are *all* producers. How do we track everything?

Undaunted, an unofficial alliance of technologists, entrepreneurs, artists, musicians, lawyers, and disruption-wary music executives is now exploring a blockchain-led approach to the entire enterprise of human expression. The essential idea is that by attaching metadata about the artist, the date of creation, the title of the piece, and other details to the digital work and then immutably registering it to a block-chain transaction, it's possible to turn something that's now completely replicable and untraceable into a uniquely defined piece of property whose journeys around the Internet can be followed and managed. That, hopefully, would empower both creators of artistic works and those who consume them.

We were fairly early experimenters in this field. At 7:57 p.m. on February 2, 2015, we took a hash of our first book, *The Age of Cryptocurrency*, and inserted that information into block number 341705 on the bitcoin blockchain. Dan Ardle, the director of curriculum at the Digital Currency Council, whose blockchain recordation tool we used for the transaction, described its relevance this way: "This hash is unique to the book, and therefore could not have been generated before the book existed. By embedding this hash in a bitcoin transaction, the existence of the book on that transaction date is logged in the most secure and irrefutable recordkeeping system humanity has ever devised." In some respects, it's a much more sophisticated version of the old trick that writers used to assert their rights to a work: they would mail themselves a copy of the manuscript, using the postal service to implicitly record, with a trusted time stamp, their authorship.

Truth be told, we really don't doubt that U.S. courts would uphold our copyright. We registered the book into the blockchain just to make a point. Also, most copies of our book were sold in physical form—that is, non-replicable, but also non-traceable—where the exercise of blockchain recording is less powerful. Where this idea really opens up possibilities is in its application to the digitally reproduced art and music that's currently being replicated willy-nilly across the Internet. The hope now is that blockchains could fulfill the same function that photographers carry out when they put a limited number of tags and signatures on reproduced photo prints: it turns an otherwise replicable piece of content into a unique asset, in this case a digital asset.

The Grammy Award–winning British singer-songwriter Imogen Heap has been a blockchain trailblazer. Heap worked with Ujo, another offshoot of the Ethereum-based lab ConsenSys, to register "Tiny Human," the song she wrote in dedication to her baby daughter, on the Ethereum blockchain. For 60 cents, people could download the song and know that their funds would be automatically divvied up by smart contracts and delivered directly to the contributors, including Heap herself, but also the sound engineer and other musicians. For $45, musicians making non-commercial projects could download the different "stems" within the music—including the vocals, the drum track, the bass, and the strings—to sample and incorporate them into their own work. It's fair to say the marketing exercise was not a rip-roaring success.

What excites Heap is not so much the revenues from selling her music directly but the potentially richer information that would be widely available once an immutable link to the musician makes a music file traceable. And rather than treating that data as a way for musicians to compete for a finite pool of funds, protectively copyrighting their work to do so, she focuses on the opportunities for discovery, collaboration, and innovation when more information about artists is available. "There are millions of artists on the planet and we don't know about them; we don't know about their music. We don't know what they can do; we don't know their skill sets," Heap says. "This is about bringing those people up and bringing them out in the open so that we don't just celebrate and pay very well the tiny, tiny percent, that we allow everyone to come up. . . . I'm excited because the music industry is ripe for change and I feel like this is the real beginning."

As it is now, music studios monopolize marketing data for their artists' tracks. They use that power in a predatory manner via the digital rights management (DRM) legal framework that has evolved for enforcing breaches of copyright in the Internet era. That system is decried by consumers of art for the onerous restrictions it imposes on creativity. (Documentary filmmakers, for example, are forced to stop filming if they hear music in the background, since they don't want a lawsuit from the rights-owning label.) But the DRM system is also often attacked by artists themselves, who see so little of the payoff. "I'd prefer that fans got hold of the music and shared it because of the love of music rather than be vilified and criminalized for doing that," says Heap.

Here's the thing, though: the DRM framework was created to deal with the problem of uncontrolled replicability in the digital world, and that's a problem we may now have solved. The outdated idea is that, unlike physical containers of content such as books and VHS videos, digital files cannot be treated as unique, isolated assets, not when perfect copies can be made at virtually zero cost. But that means that, via DRM, the creative industry was shaped by policies that actively restrict, rather than promote, widespread use. It also means that our options as consumers are, in many ways, more constrained than they were previously. As streaming has become the default means of accessing—and monetizing—music and film, we've seen a deterioration in the quality of the recordings, for example, in order to optimize bandwidth usage. That would be fine if consumers could pay more to get higher-quality content delivered over different platforms, but they can't. (This partly explains, just as much as does nostalgia and the Brooklyn hipster movement, the resurgent popularity of vinyl.)

With blockchain technology, however, we could relive the old experience of art as a distinct asset. What a blockchain could do, argues Lance Koonce, a lawyer from Davis Wright Tremaine, is create a digital version of the "first-sale doctrine," a concept that's best understood in the context of books. Because both ownership *and* possession of a physical asset are transferred when a sale takes place, secondhand booksellers are allowed to resell books at will. The seller can't hang on to a copy for themselves—not without the expensive, time-consuming, low-quality (and illegal) work of running the book through a photocopying machine before handing it to the buyer. But for e-books and all other digital files, the same problem exists that dogged digital currencies in the pre-bitcoin years: the double-spend problem. Copying a digital file of text, music, or video has always been trivial. Now, with blockchain-based models, Koonce says, "we are seeing systems develop that can unequivocally ensure that a particular digital 'edition' of a creative work is the only one that can be legitimately transferred or sold." Recall that the blockchain, as we explained in chapter three, made the concept of a *digital asset* possible for the first time.

We still have some way to go before a viable economy exists around truly non-replicable digital assets. The technology to copy files won't go away, regardless of whether the first customer obtained the work from an artist who'd registered it in the blockchain, and incumbents that make money from the old system won't give up the golden goose quickly. Nonetheless, the mere presence of metadata in an immutable structure gives power to artists to manage their creative assets without relying on intermediaries such as record labels to handle DRM for them. Users of media do want to properly attribute the work of the creator. This could help them do that fairly and seamlessly.

Ujo is by no means the only startup exploring how blockchains can help players in the digital content industry manage their businesses.

The growing field includes Monegraph, which helps artists build unique licensing businesses using blockchain-based assertions of their rights; Stem, which uses smart contracts and time-stamped records of collaboration agreements to help band members and other contributors to tracks automatically share royalty payments from YouTube and other platforms; and dotBlockchain Music Project, which plans to introduce a unique codec file with a ".bc" extension to contain a song's blockchain-proven provenance data.

Notwithstanding such efforts and partnerships, we can expect slow going from the heavyweights in the creative industries, whose cooperation, to a large extent, is still needed. That said, some are exploring these technologies. Among the 170-plus members of the Berklee College of Music–sponsored Open Music Initiative you can find big labels like Sony Music Entertainment, Universal Music Group, and Warner Music Group, as well as streaming services such as Spotify, Napster, and Netflix. The non-profit project's ability to get these big incumbents to accept new rules, however, will depend on how well it lives up to its mission to create "an open-source protocol for the uniform identification of music rights holders and creators." Don't hold your breath on the labels embracing such a thing, however. There's a danger that the Open Music Initiative will become nothing more than a talkfest as the incumbent companies use it to forestall change that challenges their ownership stake in mountains of old records.

Inevitably, then, much of the action in this arena will be applied to new music, new movies, and new artwork, rather than to the giant stack of previously copyrighted works on which the record labels and movie studios sit. Still, a push is under way to give order and enforceable claims to a great swath of already-published material, to create an infrastructure of identifiable information about creative works, their history, and their creators. That includes figuring out who has rights to much of the non-professional, or would-be-professional, content that's published in places such as Facebook and Instagram, Google's YouTube, Yahoo's Flickr, and Pinterest. There, our collective content has generated great value for the corporate owners of those platforms but rarely converts into the same for us, the creators.

Building the Metadata Bank

Identifying content is a necessary first step if we are to restructure how society engages with creative output and attaches value to it. (You'll note, once again, this concept of "identity" popping up—in this case the identity of digital artistic artifacts.) It's a gargantuan task, one that's fraught with subjective dilemmas. What makes a photo materially different from, or the same as, another one? What degree of confidence is required for claims of authorship? What mechanism would we use for dispute resolution?

Still, the process has to start somewhere. Brooklyn-based Mediachain has been busily attaching artists' metadata—details such as the name of the artist, the title of the work, and the date it was produced—to existing digital images on the Internet, all in a way that can be stored, registered, and proven in a system of decentralized trust. Mediachain has built a giant, distributed, openly accessible database of more than 125 million images, all searchable on various fields, including descriptors generated by an intelligent image-reading system. Most of these are drawn from the rich datapool of works that use Creative Commons licenses in a bid to make that system more powerful for creators. "The Creative Commons dataset is incredibly fractured across multiple, siloed databases on different platforms," says Mediachain cofounder Jesse Walden. "When your work goes outside of them there is no dopamine drip of satisfaction when someone new uses your work or shares your work. You don't get any notifications, any information." To fix this, Mediachain's distributed data structure is aimed at cutting across all platforms, making each image's metadata accessible and readable to all.

Mediachain is not, however, using a blockchain for this metadata—not for the core registry components, at least. That's because the current scalability limits on public, permissionless blockchains such as Bitcoin or Ethereum are especially acute for this kind of data. There's enough of it to fill bitcoin's 1MB block limit for decades to come, and creators have virtually no capacity to pay miners the hundreds of millions of dollars in fees that would be needed to ensure their information is included and confirmed in blocks. Yet, given the massive, multitudinous, and heterogeneous state of the world's content, with hundreds of millions of would-be creators spread all over the world and no way to organize themselves as a common interest, there's likely a need for a permissionless, decentralized system in which the data can't be restricted and manipulated by a centralized institution such as a recording studio.

In response, Mediachain, like other players across various industries that are creating immutable, decentralized repositories for non-financial information, has come up with an "off-chain" solution to the data storage problem. It uses a hierarchy of verifiable cryptographic links to organize the data in an efficient yet verifiable manner and then stores it across the Internet using the IPFS file-management system, a new decentralized system for hosting Web sites that spreads files out across multiple, participating computers. Mediachain then provides free, open-source software with which any user can search the database and that developers can use to build new apps. The cryptography keeps the database tamper-proof and reliable so long as people trust artists' assertions about their authorship—as is the case for most copyright claims. It's only when digital assets, or rights to those assets, need to be transferred from one owner to another that a blockchain-like consensus mechanism is needed.

The end goal is to fix the "broken loop" so that the value generated in the commons isn't disproportionately captured by advertising-driven social media platforms like Facebook and professional Web sites like BuzzFeed. Those services can monopolize—and therefore monetize—the data they generate on audience behavior within their sites' walled gardens. Since most of the images in Mediachain's collection carry a free-usage Creative Commons license, the answer to combatting the monopoly is not to demand direct payments from the user that would go to the creator. That would likely meet with consumer resistance and kill the very idea of the commons. Rather, the focus is on commons-friendly solutions.

One of the Mediachain team's ideas is a "CC Gratitude" license. Developed with the help of lawyer Lance Koonce, this tweaked the Creative Commons license to require users to share with the creator information about the locations in which they are publishing his or her works. It speaks to Imogen Heap's desire for artists to receive data on their customers' behavior. Initial responses from the Creative Commons foundation weren't encouraging, however, as there were concerns it would require added work, by either end-users or by platforms that would have to build systems to automate the function, and thus constrain the natural growth of the commons. Those concerns could presumably be ameliorated if platforms like Flickr charged artists a small fee to opt in for the service. But in general, says Mediachain's Walden, those big managers "don't want to share their data into an open, permissionless database, in spite of the fact that we are talking about Creative Commons licenses. . . . It's too disruptive an idea for a platform to impose on itself." Flickr, in this sense, is like so many other centralized providers on the Web—it wants to keep people inside its site, not ranging off across the Net to wherever Mediachain takes them. This way it generates data that it can sell to advertisers and other users. In other words, it is itself in line for disruption by decentralized, blockchain-based solutions.

One way that disruption could happen is via an idea that Mediachain has floated but hasn't followed through on. At one stage, Mediachain was about to join the token craze, and the company wrote up plans to issue a native cryptocurrency, called the CCcoin, for Creative Commons content. The coin would be issued to owners of Creative Commons–licensed content if they uploaded their works to Mediachain and earned votes from other users for the quality of their work. Think of it as a merit-based concept like the group moderation model at social media platform Reddit, except that it involved a currency. CCcoin was an experiment with the idea of a "proof of creative work," says Walden. It foresaw a world in which creators got some measurable stake attached to their contribution to the commons, while those who purchased and used coins could treat it as an act of "benevolent support for the public good," not dissimilar to the motives of those who donate to the Creative Commons foundation.

There hasn't been much follow-through on CCcoin after it was floated in early 2017. And that may be because Mediachain's corporate status has changed—rather dramatically. In the spring, it was bought by Spotify, the world's leading music streaming service, which integrated Walden and his team into its New York offices. There was one good reason for the deal: in 2016, Spotify had to pay out about $20 million to music publishers to settle a lawsuit over unpaid royalties. It seems Spotify bought Mediachain as part of its effort to come up with a better way to track copyright claims and royalties. In that sense, it's a validation of what Mediachain was trying to do. On the other hand, this could result in a private company taking a technology that could have been used publicly, broadly for the general good, and hiding it, along with its innovative ideas for tokens and other solutions, behind a for-profit wall. Let's hope it's not the latter.

With these ideas, we at least have a framework for thinking about how to better protect the rights of the Internet's all-important content producers and creative concept developers. But if we are to truly reclaim the Internet for all of us, the great mass of humanity that, in our many different ways, provides all of that information, entertainment, and ideas, then we also need to think about the governance of the Web itself.

The concepts that underpin blockchains force us to think about this challenge because, at its core, this technology is a governance system. And that, by default, makes it a political project—not in the sense that traditional politicians will define how the tech develops, though congressmen and law enforcement agents are a factor, but in how the stakeholders in this process will set the precepts of a program that will rule their lives. Both the question of who writes the algorithms and the debate over the external standards and regulations that might constrain this technology come down to politics. It's critical that representatives of all interest groups who are destined to be affected have their say in the design of blockchain systems and applications. How these different stakeholders work out their different priorities is always a matter of politics.

Ten

A NEW CONSTITUTION FOR THE DIGITAL AGE

The ideas behind America's Constitution, including its forceful opening declaration that "we hold these truths to be self-evident, that all men are created equal," developed over the course of generations. More than a century earlier, in 1647, a group of religious dissenters in England called the Levellers pushed for what they termed an "Agreement of the People." It called for freedom of religion, extensive suffrage, and equality under the law. And long before the Levellers, the Romans were working out these concepts as well. The Twelve Tables, from 450 BCE, sought to codify the laws of the day, to establish equality under the law between the ruling class and the common people. It wasn't exactly the most enlightened set of laws—women were by law subject to men, and violent death was a common punishment—but it does show men trying to come up with a working set of rules that bound people within a civil society. Bitcoin, with its new model of decentralized governance for the digital economy, did not spring out of nowhere, either. Some of the elements—cryptography, for instance—are thousands of years old. Others, like the idea of electronic money, are decades old. And, as should be evident in Bitcoin's block-size debate, Bitcoin is still very much a work in progress. The right conflagration of components that will allow this technology to be viable for the entire world is still being worked out.

As blockchain technology matures, we have much to learn from the political solutions that society has turned to in the past. And the U.S. Constitution, which has functioned for 229 years, is as good a reference as any—the Founding Fathers gave deep thought to how best to manage the kinds of economic and political tensions that have riven both Bitcoin and Ethereum. It must be said, though, that the foundational documents of Western democracy, including the U.S. Constitution, are having their relevance severely questioned in a rapidly changing, digitally interconnected world.

Globalization, air travel, and computerization have erased the borders within which governments can exercise the power bestowed upon them by these otherwise weighty social contacts. This impotency has fostered a sense of lost sovereignty and a fear of outside, uncontrolled forces, now manifest in the politics of xenophobia and protectionism. Politicians like Donald Trump are trying to revive the old powers of nationalism, reversing free trade initiatives, touting the rhetoric of homegrown capitalism, getting tough on immigration, and stoking the flames of ethnic conflict.

Yet most sophisticated analyses of economic, technological, and demographic trends will tell you that these actions cannot halt the zeitgeist of technological change—not when companies can simply move operations offshore to friendlier regulatory environments. If anything, nationalism will ensure that the wins and losses from change are even more inequitably distributed. Addressing the discontent that has fed the Trump phenomenon requires a different approach. And we believe that the place to start is to work out how to better align the governance rules by which society manages economic exchanges with the decentralizing forces unleashed by new information technology.

This does not mean that traditional government is going away—not by any stretch. In fact, even as these new online technologies are enabling borderless communities to operate somewhat beyond the oversight of traditional, geographically defined governments, they are also giving those governments new tools with which to exercise their power. Bitcoin and other systems governed by distributed consensus are built expressly not to have any one central point of control, in a deliberate effort to avoid giving centralized authority too much power. But other systems aren't so egalitarian. The Snowden leaks showed how willing the U.S. government's intelligence agencies are to use new machines that trace people's ever-growing online trails to pry into their lives without their knowledge. Yet, for now at least, governments can also play a vital role in protecting our privacy. That can be found in the individual freedom principles that guide the best elements of Europe's new General Data Protection Regulation, or GDPR. Americans, meanwhile, are learning what happens when governments vacate that role. In 2017, Congress rolled back Obama-era rules that prevented Internet service providers from sharing or selling their users' data without consent.

There's only so much governments can and should do. Yet they neither can nor should sit idly by and let powerful corporate entities dictate how new technologies are deployed—certainly not in an environment of accelerating job losses and mounting social and political tension. We need a system that shares the benefits of these new technologies. We're not talking about reviving the failed experiment of communism, of course, but rather ensuring that those with most access to these tools don't abuse others and that the opportunity to harness innovation and new ideas is spread as widely as possible.

The future is going to be greatly influenced by the three great power centers of our day: technology, finance, and government. In the United States that triumvirate plays out, at least metaphorically, as Silicon Valley, New York, and Washington, but the divide is basically the same around the world. It seems to us, moreover, that each of these power centers is primarily concerned with how it can bend the future to benefit its own interests. We seem to be stuck with bankers who don't really understand technology, technologists who don't understand economics, and politicians who understand only politics. If we're going to leverage technology so it can provide the greatest good for the greatest number, we must break down a lot of walls. Because the preeminent schism that they will jostle over isn't between left and right, conservative and liberal. It isn't between occidental and oriental, East and West. It is between centralized and decentralized systems. We need to understand how to harness the latter to overcome the deficits inherent in the former. To do that, we're going to need a lot more people who have at least a working understanding of technology, economics, and politics. We may need a philosopher or two, as well.

Though a major point of this book has been to show the possibilities presented by Bitcoin and other manifestations of blockchain technology, we will be among the first to admit that, as currently designed, they don't hold all the answers. The experience so far with Bitcoin itself has been one of narrowly concentrated wealth accumulation by the earliest adopters and by a small group of three or four large mining pools that control the bulk of the network's computing power. A great deal of work needs to be done to scale the technology for Bitcoin, Ethereum, and other blockchain protocols in a way that lives up to the decentralization imperative. But as we've sought to emphasize, Bitcoin and the blockchain's greatest contribution to the challenge of governance in the Internet age has been to change our way of thinking about society's problems. Bitcoin and the blockchain have introduced a new model for confronting these obstacles. What matters most is the innovation and ideation that the blockchain concept has unleashed, primarily among software engineers and entrepreneurs, but also among political scientists and economists. As for the rest of us, we must demand a social and political framework that gives this open-ended inventive process the best chance of forging a system of open access and opportunity. And for that, we would contend that, whatever software system wins out, the common social goal of managing our trust relations should be significantly more decentralized and disintermediated. Given all the imagination and frenetic, open-source innovation that these ideas have unleashed, we don't believe it is unreasonable or overly utopian to envisage that this approach can foster a better world.

Decentralization isn't the be-all-and-end-all for every problem. It's not an end in itself, but rather a means of achieving certain goals: equal opportunity, wider inclusion, greater shared prosperity and collaboration, etc. Where those goals can be better served by decentralization, that approach should be promoted. But in many cases, especially where the intermediating institution is trusted and reliable, a centralized structure will be an inherently more efficient way of processing information.

One question we often hear from businesses exploring this technology is, "Do I need a blockchain for this?" Our answer to that would be, "If the cost of centrally maintaining trust within the economic relationship in question is higher than the cost of installing a network of computers to manage trust in a decentralized manner, then yes. If not, no." Since a community must spend significant resources to prove transactions on a blockchain, that type of record-keeping system is most valuable when a high degree of mutual mistrust means that managing agreements comes at a prohibitively high price. (That price can be measured in various ways: in fees paid to middlemen, for instance, in the time it takes to reconcile and settle transactions, or in the fact that it's impossible to conduct certain business processes, such as sharing information across a supply chain.) When a bank won't issue a mortgage to a perfectly legitimate and creditworthy homeowner, except at some usurious rate, because it doesn't trust the registry of deeds and liens, we can argue that the price of trust is too high and that a blockchain might be a good solution.

The broader matter of whether to decentralize an industry could come down to the question of whether doing so would level the playing field, of whether the existing centralized structure imposes unreasonable costs on users and limits the ability of innovators to introduce better ideas. As a reference point, we can go back to Teddy Roosevelt's landmark anti-trust legislation at the start of the twentieth century, which gave us the lasting principle that it was in the public interest for the U.S. government to proactively enforce a competitive marketplace. The problem with that model, though, is that the industrial-era definitions of a monopoly don't easily apply to the world of software and information networks, where value for the consumer is a direct function of network size and where the cost to the consumer is not paid in dollars but in valuable personal data. The dominant players, who argue that ongoing product improvements and "free" services represent a constantly improving customer experience, obscure the true exploitative nature of their business models, which combine secret, closed algorithms with the allure of an established network to limit the ability of competitors to challenge their dominant market position.

All this seems to escape the attention of anti-trust regulators like the Federal Trade Commission, whose outdated standards of competitiveness are blind to the ways in which centralized institutions accumulate power in the Internet era. In essence, the traditional anti-trust viewpoint fails to recognize that you are not Facebook's customer, you are Facebook's product. In an age where everyone is a creator, where everyone is managing their "brand," we need a new manifesto for citizens' rights in the information marketplace. Decentralization needs to be part of that. And the ideas behind blockchain design are as good a place as any to start.

Every centralized system should be open for evaluation—even those of government and the political process. Already, startups such as Procivis are working on e-voting systems that would hand the business of vote-counting to a blockchain-based backend. And some adventurous governments are open to the idea. By piloting a shareholder voting program on top of Nasdaq's Linq blockchain service, Estonia is leading the way. The idea is that the blockchain, by ensuring that no vote can be double-counted—just as no bitcoin can be double-spent—could for the first time enable reliable mobile voting via smartphones. Arguably it would both reduce discrimination against those who can't make it to the ballot box on time and create a more transparent, accountable electoral system that can be independently audited and which engenders the public's trust.

What about the function of government itself? Should it be disintermediated? Well, in some cases, yes. We've already talked about how property titles could be registered in a blockchain-based immutable ledger. Some crypto-libertarians have their eyes on an even bigger goal, however, and hope to supplant what they see as a failed, obsolete model of nation-state–led government. The startup BitNation, for example, touts blockchain-based "world citizenship ID," "embassies," "nations," and "allies" for online communities that create new models of self-government. The Bitcoin blockchain, its Web site argues, "allows us to choose to govern ourselves for the way we want to live now: peer-to-peer, more locally and globally." To expect such ideas to gain traction on a large scale, at least at this stage of human history, is far-fetched. For one, they ignore the deep-seated role that our national legal systems play in our sense of justice. The law is a deep concept, ingrained into our collective and cultural thinking over centuries of development; most people won't buy the illusion that "code is law" and won't want to abandon that rich element of our social fabric for a software system they don't understand. While it's undoubtedly true that some elements of nation-states' powers have waned in the era of the globalized, digital economy, we would say that the formal disintermediation of national governments is a long way off. In any case, we have big enough challenges to tackle before we go after that one!

Re-Decentralizing the Web

The first challenge we must address: fixing the Internet. There's a concerted effort under way to "re-decentralize" the Internet, to rearrange the hierarchy of how files and information are hosted and shared on the Web so that Web site creators have more control over what is published and where. This effort is being framed, ideologically, as a return to the early vision of the Net as an open forum in which everyone would have an unfiltered voice, a way to dismantle the centralized, siloed control over our data and lives that behemoths like Google and Facebook have seized. If we don't do it, people say, if we can't bring greater interoperability to the Web, we won't achieve the true promise of "open data," with all the rich analytic information that it could unlock about life on this planet.

A great deal of high-powered thought and development is going toward these goals. There are blockchain-based offerings looking to disintermediate the business of outsourced storage and computing, for example, to break the expensive, wasteful, and environmentally harmful dominance of corporate-owned data centers. With names such as Storj, Sia, and Maidsafe, these new platforms reward you with tokens if you offer up your spare hard-drive space to other computer users in a global network of users. You could say these "cloud" services are much truer to that name than those of Amazon Web Services, Google, Dropbox, IBM, Oracle, Microsoft, and Apple, the providers with which most people associate that word.

But even bigger changes are being considered, including projects to entirely re-architect the Web itself. There's Solid, which stands for Social Linked Data, a new protocol for data storage that puts data back in the hands of the people to whom it belongs. The core idea is that we will store our data in Pods (Personalized Online Data Stores) and distribute it to applications via permissions we control. Solid is the brainchild of none other than Tim Berners-Lee, the computer scientist who perfected HTTP and gave us the World Wide Web. Another one that gets a lot of people excited is the Interplanetary File System, designed by Juan Benet. The principle behind it is similar to that of the popular file-sharing system BitTorrent, which unlike Napster has defied music- and movie-studio efforts to have it shut down on piracy grounds. As with BitTorrent, IFPS's system distributes Internet files around a network of independent computers so that they don't reside together in single servers owned by hosting services but are scattered everywhere, sitting on regular people's hard drives, with multiple copies as backups. Web hosting, in this way, becomes a collective exercise in sharing storage resources across the Internet.

Potentially even more transformative are the radical proposals of a group calling itself the Economic Space Agency, or ECSA. It takes some of its inspiration from cryptotokens, decentralized trust systems, and smart contracts, but its approach to decentralizing the economy and re-empowering individuals is very different from Bitcoin's and Ethereum's. Rather than having every single transaction or smart contract instruction processed by the entire network of a single blockchain,

ECSA has a bottom-up approach to decentralization. ECSA has a tool-kit of programs called Gravity that builds on the decades-old "object capabilities" computer security work of Cypherpunk Mark S. Miller. Gravity allows computers in a local network to safely enter into smart contracts together. ECSA also emphasizes that communities should be able to autonomously set their own governance models. The idea, sup-ported by an eclectic team of technologists, economists, political scien-tists, and anthropologists, is to empower people to build new "economic spaces" in which their communities can issue and trade cryptotokens in support of collaboration and cooperation. Unlike Ethereum, their transactions won't need to be validated by a high-powered global blockchain network. Yet by allowing for trading and interaction across communities without the intermediation of a trusted third party, Grav-ity purports to be able to build, from this bottom-up starting point, an interoperable, decentralized global economy.

If it works, ECSA's approach might not only help resolve Bitcoin's and Ethereum's problems of excessive computing power, contentious governance, and scaling limitations, but could also avoid what Lucian Tarnowski, founder of community-based learning and collaboration platform Brave New, warns is the risk that humans become "slaves to the algorithm." By focusing on monolithic software solutions like Bit-coin and Ethereum, Tarnowski and others argue that we risk succumb-ing to a kind of dictatorship of the software itself—and, by extension, of the narrow subset of human beings who have input into its design. To be sure, the use of open-source licenses for most blockchain models is intended to widen the input into how they are designed. But the reality is that the algorithms' rules can become quite rigid and the capacity to change them limited to a small group with specialized knowledge.

Here we are compelled to revert to the usual caveat: all of this is experimental. We have no idea whether any of these ideas will work. And with people throwing money at these projects via fund-raising events like ICOs, it's very likely that a great deal of money will be lost during this experimentation phase. But the point we want to stress, as we have elsewhere, is that the combination of all these projects happening at the same time, all in an almost entirely open-source, data-sharing manner, dramatically increases the chances of success. We can't look at each of these in isolation. They are occurring amid a massive exchange of multiple innovative ideas across a global pool of very smart people, a "wisdom of the crowd" force for change that creates positive feedback loops of creativity and progress. No one can know where all this ends up, just as the early architects of the Internet could not imagine music streaming, VOIP phones, or e-marketplaces being built on top of their invention. But it is safe to conclude that the Internet—and the broader economy with it—will look very different and markedly less centralized in the years to come.

Lightbulbs Going Off in the Halls of Power

During the 2016 presidential campaign, Hillary Clinton likely mystified many of her supporters when she announced her support for "public service blockchain applications." Clinton used those words on the advice of Brian Forde, a former Obama White House technology advisor and the first director of the Digital Currency Initiative at MIT Media Lab who in 2017 decided to run for Congress. He later described the effort to get her team to adopt it as "challenging." And while it was impressive that Clinton's focus was on how blockchain applications might be useful for government rather than on how to regulate them, it's worth noting that the word "blockchain" never popped up again in the rest of the campaign.

Still, lightbulbs are going off in some parts of officialdom. We've highlighted the research under way at dozens of central banks. We're hearing of pilots and exploratory investigations into blockchain applications by government agencies worldwide, not just in the big economies of the United States, the European Union, Japan, and China, but also in countries as diverse as Dubai, Georgia, Sweden, Estonia, Mexico, Singapore, and Luxembourg. In Japan, for example, the Financial Services Agency put in anti–money laundering and capital requirements for bitcoin exchanges, and categorized bitcoin and other digital currencies as a payments system—in effect, it codified these currencies, giving them an official status within the traditional capital markets. The effect was immediate: bitcoin trading in Japan skyrocketed, a big part of 2017's price spikes, and myriad Japanese companies started accepting bitcoin. Meanwhile, Blockchain startup Neocapita is working with Papua New Guinea and Afghanistan to record those governments' expenditures in a blockchain in a bid to boost transparency, restore the confidence of foreign donors, and unlock frozen aid money. At the international level, the IMF is studying blockchain technology, as is the World Bank. The Inter-American Development Bank is gung-ho about it, and the United Nations, which now has a blockchain-dedicated team of experts, has, as we've mentioned, sponsored a conference on blockchain-based personal identity.

Even on Capitol Hill, a few legislators are starting to take notice. In February 2017, Representative Jared Polis, a Democrat from Colorado, and David Schweikert, a Republican from Arizona, launched the "Blockchain Caucus" of legislators, which will advocate for "sound public policy toward blockchain-based technologies and digital currencies." Things are happening at the state government level, too. Delaware is working with Symbiont to transfer its corporate registry and share certificate management system to a distributed ledger system. And in March 2017, Illinois's government announced that it had joined R3 and launched the Illinois Blockchain Initiative, a public-private partnership to connect much of the state's bureaucratic infrastructure using a distributed ledger.

With all this activity, new ideas for what's being called "regtech"—regulatory technology—are bubbling up fast. Blockchains are a subset of that, but already we're seeing international law enforcement agencies like Europol partner with blockchain analytics firms like Chainanalysis to map out global flows of funds. And in places like Estonia, a country that has turned itself into a veritable living lab for civic tech, the government is warming to the idea of blockchains as a more reliable notarization service, ensuring that trusted documents can much more easily be submitted for applications for services. All manner of government records could soon be transferred into this immutable environment. And the more that access to that data can be put under the control of citizens themselves, rather than locked in the siloed departments that Tim Berners-Lee complains about, the closer we'll come to the great information-processing power of a longed-for open-data age.

Yet, despite these strides, the readiness of the regulatory machinery to address the changes that are coming is woeful. One problem is that before we get lawmakers and regulators to understand blockchains, we need them to focus on everything else that's going on in the digital transformation of our age: the other paradigm shifts that AI, virtual reality, 3D printing, the Internet of Things, and network analytics are bringing to the economy. As New Jersey senator Cory Booker said during a tech-related conference in Washington two years ago, "Most people can't really even think of what is the Republican view of technology and the Democratic view of technology, because there is none."

So, there are some extremely inadequate rules in place. Take the know-your-customer and anti–money laundering requirements for money transmitters handling cross-border remittances, for example. Solid privacy-protecting digital identity tools have been available for sometime that, when combined with blockchain analysis, could both make it easier for poor people to share money with each other *and* help regulators conduct financial surveillance of illicit fund flows. Yet within the Group of 20 nations' Financial Action Task Force, there is an unwavering view that the only way to battle money laundering and terrorism financing is through ever-tougher requirements for traditional, state-backed identity. This non-solution leads remittance firms to turn away more and more people, which starves poor countries of funds, creating fertile grounds for terrorists and encouraging them to use untraceable black-market systems to send money home. Says Juan Llanos, an expert in technology and payment system compliance, "The regulatory framework isn't ready for the digital age, let alone the blockchain age."

Yet, as we've demonstrated, blockchain products are being developed en masse—with or without the support of governments. Changes *are* coming. We need our regulatory framework to be ready for them. That doesn't, by the way, mean that we need new rules per se. The instinct to regulate is perhaps the fastest way to kill innovation. Rather, it's important that there is a well-reasoned and understood strategy in place, even if that strategy is to do nothing.

Here's one reason why: blockchain technologies, like so many other software-based ideas, are global in nature. That means startups using them will gravitate to friendlier jurisdictions. A case in point can be found in Zug, Switzerland, nicknamed "Crypto Valley," where Ethereum developers and a host of new smart-contract, cryptocurrency, and blockchain outfits have set up shop. One reason they've done so is because Swiss law makes it easier to set up the foundations needed to launch coin offerings and issue digital tokens. Similarly, the UK Financial Conduct Authority's "sandbox" strategy, which sets a relatively lightweight regulatory environment for startups to develop and test new fintech products, has been applauded by technologists as a way to drive innovation. It's also smart for Britain's economy: after Brexit, the city of London's all-important financial district needs to make sure it can stay ahead of New York and competing money hubs in Europe. Establishing itself as a fintech leader offers the best bet at sustaining dominance. Under pre-Brexit prime minister David Cameron, the UK government even saw fit to dedicate £10 million to digital currency research. The next question is: what will it take for U.S. policymakers to worry that America's financial and IT hubs are losing out to these foreign competitors in this vital new field?

Bringing "Trustless" Software to Communities of Trust

Trust is integral to every transaction we make, including in bitcoin. When bitcoins are sent from one person to another, we must still trust that the goods or services they're promising in return are delivered. We also have to trust that the computer or smartphone with which we are sending those bitcoins, and the Wifi network, as well as the Internet Service Provider that's carrying the data, haven't been compromised.

We return to this topic here because if we're going to design a fully integrated system of distributed ledgers and blockchains for something as mind-bogglingly complex as the global economy, it will be vital to figure out how to unite decentralized ledgers with the trusted people or entities engaged in the transactions. To get that design right, we also must come to terms with how trust defines who we are, how it builds the relationships of mutual support upon which communities are formed.

Consider an institution like France's 200-year-old Caisse des Dépôts et Consignations. This constitutionally established, overarching agency has sweeping powers. Overseen by the parliament rather than operating as an agent of the executive branch, the Caisse des Dépôts plays a central role in coordinating investments in the affairs of the nation. It manages property title records. It invests in infrastructure. It administers public savings and pension plans. And it ensures that funding goes to the judiciary and other agents of justice, as well as to universities and state research projects, all in a way that's meant to be free from political influence. If it existed within a more dysfunctional political context, the Caisse des Dépôts could become a cesspit of corruption and an agent of political interests that would lose the trust of the people. But in France, it is considered a great honor to work for the Caisse des Dépôts. And that culture of honor helps build a deep wellspring of trust. The question here is: even if it's possible to replace something like the Caisse des Dépôts with an algorithm that creates a system of distributed trust, would we want to? Might we undo centuries of cultural and social formation that goes into the creation of institutions like this?

Many of the institutions on which Western societies depend to intermediate our exchanges and interactions—be they public bodies such as government agencies and courts or private entities such as notary publics and utility companies—similarly are products of centuries of society-building. The smooth functioning of these institutions depends not only on the systems of governance and jurisprudence we've developed to hold them to account but also on some vital cultural norms.

With those mores in place, we willingly defer trust to these powerful gatekeepers at the same time that the people in charge of them routinely feel compelled to honor that trust. It's an extension of the deep sense of civic responsibility that leads people to line up for things, to hold doors for strangers, or simply to say "please" and "thank you." Institutionalized trust is a societal virtue, a form of social capital that's in short supply elsewhere in the world. In those places where we have it, it's not clear that we should be doing away with it. In each case where trust has been built up in this way, its value to society is arguably greater than the specific purpose that the institution plays.

Cryptography enthusiasts have a saying: "don't trust, verify." That's wise advice for someone running security on a mission-critical computing system that's at risk of cyber-attack. And it's the right approach for guarding your money, at least when dealing with strangers. But when applied more broadly, that maxim diminishes the core element of what brings a society together. It's not for nothing that trust is seen as a positive thing and why early cryptographers' descriptions of Bitcoin as a "trustless" system weren't embraced by non-crypto folks. We should look upon the distributed trust solutions blockchains offer as a way to enable communities to strengthen their bonds of trust in other environments, not as a replacement for them.

Functioning as a kind of societal glue, trust makes possible the multiple exchanges we enter into every day, little deals that we can't imagine taking to court but which nonetheless carry some agreed expectation of mutual exchange: when we don't butt in on a line of fellow commuters at the bus ticket vending machine; when we get on the bus, swipe our ticket, and expect that the driver and the vehicle will safely get us to our destination within some reasonably expected time frame; when we get off the bus and walk down a busy street, believing that the oncoming people aren't going to walk into us. The cultural, sociological, and psychological factors that lead us to develop these and countless other trust bonds must be treated as vital components of whatever decentralized governance system we end up designing for our rapidly

evolving, digitizing society. They will help us form the connective tis-
sue between our "on-chain," software-regulated transactions and the
human-regulated world in which we otherwise live.

One big reason to work out the human element to this technological development stems from that key limitation of the early blockchains that we've discussed repeatedly: their scalability. As currently
designed, Bitcoin and Ethereum are inherently complex and expensive to run, with all those computers having to engage in the same act
of computation, all validating the same transaction, identity assertion,
asset transfer, or smart contract. Although their respective consensus
mechanisms, incentive models, and protocol designs result in different
computational efficiencies and inefficiencies, Bitcoin and Ethereum,
and most other permissionless, public blockchains, inevitably chew up
computing and energy resources as their networks grow.

The good news, again, is that a great deal of thought and investment is going into overcoming these challenges. Consider these ideas,
addressed earlier in the book: the Lightning Network is adding a new
payment channel layer to Bitcoin to free up transactions; EOS is a permissionless blockchain that startup block.one claims can process millions of transactions a second; Tezos is reinventing governance to allow
a more fluid, democratic system of ongoing blockchain protocol improvement; and Zcash and Monero are striving to resolve privacy concerns. There's also James Lovejoy's Cryptokernel project, whose K320
application addresses Bitcoin's bugaboos of currency hoarding and
the inequitable dominance of high-powered "ASIC" mining equipment.
And to these you can add a project called Algorand, the sweeping new
blockchain proposal from an MIT team including Turing Prize laureate
Professor Silvio Micali, which addresses many of these challenges at once.
If we assume that one or more of these can one day surpass Bitcoin
and Ethereum's adoption rate and at least match Bitcoin's proven economic security—or, alternatively, that those two established blockchains end up incorporating their ideas—this process of invention is a
source of great hope. Together they increase the likelihood that the global,
digital economy can be managed by a decentralized trust architecture

that is open, permissionless, and dynamic yet also more manageable, scalable, secure, and safe for the environment.

One thing that's also badly needed, however, is a lot more engineering talent. The complexity, and the overriding need for rock-solid security on a global level, mean that blockchain systems currently depend on highly specialized, deep knowledge. Without these specialists maintaining, updating, and de-bugging the core software protocols, the entire blockchain ecosystem could not function. As they are now designed, blockchains have an all-in-one mix of features, from cryptography to consensus algorithms, and demanding security features, all of which make them very clunky, complicated, and labor-intensive to work on. It takes a special type of software coder to deal with all of that.

Services such as EOS are designed to create a more user-friendly toolkit so that enterprises can build their own blockchain solutions. That could alleviate some of the recruiting pressure on blockchain specialists. However, if society as a whole is to have a say in how this new economic governance system evolves, we're still going to need to build up that pool of protocol developers. We'll also need to tap this talent from the widest, most diverse swath of humanity—crossing gender, racial, and ethnic lines—so that the values and biases that are inevitably baked into the algorithms that rule our lives don't come from an overly narrow subset of society. The moral of the story: invest in coding education for all.

The Rise of the Citizen

Yet there's something more fundamental than financial stability behind the value of decentralization. It relates to the foundational idea of citizenship. This book has explored ways in which individuals might, for the first time, be empowered as economic agents to exercise their rights to commerce, unhindered self-expression, and creative thought, and at the same time take charge of the property that's rightfully theirs. Now, more than ever, this idea of a citizenship defined by these fundamental rights, an idea that began in the Enlightenment, hinges on control over information. How we govern information, the right to access and use it, will define the boundaries of freedom. That's why the idea of an unbreakable truth machine that no one person or institution can break is so empowering.

Don't take our word for it. Listen to this January 2016 report from the UK's Government Office for Science on blockchain technology and its myriad uses. "The technology could prove to have the capacity to deliver a new kind of trust to a wide range of services," two members of Parliament, Matthew Hancock and Ed Vaizey, wrote in a foreword. "As we have seen open data revolutionize the citizen's relationship with the state, so may the visibility in these technologies reform our financial markets, supply chains, consumer and business-to-business services, and publicly-held registers." Then, further on, in a section entitled "Applications in Government," Catherine Mulligan of the Imperial College London wrote that "the eventual impact of [digital ledger technologies] on British society may be as significant as foundational events such as the creation of Magna Carta." That's right. Magna Carta.

How, exactly, is this record so important from a constitutional perspective? Well, we've said elsewhere that the blockchain could represent the very first time that human society has a system for creating an unbroken historical record. We've also talked about what that might mean for the potential to end a millennia-old model in which power stems from control over our information. This is as important as ever now, with a U.S. president who believes he alone can define the boundaries of what constitutes "fake news" and publishes dubious official information that his minders describe as "alternative facts." Seen from that context, the very prospect that we could build a truth machine—whether it resides on a blockchain or lives across a patchwork of Gravity-based economic spaces—is incredibly enticing. There's something profoundly empowering about letting self-sovereign individuals record data to a publicly verifiable record, without requiring anyone's permission to do so. If you've created something of value, such as a popular piece of digital art or an idea that could be translated into a profitable venture, it can be a game-changer if you can stake your claim to it without the approval of a business name registrar or some other certifying entity. That's especially true for people in countries where such institutions are dysfunctional or don't even exist. And when you add in the fact that this record can't be destroyed, the possibilities become quite large indeed. Permanence of information is an essential component of democracy.

I Was Here, My Humanity Matters

If you doubt that something as utilitarian as a ledger composed of alphanumeric codes could help preserve our humanity, with all its quirks, charm, and madness, we invite you to dig into a little-discussed aspect of the Bitcoin blockchain: the phenomenon of block graffiti. Bitcoin users will often inscribe messages into transactions, following a tradition that dates back to the very first Bitcoin transaction, when Satoshi took a headline from a UK paper of the day and inscribed into a transaction data field the words "The Times 03/Jan/2009 Chancellor on brink of second bailout for banks." Ever since, people have treated the ledger as an immutable, time-stamped journal in which to make declarations that, for whatever reason, they want to pass the test of time.

When we took a look at a few months of Bitcoin graffiti managed by the site CryptoGraffiti.info, starting with the spring of 2017 and then scrolling back in time, we found a rich trove of all manner of statements. Many were love notes, like this one on March 20, which came from address 1GRtrEGKPwXJTqS3jp8JbZDkLNpZjagCCb, cost the person BTC 0.00055039 ($0.57 at the time), and found permanent representation in Block #458160:

> My love to all creatures in this reality is infinite. My love to one of these creatures reaches beyond this reality. You are everything to me Jana Sedlackova.-Petr.

There were also photographic images viewable on the CryptoGraffiti.info site, if not directly on the blockchain, including the famous

1989 image of the man in front of the Tiananmen Square tank, posted on March 17, also in 2017. It was preceded by a text message, first in Chinese, then in English, calling President Xi Jinping of China to "Tell the Truth About Tiananmen" on the forthcoming anniversary of the massacre. There was a photo of a couple, accompanied by a love poem in Spanish. There was this one, too: "In loving memory of Georges Fraiponts (16/01/1946-19/02/2017). Awesome man, father and friend. We will miss you."

Scrolling back through prior transactions, we found remarks in multiple languages conveying a varied mix of similarly sentimental comments, but also trading tips, motor vehicles for sale, statements about the oil pipeline protests at Standing Rock, some farewell message to a guy called Tobias by his team members from "Blockchain at Berkeley," the occasional conspiracy theory, and, perhaps unsurprisingly, commentary about time travel. Then, we looked at October 2016, when the Bitcoin blocks were coinciding with the final siege of Aleppo by Syrian government forces, a year after Najah Saleh Al-Mheimed, whom we met in the introduction, had already fled for Jordan. The people of Aleppo were all but cut off from the outside world, except for the few holdout freelance bloggers who used rudimentary Internet connections to file stories about the people now trapped there. In that month, three messages jumped out:

Need 30 btc. Please! Dream to leave Syria

http://syria.mil.ru/syria/livecam.htm

Help get out of Syria. I live in Aleppo. I am 14 years old. I do not cheat. Community help!!!!!!

With that turn, the graffiti scroll started to feel a bit haunting. It also reminded us of another time and place when an oppressed community longed to communicate with the outside world: during the Cold War, at the Berlin Wall. There, too, the graffiti—all on the West

German side—was a mix of pleas to respect people's rights, of love notes, of messages of peace and hope, and of straightforward statements that so and so had visited that place—the classic "I Was Here" proof of existence, proof of humanity. Yet if a Cold War graffito is read as a statement of defiance against a wall that sought to constrain and restrict human connections, the messages here in this strange digital accounting system are powerful because it is *not* a wall. No state or corporation can put bricks around the Bitcoin blockchain or whitewash its record. They can't shut down the truth machine, which is exactly why it's a valuable place to record the voices of human experience, whether it's our love poems or our cries for help. This, at its core, is why the blockchain matters.

Acknowledgments

It's hard for anyone to keep up with the frenetic pace at which cryptocurrency and blockchain development evolves. For an author, it can be downright exhausting. The rhythms of the community attached to this technology run on a cycle multiple times faster than those of the book publishing industry. It creates special challenges for those who write for the latter and leaves them dependent on a team of supporters who understand those challenges, are flexible with the constant demands for last-minute updates, and can put up with you when it all gets a bit stressful. In our case, the task was further complicated by the fact that each of us was engaged in a separate, unconnected book project while this one was under contract. So, in that spirit, we want to thank the many people who've helped us pull this project together. They are, as always, too numerous to name in full.

Among those who must be mentioned, we'll first cite our agent, Gillian MacKenzie, who has continued to believe in us and has been a tireless supporter of our work. Gillian is a reliable source of good advice on all matters of life as an author. We count her as a vital business partner and friend.

Our editor at St. Martin's Press, Tim Bartlett, is truly one of the best in his business. Once again, he proved to be a tough, exacting editor, constantly pushing us to clarify our sometimes-hard-to-explain ideas. The book is immeasurably better for his tough love. He was also supremely generous in allowing for a flexible production time frame as the circumstances of both the story and our work schedule changed over time. Helping Tim was a big crew at St. Martin's. They pulled this together within the tight time frame that our erratic work habits demanded. Among those deserving particular thanks are Tim's assistant, Alice Pfeifer, who has been tremendously helpful in guiding us as we prepared the manuscript for production; Managing Editor Alan Bradshaw, who kept us on schedule; copy editor Jennifer Simington for her meticulous work; Associate Publisher Laura Clark, who has championed both of our books with SMP; and last but certainly not least, the one-two punch of publicist Katie Bassel and marketer Jason Prince.

Michael

My colleagues at MIT are a constant source of inspiration. They shaped much of the thinking behind this book, probably without knowing it. Special thanks go to Media Lab Director Joi Ito, Digital Currency Initiative Director Neha Narula, and my Sloan School co-lecturer Simon Johnson, as well as to Robleh Ali, Mark Weber, Tadge Dryja, Chelsea Barabas, Prema Shrikrishna, Alin Dragos, James Lovejoy, Sandy Pentland, Dazza Greenwood, Harvey Michaels, David Birnbach, and Christian Catalini. Also, a special shout-out to Brian Forde, the first director of the DCI, who is now aiming to bring blockchain technology into Congress and who convinced me to give up journalism for a life of academic research. Meanwhile, at CoinDesk, I'd like to thank Kevin Worth, Marc Hochstein, Pete Rizzo, and the rest of the team for giving me a new platform upon which to express my point of view. It has been fun getting my teeth back into journalism, albeit as a side-gig.

Others who deserve gratitude for their insights, support, and friendship include: Rik Willard, Nii Nortei Lokko, Lance Koonce, Patrick Murck, Juan Llanos, Mariana Dahan, Maja Vujinovic, Kyle Burgess, Joe Colangelo, Yorke Rhodes, Balaji Srinivasan, Joel Telpner, and Don Tapscott. And a special thanks to the camaraderie and encouragement of my Blockchain Summit family, including but by no means limited to: Valery Vavilov, George Kikvadze, Bill Tai, Jamie Smith, Tomicah Tilleman, Dante Disparte, Vinny Lingham, Hernando de Soto, Gabriel Abed, Imogen Heap, Erick Miller, Heidi Pease, Laura Shin, Jim Newsome, Roya Mahboob, Eva Kaili, Suna Said, Beth Moses, Joby Weeks, Jen Morris, and many more.

Last but not least, my nearest and dearest, without whom none of this is ever possible. Zoe, Lia, and, of course, Alicia, the love of my life, thank you for sticking by me and encouraging me to do what interests me.

Paul

As always, my colleagues at *The Wall Street Journal* have been encouraging and generous in their support. I am indebted to Stephen Grocer and Erik Holm, Aaron Lucchetti and David Reilly, Neal Lipschutz, Karen Pensiero, and our editor-in-chief, Gerard Baker.

My family remains my inspiration and motivation, and without their support and encouragement, I wouldn't be able to do this. So, thank you, Elizabeth, and thank you, Robert. I love you both.

Notes

INTRODUCTION

2   *"It was an ordeal . . . ":* Interview conducted by World Food Program staff. Email to Michael J. Casey, August 7, 2017.

5   *According to WFP spokesman:* Phone interview with Michael J. Casey, July 20, 2017.

7   *Why do we even need this particular company:* Kashmir Hill, " 'God View': Uber Allegedly Stalked Users for Party-Goers' Viewing Pleasure," *Forbes,* October 3, 2014, https://www.forbes.com/sites/kashmirhill/2014/10/03/god -view-uber-allegedly-stalked-users-for-party-goers-viewing-pleasure /#2aa731af3141.

9   *the promise of "Internet 3.0,":* For an explanation of Internet 3.0 architecture, see: Jeff Hussey, "Internet 3.0: Welcome to the Future of Secure Networking," *Tempered Networks,* https://www.temperednetworks.com/resources/blog /internet-3.0-welcome-to-the-future-of-secure-networking.

10   *R3 CEV, a New York–based technology developer:* Jonathan Shieber, "Blockchain Consortium R3 Raises $107 Million," *TechCrunch,* May 23, 2017, https://techcrunch.com/2017/05/23/blockchain-consortium-r3-raises-107 -million/.

10   *It went from a turnout of 600:* Figures provided to Michael Casey by CoinDesk, e-mail received August 22, 2017.

12   *Such results give credence to crypto-asset analysts:* Chris Burniske and Jack Tatar, *Cryptoassets: The Innovative Investor's Guide to Bitcoin and Beyond* (McGraw Hill, 2017).

13   *Blockchains point the entire digital economy:* The term "Internet of Value"

has been popularized by the team at Ripple Labs, which manages the Ripple protocol for peer-to-peer payments and transactions. An early reference appears in: Stefan Thomas, "The Internet's Missing Link," *TechCrunch*, September 27, 2014, https://techcrunch.com/2014/09/27 /the-internets-missing-link/.

CHAPTER ONE

18   *most of the kings had their own rules set out as well:* Douglas Garbutt, "The Significance of Ancient Mesopotamia in Accounting History," *Accounting Information* 11, no. 1 (1984), http://www.accountingin.com/accounting -historians-journal/volume-11-number-1/the-significance-of-ancient -mesopotamia-in-accounting-history/.

21   *The firm, founded 167 years earlier:* Lehman Brothers Holdings, Inc., "Annual Report Pursuant to Section 13 or 15(d) of the Securities Exchange Act of 1934 for the Fiscal Year Ended November 30, 2007," United States Securities and Exchange Commission, https://www.sec .gov/Archives/edgar/data/806085/000110465908005476/a08-3530_110k .htm.

22   *This is clear in Pew Research's:* Pew Research Center, "Public Trust in Government: 1958–2017," May 3, 2017, http://www.people-press.org/2017/05 /03/public-trust-in-government-1958-2017/.

22   *A separate survey by Gallup:* Gallup, "Confidence in Institutions," http:// www.gallup.com/poll/1597/confidence-institutions.aspx.

24   *Lehman's accountants would move billions:* For a straightforward explanation of how Lehman Brothers used the "repo 105" facility, see: Jacob Goldstein, "Repo 105: Lehman's 'Accounting Gimmick' Explained," *NPR Planet Money*, March 12, 2010, http://www.npr.org/sections/money /2010/03/repo_105_lehmans_accounting_gi.html.

25   *Double-entry accounting was popularized in Europe:* Mary Poovey, *A History of the Modern Fact* (University of Chicago Press, 1998).

25   *It was only during the twelfth century and the Crusades:* Ibid.

25–26   *In the thirteenth century, an Italian merchant named Fibonacci:* L. E. Sigler, *Fibonacci's Liber Abaci: A Translation into Modern English of Leonardo Pisano's Book of Calculation* (Springer, 2003).

26   *Pacioli's* Summa de arthmetica, geometria, proportioni et proportionalita: Jeremy Cripps, *Particularis de Computis et Scripturis: A Contemporary Interpretation* (Pacioli Society, 1994).

26   *"Without double entry, businessmen would not . . .":* ibid., p. 2.

27   *During the Middle Ages, writes author James Aho:* James Aho, *Confession and Bookkeeping: The Religious, Moral, and Rhetorical Roots of Modern Accounting* (State University of New York Press, 2006).

27   *Aho writes:* Ibid.

27   *"Businessmen should begin their business records . . .":* Quoted in Jeremy Cripps, *Particularis de Computis et Scripturis: A Contemporary Interpretation* (Pacioli Society, 1994).

28–29   *In a comprehensive dissection in 2014:* Matt Levine, "Bank of America Made $168 Million Last Quarter, More or Less," *Bloomberg View*, October 15, 2014, https://www.bloomberg.com/view/articles/2014-10-15/bank-of-america-made-168-million-last-quarter-more-or-less.

29   *On October 31, 2008, while the world:* Satoshi Nakamoto, "Bitcoin: A Pear-to-Pear Electronic Cash System," https://bitcoin.org/bitcoin.pdf.

30   *In 2005, a computer expert named Ian Grigg:* Ian Grigg, "Triple Entry Accounting," 2005, http://iang.org/papers/triple_entry.html.

31   *Szabo's system—he called it the "God Protocol":* Nick Szabo, "The God Protocols," http://www.fon.hum.uva.nl/rob/Courses/InformationInSpeech/CDROM/Literature/LOTwinterschool2006/szabo.best.vwh.net/msc.html.

33   *For society to function, we need a "consensus on facts":* Tomicah Tilleman's comments made during the 2017 Blockchain Summit at Necker Island, British Virgin Islands, July 27.

34   *If we think about this as the Israeli historian:* Yuval Noah Harari, *Sapiens: A Brief History of Humankind* (Harper, 2015).

CHAPTER TWO

37   *It happened that this was exactly:* Full account of the incident included in Sims's blog post: Peter Sims, "Can We Trust Uber?" *Silicon Guild*, September 6, 2014, https://thoughts.siliconguild.com/can-we-trust-uber-c0e793deda36.

37   *In November 2014, Uber launched an investigation:* Johana Bhuiyan and Charlie Warzel, "'God View': Uber Investigates Its Top New York Executive for Privacy Violations," *BuzzFeed*, November 18, 2014, https://www.buzzfeed.com/johanabhuiyan/uber-is-investigating-its-top-new-york-executive-for-privacy.

38   *a settlement with New York Attorney General Eric Schneiderman:* Kaja Whitehouse, "Uber Settles 'God View' Allegations," *USA Today*, January 6, 2016, http://www.usatoday.com/story/tech/2016/01/06/uber-settles-god-view-allegations/78383276/.

39   *It's why during the 2016 U.S. presidential campaign:* Craig Silverman and Law-rence Alexander, "How Teens in the Balkans Are Duping Trump Supporters with Fake News," *BuzzFeed*, November 3, 2016, https://www.buzzfeed.com /craigsilverman/how-macedonia-became-a-global-hub-for-pro-trump-misinfo.

39   *Others have said this, of course:* See, for example, Bruce Schneer's remarks, cited in Barton Gellman, "Facebook: You're Not the Customer, You're the Product," October 15, 2010, *TIME*, http://techland.time.com/2010/10/15 /facebook-youre-not-the-customer-youre-the-product/, or *The Economist*'s take in "The World's Most Valuable Resource Is No Longer Oil, but Data," *Economist*, May 6, 2017, https://www.economist.com/news/leaders/21721656 -data-economy-demands-new-approach-antitrust-rules-worlds-most -valuable-resource.

39   *In the wake of the 2016 legal battle:* For a useful analysis of this dispute, see: Arash Khamooshi, "Breaking Down Apple's iPhone Fight with the U.S. Gov-ernment," *The New York Times*, March 21, 2016, https://www.nytimes.com /interactive/2016/03/03/technology/apple-iphone-fbi-fight-explained.html.

40   *Even though the world spent:* "Gartner Says Worldwide Information Security Spending Will Grow Almost 4.7 Percent to Reach $75.4 Billion in 2015," *Gart-ner*, September 23, 2015, http://www.gartner.com/newsroom/id/3135617.

40   *were running at $400 billion:* Stephen Gandel, "Lloyd's CEO: Cyber Attacks Cost Companies $400 Billion Every Year," *Fortune*, January 23, 2015, http:// fortune.com/2015/01/23/cyber-attack-insurance-lloyds/.

40   *That's the estimated fraud loss Juniper Research:* Juniper Research, "Cyber-crime Will Cost Businesses over $2 Trillion by 2019," *Juniper*, May 12, 2015, https://www.juniperresearch.com/press/press-releases/cybercrime-cost -businesses-over-2trillion.

40   *To put that figure in perspective:* Based on World Bank Estimates taken from: "Global Economic Prospects: A Fragile Recovery," World Bank Group, June 2017, https://www.worldbank.org/content/dam/Worldbank/GEP/GEP 2015a/pdfs/GEP15a_web_full.pdf.

41   *The risks contained in these contradictory trends:* For a good explanation of the Dyn attack, see: Peter Tran, "The Dyn Attack—How IoT Can Take Down the "Global Information Grid" Back Bone (Part I)," RSA, October 25, 2016, https://www.rsa.com/en-us/blog/2016-10/the-dyn-attack-how-iot-can-take -down-the-global-information-grid-back-bone-part-i.

41   *IBM estimated that human beings:* Ralph Jacobsen, "2.5 Quintillion Bytes of Data Created Every Day. How Does CPG & Retail Manage It?" IBM, April 14, 2013, https://www.ibm.com/blogs/insights-on-business/consumer-products /2-5-quintillion-bytes-of-data-created-every-day-how-does-cpg-retail -manage-it/.

42   *Online identity theft has been linked:* "Identity Theft: The Aftermath 2013," Identity Theft Resource Center, http://www.idtheftcenter.org/images/surveys _studies/Aftermath2013.pdf.

42   *speculation that the mysterious disappearance of Malaysian Airlines flight MH370:* Sometime after that attack, various reports emerged of the Asia-Pacific-based hacking group Naikon hacking into Malaysian government servers. See: Elsie Viebeck, "Cyberattacks Followed Malaysia Airlines Flight Disappearance," *The Hill,* April 21, 2015, http://thehill.com/policy/cybersecurity /239529-cyberattacks-followed-malaysia-airlines-flight-disappearance.

43   *data on 18 million people was compromised:* Brendan I. Koerner, "Inside the Cyberattack That Shocked the US Government," *Wired,* October 23, 2016, https://www.wired.com/2016/10/inside-cyberattack-shocked-us-government/.

44   *On stage at the time, Adam Ludwin:* Ludwin was speaking at the DTCC's "Blockchain Symposium" on March 29, 2016.

46   *Let's compare our current:* See two paired articles by John Crossman: "The 'Shared Secret' Identity Model Is Finished," *Medium,* February 24, 2016, https://medium.com/@john_17722/the-shared-secret-identity-model-is -finished-59bd30e1da6a, and "The Device Identity Model," *Medium,* February 26, 2016, https://medium.com/@john_17722/the-device-identity-model -6444ca6328f9.

47   *A 2016 cyber-attack on insurer Anthem Health:* Anna Wilde Mathews, "Anthem: Hacked Database Included 78.8 Million People," *The Wall Street Journal,* February 24, 2015, https://www.wsj.com/articles/anthem-hacked -database-included-78-8-million-people-1424807364.

47   *the so-called WannaCry ransom attacks:* Ian Scherr, "WannaCry Ransomware: Everything You Need to Know," *CNET,* May 19, 2017, https://www.cnet.com /news/wannacry-wannacrypt-uiwix-ransomware-everything-you-need-to -know/.

47   *That's why initiatives like MedRec:* Ariel Ekblaw and Asaf Azaria, "MedRec: Medical Data Management on the Blockchain," *PubPub,* September 19, 2016, https://www.pubpub.org/pub/medrec.

48   New York Times *columnist Thomas Friedman:* Thomas Friedman, *The World Is Flat: A Brief History of the Twenty-First Century* (Farrar, Straus and Giroux, 2005)

49   *In* The Age of Cryptocurrency, *we reported:* Paul Vigna and Michael J. Casey, *The Age of Cryptocurrency* (St. Martin's Press, 2015), pp. 57–60.

51   *This was not the dream conveyed:* Timothy C. May, "The Crypto Anarchist Manifesto," https://www.activism.net/cypherpunk/crypto-anarchy.html.

51   *Ideas like Ted Nelson's ill-fated Xanadu project:* For a detailed analysis of the Xanadu Project's sweeping vision but failed implementation, see: "The Curse of Xanadu," *Wired,* June 1, 2015, https://www.wired.com/1995/06/xanadu/.

52   *These people included Marc Andreessen:* Don Tapscott and Alex Tapscott,
      Blockchain Revolution: How the Technology behind Bitcoin Is Changing Money,
      Business and the World (Portfolio, 2016), p. 5.

54   *used by Harvard professor Lawrence Lessig:* Lawrence Lessig, "Code Is Law:
      On Liberty in Cyberspace," *Harvard Magazine,* January 1, 2000, http://
      harvardmagazine.com/2000/01/code-is-law-html.

55   *from what Carl Jung called:* C. G. Jung, *The Structure and Dynamics of the*
      Psyche (Collected Works of C. G. Jung, Vol. 8) (Princeton University Press,
      1970, 2nd edition), p. 325.

56   *grave warnings about flaws in the code:* See: Emin Gun Sirer, "Caution: The
      DAO Can Turn Into a Naturally-Arising Ponzi," *Hacking, Distributed,*
      June 13, 2016, http://hackingdistributed.com/2016/06/13/the-dao-can-turn
      -into-a-naturally-arising-ponzi/, and Drew Hinkes, "A Legal Analysis of the
      DAO Exploit and Possible Investor Rights," *Bitcoin Magazine,* June 21, 2016,
      https://bitcoinmagazine.com/articles/a-legal-analysis-of-the-dao-exploit
      -and-possible-investor-rights-1466524659/.

56   *In the pitch documents explaining the terms of the deal:* The online documents
      have since been deleted, but are summarized on an Ethereum reddit post:
      https://www.reddit.com/r/ethereum/comments/4oo0ql/the_dao_terms
      _and_conditions/, accessed September 8, 2017.

57   *"I'm not even sure that this qualifies as a hack":* Emin Gun Sirer, "Thoughts on
      The DAO Hack," *Hacking, Distributed,* June 17, 2016, http://hackingdistributed
      .com/2016/06/17/thoughts-on-the-dao-hack/.

57   *As many lawyers argued:* Preston Byrne, "#THEDAO: Broken, but Worth Fix-
      ing," May 17, 2016, https://prestonbyrne.com/2016/05/17/thedao-dont-walk
      -away-restructure/.

58   *Conducting an investigation into the affair:* "SEC Issues Investigative Report
      Concluding DAO Tokens, a Digital Asset, Were Securities," U.S. Securities
      and Exchange Commission, July 25, 2017, https://www.sec.gov/news/press
      -release/2017-131.

CHAPTER THREE

64   For more technically minded people looking for greater detail on how Bitcoin
      works, we recommend: Andreas M. Antonopoulos, *Mastering Bitcoin: Un-*
      locking Digital Cryptocurrencies (O'Reilly Media, 2014).

72   *Visa, whose network handles about 65,000 transactions per second:* "Visa Inc.
      Overview," Visa, April 2017, https://usa.visa.com/dam/VCOM/download
      /corporate/media/visanet-technology/visa-net-fact-sheet.pdf.

73   *By June 2017, the average fee on the Bitcoin network:* Paul Vigna, "Why You
        Won't Be Buying a Coffee with Bitcoin Anytime Soon," *The Wall Street Jour-
        nal*, July 2, 2017, https://www.wsj.com/articles/why-you-wont-be-buying-a
        -coffee-with-bitcoin-anytime-soon-1498996800#.

73   *"I've become a trusted third party":* Interview with Michael J. Casey, New
        York, September 27, 2016.

74   *Then, out of the creative mind of Bitcoin developer Pieter Wuille:* The Segre-
        gated Witness proposals and source code can be found at https://github.com
        /bitcoin/bips/blob/master/bip-0141.mediawiki.

75   *It allows people to jointly sign:* Joseph Poon and Thaddeus Dryja, "The Bitcoin
        Lightning Network: Scalable Off-Chain Instant Payments," January 14,
        2016, https://lightning.network/lightning-network-paper.pdf.

76   *after lining up with early Bitcoin investor and prominent libertarian Roger Ver:*
        Laura Shin, "Is This Massive Power Struggle About to Blow Up Bitcoin?"
        Forbes, March 21, 2017, https://www.forbes.com/sites/laurashin/2017/03/21/is
        -this-massive-power-struggle-about-to-blow-up-bitcoin/#9872e4873250.

76   *Barry Silbert came up with the SegWit2x compromise:* "Bitcoin Scaling Agree-
        ment at Consensus 2017," Digital Currency Group, *Medium*, May 23, 2017,
        https://medium.com/@DCGco/bitcoin-scaling-agreement-at-consensus
        -2017-133521fe9a77.

80   *When Buterin released his white paper in December 2013:* Vitalik Buterin,
        "Ethereum White Paper: A Next Generation Smart Contract & Decentralized
        Application Platform," http://www.the-blockchain.com/docs/Ethereum_white
        _paper-a_next_generation_smart_contract_and_decentralized_application
        _platform-vitalik-buterin.pdf.

80   *"You're just as likely to find a web developer . . .":* "An Ode to the Ethereum
        Community," *Steemit*, October 2016, https://steemit.com/ethereum/@owaisted
        /an-ode-to-the-ethereum-community.

81   *After launching Ethereum at the North American Bitcoin Conference:* Inter-
        view with Michael J. Casey, Miami, January 26, 2014.

83   *For example: the Parity Wallet:* Wolfie Zhao, "$30 Million: Ether Reported
        Stolen Due to Parity Wallet Breach," *CoinDesk*, July 19, 2017, https://www
        .coindesk.com/30-million-ether-reported-stolen-parity-wallet-breach/

84   *In what was then one of the biggest crowd sales of its kind:* "The History of Ethe-
        reum," http://www.ethdocs.org/en/latest/introduction/history-of-ethereum
        .html#the-ethereum-foundation-and-the-ether-presale.

86   *Plasma, personally created by Buterin:* Joseph Poon and Vitalik Buterin,
        "Plasma: Scalable Autonomous Smart Contracts," August 11, 2017, http://
        plasma.io/plasma.pdf.

87   *As Zooko Wilcox-O'Hearn, founder of a new cryptocurrency called Zcash:* Presentation recorded by "Triangle Bitcoin & Business Meetup," April 4, 2017, available on YouTube at https://www.youtube.com/watch?v=OZu4u_5L0l8.

87   *When the FBI auctioned the 144,000 bitcoins:* Commentators on one forum speculated that the premium related to "clean coins" was about 3.5 percent. See the thread for "US Marshalls to Auction off 29,656 Bitcoins" at https://texags.com/forums/16/topics/2488176.

88   *In February 2017, seven of the world's biggest banks:* Robert Hackett, "Big Business Giants from Microsoft to J.P. Morgan Are Getting behind Ethereum," *Fortune,* February 27, 2017, http://fortune.com/2017/02/28/ethereum-jpmorgan-microsoft-alliance/.

88   *Over the course of twelve days in July, they raised $232 million and $185 million:* James Mosher, "Initial Coin Offerings Going Way beyond Small Change," American Institute for Economic Research, July 26, 2017, https://www.aier.org/research/initial-coin-offerings-going-way-beyond-small-change.

89   *With easier computation demands:* See Vincent Everts's interview with Ian Grigg, "Millions of Transactions Per Second on EOS.IO Blockchain | Interview Ian Grigg of Block.One," available on YouTube at https://www.youtube.com/watch?v=UC6RYwYPnpU.

89   *their own governance model:* Tezos CEO Kathleen Breitman and CTO Arthur Breitman interviewed by Michael J. Casey, June 29, 2017.

CHAPTER FOUR

91   Various passages in this chapter were taken from a report written by Michael J. Casey for the Blockchain Research Institute (BRI). That article, entitled "The Token Economy: When Money Becomes Programmable," was distributed to BRI members on September 29, 2017, and was due to be made available publicly in the early spring of 2018. The passages included here were done so with the explicit permission of the BRI.

91   *On May 31, 2017, at 2:34 p.m. GMT, Brave Software Inc.:* Jon Russell, "Former Mozilla CEO Raises $35M in under 30 Seconds for His Browser Startup Brave," *TechCrunch,* June 1, 2017, https://techcrunch.com/2017/06/01/brave-ico-35-million-30-seconds-brendan-eich/.

91   *almost $1.5 billion flowed into this new investment class:* According to CoinDesk's ICO Tracker service: https://www.coindesk.com/ico-tracker/.

92   *By one estimate, $23 a month:* Rob Leathern, "Carriers Are Making More from Mobile Ads Than Publishers Are," *Medium,* October 4, 2015, https://medium.com/@robleathern/carriersare-making-more-from-mobile-ads-than-publishers-are-d5d3c0827b39.

92   *resulting in $7.2 billion in losses for the industry in 2016:* Margaret Bo-
        land, "Cyber Criminals Are Stealing Billions from the Ad Industry
        Each Year," *Business Insider*, May 28, 2016, http://www.businessinsider
        .com/the-ad-fraud-report-bot-traffic-2016-3.

92   *Perhaps inevitably, consumers are turning to ad-blocking software:* "Basic
        Asset Token (BAT): Blockchain Based Digital Advertising," May 29,
        2017, p. 9, https://basicattentiontoken.org/BasicAttentionTokenWhite
        Paper-4.pdf.

93   *The idea is to create price signals:* ibid.

93   *The Tragedy of the Commons concept stems from a 1968 essay:* Garrett
        Hardin, "The Tragedy of the Commons," *Science*, December 13, 1968,
        162 (3859): pp. 1243–1248.

94   *The Economist described as a twenty-first century resource:* "The World's
        Most Valuable Resource Is No Longer Oil, But Data," *The Economist*, May 6,
        2017, https://www.economist.com/news/leaders/21721656-data-economy
        -demands-new-approach-antitrust-rules-worlds-most-valuable-resource.

96   *Fans of the* Freakonomics *book series:* Steven D. Levitt and Stephen J.
        Dubner, *Freakonomics: A Rogue Economist Explores the Hidden Side of
        Everything* (William Morrow, 2005).

96   *Currently, Gamecredits says fraudulent sales:* Per the company website
        home page: https://gamecredits.com/, accessed September 8, 2017.

97   *"Early on we saw this as something that would . . .":* Phone interview with
        Michael J. Casey, June 29, 2017.

98   *Some argue that the pre-set fund-raising cap:* Critics included Ethereum
        founder Vitalik Buterin, per Twitter: https://twitter.com/VitalikButerin
        /status/869972830191984641.

98   *But others say Brave, which decided to limit how much:* For example:
        Dustin Byington, "Why We Need a Cap on Every ICO—Looking at You
        Tezos," *Medium*, May 7, 2017, https://medium.com/@dustin_byington
        /why-we-need-a-cap-on-every-ico-looking-at-you-tezos-90d412f34b88.

98   *As for Eich, he complained to CoinDesk:* Michael del Castillo, "Why
        Brave's $35 Million ICO May Not Be Enough for a High-Tech Hiring
        Spree," *CoinDesk*, July 12, 2017, https://www.coindesk.com/braves-35
        -million-ico-may-not-enough-high-tech-hiring-spree/.

99   *at one stage nearly burning through all its:* Pete Rizzo, "Ethereum: Bit-
        coin Price Decline Created $9 Million Funding Shortfall," *CoinDesk*,
        September 28, 2015, https://www.coindesk.com/ethereum-bitcoin-decline
        -9-million-funding-shortfall/.

102–03 *When Stephan Tual, the founder of Slock.it:* Paul Vigna, "Chiefless
        Company Rakes in More Than $100 Million," *The Wall Street Journal*,

May 16, 2016, https://www.wsj.com/articles/chiefless-company-rakes-in
-more-than-100-million-1463399393.

103   *in November 2016, when a site called Golem:* Roger Aitken, "Fintech Golem's
'Airbnb' For Computing Crowdsale Scores $8.6M in Minutes," *Forbes,*
November 12, 2016, https://www.forbes.com/sites/rogeraitken/2016/11/12
/fintech-golems-airbnb-for-computing-crowdsale-scores-8-6m-in-minutes
/#324579c73583.

104   *An initial high-water mark came:* Alyssa Hertig, "ICO Insanity? $300 Million
Gnosis Valuation Sparks Market Reaction," *CoinDesk,* April 25, 2017, https://
www.coindesk.com/ethereum-ico-irrationality-300-million-gnosis
-valuation-sparks-market-concerns/.

105   *Santori later told us that he:* Phone interview with Paul Vigna, June 29, 2017.

105   *CoinDesk's new Cointracker service:* https://www.coindesk.com/ico-tracker/.

105   *"Most of these will fail," said Olaf Carlson-Wee:* Paul Vigna, "How a Bitcoin Clone
Helped a Company Raise $12 Million in 12 Minutes," *The Wall Street Jour-
nal,* May 17, 2017, https://www.wsj.com/articles/how-a-bitcoin-clone-helped-a
-company-raise-12-million-in-12-minutes-1495018802?tesla=y&mod=e2tw.

106   *In fact, says Cornell cryptographer and cryptocurrency expert:* Phone interview
with Michael J. Casey, June 22, 2017.

107   *Big-name firms such as Andreessen Horowitz, Sequoia Capital:* Laura Shin,
"Crypto Boom: 15 New Hedge Funds Want In on 84,000% Returns," *Forbes,*
July 12, 2017, https://www.forbes.com/sites/laurashin/2017/07/12/crypto
-boom-15-new-hedge-funds-want-in-on-84000-returns/#40c3d1aa416a.

107   *When it became known that Draper:* Stan Higgins, Alex Sunnarborg, and Pete
Rizzo, "$150 Million: Tim Draper-Backed Bancor Completes Largest-Ever
ICO," *CoinDesk,* June 12, 2017, https://www.coindesk.com/150-million-tim
-draper-backed-bancor-completes-largest-ever-ico/.

108   *"In December, I had a dream . . .":* Paul Vigna, "Forget an IPO, Coin Offerings
Are New Road to Startup Riches," *The Wall Street Journal,* July 7, 2017, https://
www.wsj.com/articles/forget-an-ipo-coin-offerings-are-new-road-to
-startup-riches-1499425200.

108   *It put extra attention on some troubling:* Arthur Breitman, "The Path Forward: A Letter from Arthur & Kathleen Breitman to the Tezos Community,"
Medium, October 18, 2017, https://medium.com/@arthurb/the-path-forward
-eb2e6f63be67.

108   *That spat attracted a lot of press coverage:* Anna Irrera, Steve Stecklow, and
Brenna Hughes Neghaiwi, "Special Report: Backroom Battle Imperils $230
Million Cryptocurrency Venture," *Reuters,* October 18, 2017, https://www
.reuters.com/article/us-bitcoin-funding-tezos-specialreport/special-report
-backroom-battle-imperils-230-million-cryptocurrency-venture-idUS

KBN1CN35K; Paul Vigna, "Tezos Raised $232 Million in a Hot Coin Offering, Then a Fight Broke Out," *The Wall Street Journal,* October 19, 2017, https://www.wsj.com/articles/tezos-raised-232-million-in-a-hot-coin-offering-then-a-fight-broke-out-1508354704; Jeff John Roberts, "Tezos Rebuffs Rumors of SEC Probe Into $232 Million Crypto ICO," *Fortune,* October 28, 2017, http://fortune.com/2017/10/28/tezos-sec/; Chloe Cornish, "Acrimony over $232m ICO Set to Intensify Regulatory Scrutiny," *Financial Times,* October 26, 2017, https://www.ft.com/content/fcb16026-b45a-11e7-aa26-bb002965bce8.

108   *Consider what online meal-kit maker Blue Apron:* ibid.

109   *In September 2017, the market got a taste:* Stan Higgins, "China's Crypto Exchanges Yank Token Listings amid ICO Ban Fallout," *CoinDesk,* September 6, 2017, https://www.coindesk.com/chinas-exchanges-yank-token-listings-ico-crackdown/.

109   *As for the SEC, in its no-action opinion:* "SEC Issues Investigative Report Concluding DAO Tokens, a Digital Asset, Were Securities," U.S. Securities and Exchange Commission, July 25, 2017, https://www.sec.gov/news/press-release/2017-131.

111   *"The issuers then use the funds they raise . . .":* Phone interview with Michael J. Casey, June 26, 2017.

111   *In its first-ever application, a SAFT offering:* Stan Higgins, "$200 Million in 60 Minutes: Filecoin ICO Rockets to Record Amid Tech Issues," *CoinDesk,* August 10, 2017, https://www.coindesk.com/200-million-60-minutes-filecoin-ico-rockets-record-amid-tech-issues/.

113   *Union Square Ventures partner Fred Wilson compellingly explained:* Fred Wilson, "The Golden Age of Open Protcols," *AVC,* July 21, 2016, http://avc.com/2016/07/the-golden-age-of-open-protocols/.

115   *He raised $5 million, partially with tokens:* Interview with Michael J. Casey, March 23, 2017.

116   *Ripple Labs' Interledger project:* https://interledger.org/.

116   *Tendermint has unveiled an interoperability protocol called Cosmos:* See the white paper at: Jae Kwon and Ethan Buchman, "Cosmos: A Network of Distributed Ledgers," https://github.com/cosmos/cosmos/blob/master/WHITEPAPER.md.

117   *Because, says Peter Reuschel, whose Berlin-based Leondrino:* Interview with Michael J. Casey in Heidelberg, Germany, June 19, 2016.

117   *Well, a startup called TokenStars says:* https://tokenstars.com/.

118   *In a* Wired *article about where this idea could go:* Cade Metz, "Forget Bitcoin. The Blockchain Could Reveal What's True Today and Tomorrow," *Wired,* March 22, 2017, https://www.wired.com/2017/03/forget-bitcoin-blockchain-reveal-whats-true-today-tomorrow/.

118 *Out of this concept, Miller and a team:* Draft, pre-publication white paper shared with Michael J. Casey, August 8, 2017.

CHAPTER FIVE

123 *World Economic Forum founder Klaus Schwab says:* Klaus Schwab, *The Fourth Industrial Revolution* (Crown, 2017).

124 *Security expert Bruce Schneier laid it all bare:* Bruce Schneier, "The Internet of Things Will Turn Large-Scale Hacks into Real World Disasters," *Motherboard*, July 25, 2016, https://motherboard.vice.com/en_us/article/qkjzwp/the-internet-of-things-will-cause-the-first-ever-large-scale-internet-disaster.

125 *In a widely read paper titled "Device Democracy . . .":* Veena Pureswaran and Paul Brody, "Device Democracy: Saving the Future of the Internet of Things," September 2014, http://www-01.ibm.com/common/ssi/cgi-bin/ssialias?htmlfid=GBE03620USEN.

128 *Demonstrating the extent of this challenge, researchers at the University of Michigan:* Andy Greenberg, "This 'Demonically Clever' Backdoor Hides in a Tiny Slice of a Computer Chip," *Wired*, June 1, 2016, https://www.wired.com/2016/06/demonically-clever-backdoor-hides-inside-computer-chip/.

128 *This system is not without controversy among privacy advocates:* For a balanced look at the pros and cons of trusted computing, see: "Trusted Computing: Promise and Risk," Electronic Frontier Foundation, October 1, 2003. https://www.eff.org/wp/trusted-computing-promise-and-risk.

129 *The chip-making giant has developed a blockchain technology:* See background information at: "Hyperledger Sawtooth documentation," https://intelledger.github.io/.

132 *After the MIT group reported on its findings:* Daniel Palmer, "Broken Hash Crash? IOTA's Price Keeps Dropping on Tech Critique," *CoinDesk*, September 8, 2017, https://www.coindesk.com/broken-hash-function-iota-price-drops-on-tech-critique/.

132 *Investors in IOTA—clearly unhappy:* See an example of the comments at this thread in the IOTA subreddit: https://www.reddit.com/r/Iota/comments/6z87sw/all_of_this_fud_is_a_good_sign/?st=j8ks3khu&sh=8be3c663.

132 *attacking the integrity of a* Forbes *journalist:* Limo, "Competitors and Amy Castor: A Tale on Reputation Usage and a Campaign to Discredit IOTA," *The Tangler*, September 13, 2017, http://www.tangleblog.com/2017/09/13/competitors-amy-castor-tale-reputation-usage-discredit-campaign/.

132 *Co-founder Sergey Ivancheglo took to an IOTA-linked blog:* Misty Wind, "IOTA Cofounder Sergey Ivancheglo aka Come-from-Beyond's Responses to the Ongoing FUD about So Called 'Vulnerabilities' in IOTA Code Which Never

Really Existed," *Medium*, September 10, 2017, https://medium.com/@misty-wind/iota-cofounder-sergey-ivancheglo-aka-come-from-beyonds-responses-to-the-ongoing-fud-about-so-ea3afd51a79b.

133   *the Trusted IoT Alliance:* See https://www.trustediot.org/.

133   *Department of Homeland Security awarding:* Jamie Redman, "Dept of Homeland Security Awards $200K to Factom for ID System," *Bitcoin*, June 18, 2016, https://news.bitcoin.com/dhs-awards-200k-factom/.

134   *In October 2015, at the UN's "COP 21" conference:* G. Ananthakrishnan, "Modi Asks Rich Nations to Cut Emissions, Share Carbon Space with Poor," *The Hindu*, December 1, 2015, http://www.thehindu.com/sci-tech/energy-and-environment/cop21-paris-climate-conference-narendra-modi-cautions-against-unilateral-steps-in-combating-climate-change/article7933873.ece.

135   *a Chinese-Japanese consortium was in 2016:* Katie Fehrenbacher, "A Jaw-Dropping World Record Solar Price Was Just Bid in Abu Dhabi," *Fortune*, September 19, 2016, http://fortune.com/2016/09/19/world-record-solar-price-abu-dhabi/.

136   *Check out nighttime photos of Manhattan:* Jeff St. John, "How Microgrids Helped Weather Hurricane Sandy," *Greentech Media*, November 20, 2012, https://www.greentechmedia.com/articles/read/how-microgrids-helped-weather-hurricane-sandy.

138   *And in the summer of 2017, LO3 took the process a step further:* Draft version of the plan shared with Michael J. Casey.

139   *Grid Singularity, which has formed an alliance with the Rocky Mountain Institute:* "Energy Companies Join Forces with Rocky Mountain Institute and Grid Singularity to Launch Global Blockchain Initiative for Energy," March 8, 2017, Rocky Mountain Institute, https://www.rmi.org/about/news-and-press/press-release-energy-web-foundation-launch/.

141   *An E. coli outbreak at Chipotle Mexican Grill:* Katie Little, "One Year after Chipotle's E. coli crisis, Chain Still Struggling," CNBC.com, October 31, 2016, https://www.cnbc.com/2016/10/31/one-year-after-chipotles-e-coli-crisis-chain-still-struggling.html.

143   *Provenance, a UK-based startup:* www.provenance.org.

143   *Walmart is working with IBM and Tsinghua University:* Robert Hackett, "Walmart and IBM Are Partnering to Put Chinese Pork on a Blockchain," *Fortune*, October 19, 2016, http://fortune.com/2016/10/19/walmart-ibm-blockchain-china-pork/.

143   *Mining giant BHP Billiton is using the technology:* Pete Rizzo, "World's Largest Mining Company to Use Blockchain for Supply Chain," *CoinDesk*, September 23, 2016, https://www.coindesk.com/bhp-billiton-blockchain-mining-company-supply-chain/.

143   *The startup Everledger has uploaded:* Gian Volpicelli, "How the Blockchain Is Helping Stop the Spread of Conflict Diamonds," *Wired UK,* February 15, 2017, http://www.wired.co.uk/article/blockchain-conflict-diamonds-everledger.

144   *"How can the maintenance crew on a U.S. . . .":* Email to Michael J. Casey, March 2, 2017.

145   *The company announced that it has entered:* "Lockheed Martin Contracts Guardtime Federal for Innovative Cyber Technology," Lockheed Martin, April 27, 2017, http://news.lockheedmartin.com/2017-04-27-Lockheed -Martin-Contracts-Guardtime-Federal-for-Innovative-Cyber-Technology.

145   *Nashville-based startup Keyturn:* Meeting between co-CEOs David Bryan and Marc Howland with Michael J. Casey, March 22, 2017.

145   *McKinsey Global Institute says accounts for 13 percent of world GDP:* "Reinventing Construction: A Route to Higher Productivity," McKinsey Global Institute, February 2017, file:///Users/michaelcasey/Downloads/MGI-Reinventing -Construction-Executive-summary.pdf.

145   *Using a permissioned distributed ledger to track:* Kim S. Nash and Rachael King, "IBM Set to Launch One of the Largest Blockchain Implementations to Date," *The Wall Street Journal,* July 29, 2016, https://blogs.wsj.com/cio/2016/07 /29/ibm-set-to-launch-one-of-the-largest-blockchain-implementations-to -date/.

146   *Standard Chartered in Singapore has already developed:* "Standard Chartered Pilots Blockchain Trade Finance Tool," PYMNTS.com, April 3, 2017, http:// www.pymnts.com/news/b2b-payments/2017/standard-chartered-hong-kong -blockchain-distributed-ledger-trade-finance-banking-pilot-blockchain-hong -kong/.

146   *the company said that the prototype's use had generated $6.5 million:* Andrew Sawers, "Foxconn Uses Blockchain for New SCF Platform after $6.5m Pilot," SCF Briefing, March 17, 2017, http://www.scfbriefing.com/foxconn-launches -scf-blockchain-platform/.

147   *Blockchain-proven digital tokens point to what blockchain:* Michael J. Casey and Pindar Wong, "Global Supply Chains Are About to Get Better, Thanks to Blockchain," *Harvard Business Review,* March 13, 2017, https://hbr.org/2017 /03/global-supply-chains-are-about-to-get-better-thanks-to-blockchain.

149   *Belt and Road Blockchain Consortium:* https://www.beltandroadblockchain .org/.

149   *Some have described it as a Beijing-led Marshall Plan:* "China's One Belt, One Road: Will It Reshape Global Trade?" Podcast Transcript, July 2016, McKinsey.com, https://www.mckinsey.com/global-themes/china/chinas-one-belt -one-road-will-it-reshape-global-trade.

CHAPTER SIX

153   *As Nakamoto wrote in 2009:* Satoshi Nakamoto, "Bitcoin Open Source Implementation of P2P currency," P2P Foundation, February 11, 2009, http://p2pfoundation.ning.com/forum/topics/bitcoin-open-source.

155   *Bloomberg News estimated at $12.8 trillion:* Karen Weise, "Tallying the Full Cost of the Financial Crisis," *Bloomberg,* September 14, 2012, https://www.bloomberg.com/news/articles/2012-09-14/tallying-the-full-cost-of-the-financial-crisis.

155   *the DTCC says such "fails" run to more than $50 billion:* The DTCC keeps a tally rolling one-year record of its daily fails on its Web site: http://www.dtcc.com/charts/daily-total-us-treasury-trade-fails.

157   *an "I quit" blog post complaining about the bitter infighting:* Mike Hearn, "The Resolution of the Bitcoin Experiment," *Medium,* January 14, 2016, https://blog.plan99.net/the-resolution-of-the-bitcoin-experiment-dabb30201f7.

160   *The problem, as described in more detail:* Michael Lewis, *The Big Short: Inside the Doomsday Machine* (Norton, 2010).

161   *Warren Buffett, who in 2002 labeled derivatives "weapons of financial mass destruction":* Lawrence Lewitinn, "How Buffett Used 'Financial Weapons of Mass Destruction' to Make Billions of Dollars," Yahoo! Finance, https://finance.yahoo.com/news/how-buffett-used—financial-weapons-of-mass-destruction—to-make-billions-of-dollars-175922498.html.

161   *That thought "was like being hit on the head by an apple":* E-mailed remarks sent to Michael J. Casey, September 18, 2016.

162   *R3's Swanson has argued that the mere possibility of a 51 percent attack:* Tim Swanson, "Settlement Risks Involving Public Blockchains," Tabbforum.com, December 30, 2016, http://tabbforum.com/opinions/settlement-risks-involving-public-blockchains.

164   *Well, as of January 2017:* "Blockchain and Central Banks: A Tour de Table Part II," *Finextra,* January 9, 2017. https://www.finextra.com/blogposting/13532/blockchain-and-central-banks-a-tour-de-table-part-ii.

165   *That's vital, says Robleh Ali, a research scientist who joined MIT:* E-mailed remarks sent to Michael J. Casey, September 1, 2017.

166   *This is one reason why researchers at the BOE speculated:* John Barrdear and Michael Kumhoff, "Staff Working Paper No. 605: The Macroeconomics of Central Bank Issued Digital Currencies," Bank of England, July 2016, http://www.bankofengland.co.uk/research/Documents/workingpapers/2016/swp605.pdf.

168   *Describing the technology as "an operating system for marketplaces . . .":* http://hyperledger.org/about.

169   *As MIT Media Lab's Joi Ito:* Ito has frequently made the comparison, includ-
      ing during remarks to *MIT Technology Review*'s "Business of Blockchain"
      conference, April 18, 2017.
169   *"Signing off on the press release was the easy part . . . ":* Remarks at DTCC's
      offices, Jersey City, NJ, January 28, 2016.
170   *At that same January 2016 meeting:* "IBM Delivers Blockchain-as-a-Service
      for Developers; Commits to Making Blockchain Ready for Business," IBM,
      February 16, 2016, https://www-03.ibm.com/press/us/en/pressrelease/49029.wss.

CHAPTER SEVEN

175   *After a long multi-decade fight with the city:* Jorge Salomón, "El barrio Char-
      rúa, una pequeña Bolivia en el sur de Buenos Aires," *El País*, February 12,
      2016, http://www.elpaisonline.com/index.php/2013-01-15-14-16-26/sociedad
      /item/204708-el-barrio-charrua-una-pequena-bolivia-en-el-sur-de-buenos
      -aires.
177   *Hernando de Soto estimates that:* Hernando de Soto, *The Mystery of Capital:
      Why Capitalism Triumphs in the West and Fails Everywhere Else* (Basic Books,
      2000).
178   *7.7 percent of the population is "unbanked,":* Lori London, "The Top 10 Un-
      banked and Underbanked Cities," goEBT, March 29, 2017, https://www.goebt
      .com/the-top-10-unbanked-and-underbanked-cities/.
179   *For the more than 2 billion adults worldwide:* Global Findex Database, World
      Bank, 2014, http://www.worldbank.org/en/programs/globalfindex.
179   *UN's plan to eradicate global poverty:* Sustainable Development Goals,
      United Nations, http://www.un.org/sustainabledevelopment/poverty/.
179   *committed a combined $31 billion in 2013:* Consultative Group to Assist the
      Poor, "2014 Saw $31 Billion in International Funding for Financial Inclu-
      sion," CGAP, January 19, 2016, http://www.cgap.org/news/2014-saw-31-billion
      -international-funding-financial-inclusion.
181   *Stamps date as far back as 7600 BCE:* Joshua J. Mark, "Cylinder Seals in An-
      cient Mesopotamia—Their History and Significance," *Ancient History Ency-
      clopedia*, December 2, 2015, http://www.ancient.eu/article/846/.
182   *increasing default rates and a host of scandals shed light:* David Roodman,
      "Grameen Bank, Which Pioneered Loans for the Poor, Has Hit a Repayment
      Snag," Center for Global Development, February 9, 2010, https://www.cgdev
      .org/blog/grameen-bank-which-pioneered-loans-poor-has-hit-repayment
      -snag.
185   *"The reason people don't go around recording themselves":* Michael J. Casey,
      "Could the Blockchain Empower the Poor and Unlock Global Growth?"

Techonomy, March 7, 2016, http://techonomy.com/2016/03/blockchain-global
-growth/.

186   *He is working on a pilot in the Republic of Georgia:* Laura Shin, *Forbes*,
      April 21, 2016, "Republic of Georgia to Pilot Land Titling on Blockchain
      with Economist Hernando De Soto, BitFury," https://www.forbes.com/sites
      /laurashin/2016/04/21/republic-of-georgia-to-pilot-land-titling-on
      -blockchain-with-economist-hernando-de-soto-bitfury/#3c381e6144da.

186   *blockchain startup Ubitquity is partnering with Priority Title & Escrow:*
      "Ubitquity, the Blockchain-Secured Platform for Real Estate Transactions,
      Partners with US-Based 'Rising Barn' for Property Recording," Ubitquity.io,
      October 17, 2016, https://www.ubitquity.io/blog/ubitquity_llc_partners
      _prioritytitle_blockchain_10_17_2016.html.

186   *Here, we are sobered by the experience of:* Sierra Leone: Land Governance As-
      sessment Framework, Draft Final Report, World Bank, September 2015,
      http://siteresources.worldbank.org/INTLGA/Resources/Sierra_Leone_Final
      _Draft_Report_Oct12_v2.pdf; also see: Sierra Leone Ministry of Lands,
      Country Planning and the Environment, "Draft National Land Policy of Si-
      erra Leone," United Nations Development Programme, August 1, 2015,
      http://www.sl.undp.org/content/dam/sierraleone/docs/projectdocuments
      /environment/Land%20Policy%20SL%20151214%20FINAL.pdf.

187   *This problem was highlighted in a critical study:* Victoria Louise Lemieux,
      "Trusting Records: Is Blockchain Technology the Answer?" *Records Man-
      agement Journal* 26, no. 2 (2016): 110–139, doi: 10.1108/RMJ-12-2015-0042.

188   *In Cameroon and Senegal, Julius Akinyemi:* "Unleashing the Wealth of Na-
      tions," http://wealthofnations.media.mit.edu/node/2.

189   *In yet another project from MIT Media Lab:* Details on various projects from
      MIT's Media Lab come from Michael Casey's work with these groups; addi-
      tional information can be found on the lab's Web site: https://www.media
      .mit.edu/.

191   *there are now ninety-three countries with some form of mobile-money service:*
      GSMA's Mobile Money Deployment Tracker: http://www.gsma.com/mobile
      fordevelopment/m4d-tracker/mobile-money-deployment-tracker.

191   *"Between 60 percent and 90 percent of [mobile] accounts . . .":* Carol Realini,
      "Unbanked Consumers Strive for Better Banking Services," www.carolrealini
      .com, February 7, 2015, http://www.carolrealini.com/unbanked-consumers
      -better-banking-services/.

192   *reluctant to make their systems interoperable:* Rob Jillo, "Airtel Presses for
      Share of Safaricom's M-PESA Platform," *Capital Business*, July 3, 2015,
      http://www.capitalfm.co.ke/business/2015/07/airtel-presses-for-share-of
      -safaricoms-m-pesa-platform/.

193   *A Jamaican immigrant in Miami might find:* Remittance Prices Worldwide, World Bank, https://remittanceprices.worldbank.org/en/corridor/United-States /Jamaica.

194   *the recent success of BitPesa:* Laura Shin, "Bitcoin Payments Firm BitPesa Secures Greycroft as Lead Investor for $10 Million Total Funding," *Forbes*, August 30, 2017, https://www.forbes.com/sites/laurashin/2017/08/30/bitcoin -payments-firm-bitpesa-secures-greycroft-as-lead-investor-for-10-million -total-funding/#4dfaefb66066.

194   *20 percent of the remittances that Filipino immigrants:* Luke Parker, "Bitcoin Remittances '20 percent' of South Korea-Philippines Corridor," *Brave New Coin*, September 14, 2016, https://bravenewcoin.com/news/bitcoin-remittances -20-percent-of-south-korea-philippines-corridor/.

195   *established its precedent-setting BitLicense:* New York State Department of Financial Services, New York Codes, Rules, and Regulations, Title 23, Chapter 1, Part 200: Virtual Currencies, http://www.dfs.ny.gov/legal/regulations /adoptions/dfsp200t.pdf.

198   *Consider the Dunbar number:* Maria Konnikova, "The Limits of Friendship," *New Yorker*, October 7, 2014, https://www.newyorker.com/science /maria-konnikova/social-media-affect-math-dunbar-number-friendships.

CHAPTER EIGHT

202   *It's made more difficult by the fact that 2.4 billion people:* Mariana Dahan and Alan Gelb, "The Identity Target in the Post-2015 Development Agenda," World Bank, September 17, 2015, http://www.worldbank.org/en/topic/ict/brief/the -identity-target-in-the-post-2015-development-agenda-connections-note-19.

202   *According to . . . UNESCO:* "Trafficking and HIV/AIDS Project," UNESCO, July 4, 2017, http://bangkok.unesco.org/content/trafficking-and-hivaids-project.

204   *including at big tech firms like Microsoft:* Joon Ian Wong, "Microsoft Thinks Blockchain Tech Could Solve One of the Internet's Toughest Problems: Digital Identities," *Quartz*, June 1, 2017, https://qz.com/989761/microsoft-msft -thinks-blockchain-tech-could-solve-one-of-the-internets-toughest -problems-digital-identities/.

205   *As of this writing, this system:* Jeanette Rodrigues, "India ID Program Wins World Bank Praise Despite 'Big Brother' Fears," *Bloomberg*, March 15, 2017, https://www.bloomberg.com/news/articles/2017-03-15/india-id-program -wins-world-bank-praise-amid-big-brother-fears.

205   *In early 2017, IDFC Bank launched its Aadhaar Pay service:* Sandeep Phuken, "Aadhaar Pay: New App Does Away with Transaction Fee, Debit, Credit

Cards," NDTV, March 8, 2017, http://www.ndtv.com/india-news/aadhaar-pay-new-app-does-away-with-transaction-fee-debit-credit-cards-1667254.

206   *Nasdaq, for example, has introduced:* Shaun Waterman, "Nasdaq Says Estonia E-voting Pilot Successful," *CyberScoop,* January 25, 2017, https://www.cyberscoop.com/nasdaq-estonia-evoting-pilot/.

206   *Already, a team of data security experts from the U.S. and UK:* Drew Springall, Travis Finkenauer, Zakir Durumeric, Jason Kitcat, Harri Hursti, Margaret MacAlpine, and J. Alex Halderman, "Security Analysis of the Estonian Internet Voting System," ACM CCS 2014—21st ACM Conference on Computer and Communications Security, November 3–7, 2014, http://dx.doi.org/10.1145/2660267.2660315.

207   *This case reminds us of a stern warning:* Meeting with Michael J. Casey, New York City, June 2015.

207   *However, as identity policy expert David Birch:* David Birch, *Identity Is the New Money* (London Publishing Partnership, 2004).

208   *The World Economic Forum has contributed:* "A Blueprint for Digital Identity: The Role of Financial Institutions in Building Digital Identity," World Economic Forum, August 2016, http://www3.weforum.org/docs/WEF_A_Blueprint_for_Digital_Identity.pdf.

209   *Robust Digital Identity. Identity, whether:* "Towards an Internet of Trusted Data: A New Framework for Identity and Data Sharing," August 2016, MIT Connection Science, https://www.nist.gov/sites/default/files/documents/2016/09/16/mit_rfi_response.pdf.

213   *The sweeping goal, according to Yorke Rhodes:* Yorke Rhodes III, "What Does Identity Mean in Today's Physical and Digital World?" Microsoft.com, https://azure.microsoft.com/en-us/blog/what-does-identity-mean-in-today-s-physical-and-digital-world/.

215   *"The public [permissionless] blockchains deliberately":* Ron Miller, "The Promise of Managing Identity on the Blockchain," *TechCrunch,* September 10, 2017, https://techcrunch.com/2017/09/10/the-promise-of-managing-identity-on-the-blockchain/.

215   *cryptocurrency journalist Juan Galt:* Juan Galt, "Andreas Antonopoulos: The Case Against Reputation and Identity Systems," *Bitcoin Magazine,* December 19, 2015, https://news.bitcoin.com/andreas-antonopoulos-case-reputation-identity-systems/.

215   *Influential cryptocurrency thinker Andreas Antonopoulos:* ibid.

217   *And hackers have demonstrated:* Russell Brandon, "Your Phone's Biggest Vulnerability Is Your Fingerprint," *The Verge,* May 2, 2016, http://www.theverge.com/2016/5/2/11540962/iphone-samsung-fingerprint-duplicate-hack-security.

219   *Learning Machine CEO Chris Jagers says:* Chris Jagers, "Digital Identity and
           the Blockchain," Learning Machine Blog, July 16, 2017, https://medium.com
           /learning-machine-blog/digital-identity-and-the-blockchain-10de0e7d7734.

219   *Here's how Chris Allen, a research scientist at bitcoin infrastructure:*
           Chris Allen, "The Path to Self-Sovereign Identity," Life with Alacrity blog,
           April 25, 2016, http://www.lifewithalacrity.com/2016/04/the-path-to
           -self-soverereign-identity.html.

CHAPTER NINE

223   *"Software is eating the world":* Marc Andreessen, "Why Software Is Eat-
           ing the World," *The Wall Street Journal*, August 20, 2011, https://www
           .wsj.com/articles/SB10001424053111903480904576512250915629460.

224   *"Unless we understand better how technologies . . .":* S. Jasanoff, *The Ethics
           of Invention: Technology and the Human Future* (W. W. Norton, 2016).

225–26   *In his 1891 essay "The Soul of Man under Socialism":* Oscar Wilde, "The
           Soul of Man under Socialism," First publication in *Fortnightly Review*, Feb-
           ruary 1891, p. 292.

229   *A Wall Street Journal* report titled *"Blue Feed, Red Feed":* "Blue Feed, Red
           Feed: See Liberal Facebook and Conservative Facebook, Side by Side,"
           The Wall Street Journal, http://graphics.wsj.com/blue-feed-red-feed/.

229   *Yet here they are having to compete:* Craig Silverman and Lawrence Alex-
           ander, "How Teens in the Balkans Are Duping Trump Supporters with
           Fake News," *BuzzFeed*, November 3, 2016, https://www.buzzfeed.com
           /craigsilverman/how-macedonia-became-a-global-hub-for-pro-trump
           -misinfo.

231   *Today, there are well over a billion works:* In 2015, the Creative Com-
           mons foundation came up with an estimate of 1.1 billion licenses. Since
           that estimate was inherently linked to known platforms and repositories
           that publish CC-licensed material, and based on an accelerating rate of
           usage that saw CC licenses triple in the five years to 2015, it's reasonable
           to assume the 2017 number is much larger. For the 2015 estimate, see:
           "State of the Commons," https://stateof.creativecommons.org/2015/.

232   *An Ethereum-based service called adChain:* Robert Hof, "How MetaX
           Plans to Use Blockchain to Stop Ad Fraud," *Forbes*, March 21, 2017,
           https://www.forbes.com/sites/roberthof/2017/03/21/how-metax-plans
           -to-use-blockchain-to-stop-ad-fraud/#2e417d0e59da.

232   *"This hash is unique to the book":* "Age of Cryptocurrency, Recorded on
           the Bitcoin Blockchain," *CoinDesk*, February 3, 2015, https://www
           .coindesk.com/age-of-cryptocurrency-bitcoin-blockchain/.

234   *"There are millions of artists on the planet"*: Heap interviewed by Michael J. Casey on sidelines of the Blockchain Summit 2017, Necker Island, British Virgin Islands, July 28, 2017.

234   *"I'd prefer that fans got hold of the music and shared it"*: "Imogen Heap— Future Music—PART 1/2, London Real," YouTube channel, December 27, 2015, https://www.youtube.com/watch?v=IkLrdRx0F6w.

235   *What the blockchain could do, argues Lance Koonce:* Lance Koonce, "Copyright's 'Double Spend' Problem: Digital First Sales," *Medium*, April 27, 2016, https://medium.com/creativeblockchain/copyrights-double-spend-problem -digital-first-sales-f18c586612b9.

237   *"The Creative Commons dataset is incredibly fractured"*: Mediachain founder Jesse Walden, phone interview with Michael J. Casey, March 25, 2017.

239   *But in general, says Mediachain's Walden:* ibid.

239   *The coin would be issued to owners:* Tim Gosselin, "A New Cryptocurrency to Reward Creative Commons Creators," mediachain.io, March 9, 2017, https:// blog.mediachain.io/a-new-cryptocurrency-to-reward-creative-commons -creators-e41e1791c4c0.

240   *In the spring, it was bought by Spotify:* Sarah Perez, "Spotify Acquires Blockchain Startup Mediachain to Solve Music's Attribution Problem," *TechCrunch*, April 26, 2017, https://techcrunch.com/2017/04/26/spotify-acquires-blockchain -startup-mediachain-to-solve-musics-attribution-problem/.

240   *in 2016, Spotify had to pay out about $20 million:* Todd Spangler, "Spotify to Pay More Than $20 Million to Music Publishers in Royalty Pact for 'Unmatched' Songs," *Variety*, March 17, 2016, http://variety.com/2016/digital /news/spotify-nmpa-music-publishers-royalties-1201732879/.

CHAPTER TEN

249   *The startup BitNation, for example, touts blockchain-based:* https://bitnation.co/.

252   *During the 2016 presidential campaign:* Brian Forde, "Hillary Clinton and the Blockchain," *TechCrunch*, July 7, 2016, https://techcrunch.com/2016/07/07 /hillary-clinton-and-the-blockchain/.

253   *Meanwhile, Blockchain startup Neocapita:* Diana Ngo, "Governments, NGOs Consider Neocapita's Blockchain Pilots for E-Governance," *Bitcoin Magazine*, March 31, 2017, https://bitcoinmagazine.com/articles/governments-ngos -consider-neocapitas-blockchain-pilots-e-governance/.

253   *Even on Capitol Hill, a few legislators are starting to take notice:* Ali Breland, "Lawmakers Introduce the Blockchain Caucus," *The Hill*, February 9, 2017, http://thehill.com/policy/technology/318845-lawmakers-introduce-the -blockchain-caucus.

253   *Delaware is working with Symbiont:* Jeff John Roberts, "Companies Can Put
       Shareholders on a Blockchain Starting Today," *Fortune*, August 1, 2017, http://
       fortune.com/2017/08/01/blockchain-shareholders-law/.

253   *And in March 2017, Illinois's government:* Anna Irrera, "Illinois Watchdog
       First U.S. Regulator to Join Blockchain Consortium R3," *Reuters*, March 16,
       2017, https://www.reuters.com/article/us-blockchain-illinois/illinois-watchdog
       -first-u-s-regulator-to-join-blockchain-consortium-r3-idUSKBN16N2FN.

253   *international law enforcement agencies like Europol partner:* The Traderman,
       "Chainanalysis Partners with Europol's European Cybercrime Centre," *The
       Merkle*, February 22, 2016, https://themerkle.com/chainanalysis-partners
       -with-europols-european-cybercrime-centre/.

255   *Similarly, the UK Financial Conduct Authority's "sandbox" strategy:* Regulatory
       sandbox details at FCA Innovate: https://www.fca.org.uk/firms/regulatory
       -sandbox.

258   *And to these you can add a project called Algorand:* Yossi Gilad, Rotem
       Hemo, Silvio Micali, Georgios Vlachos, and Nickolai Zeldovich, "Algorand:
       Scaling Byzantine Agreements for Cryptocurrencies," MIT CSAIL, https://
       people.csail.mit.edu/nickolai/papers/gilad-algorand-eprint.pdf.

260   *Listen to this January 2016 report:* "Distributed Ledger Technology: Beyond
       Block Chain [*sic*]," UK Government Office for Science, January 19, 2016.

260   *dubious official information that his minders describe:* "Conway: Press Secretary
       Gave 'Alternative Facts'," per KellyAnne Conway's interview with Chuck
       Todd of NBC News, NBC News, January 22, 2017, https://www.nbcnews.com
       /meet-the-press/video/conway-press-secretary-gave-alternative-facts
       -860142147643.

Index